LOST LAND EMERGING

Walter B. Emery

EDWARDS PROFESSOR OF EGYPTOLOGY
UNIVERSITY OF LONDON

ILLUSTRATIONS BY THE AUTHOR

LOST
LAND

EMERGING

CHARLES SCRIBNER'S SONS · NEW YORK

PREFACE

THIS volume is designed to provide, for the general reader, an account of Nubia, so soon to be destroyed by the waters of the great reservoir which will be created by the High Dam blocking the Nile at Aswan.

The book is in no way intended for the specialist; its aim is to summarize a record of archaeological exploration and to present an outline of Nubian history compiled from this research and from other sources drawn both from Nubia itself and from Egypt.

For the translation of the relevant texts used in the historical outline, I have depended to a major extent on those presented by James Henry Breasted, published in his invaluable *Ancient Records of Egypt*.

WALTER B. EMERY

v

CONTENTS

ILLUSTRATIONS • PLATES   *ix*

ILLUSTRATIONS • FIGURES IN TEXT   *xi*

PART ONE. Introduction

I   A Battleground of the Ancient World   *3*

II   The High Dam   *15*

PART TWO. Exploration

I   The First Archaeological Survey   *27*

II   The Second Archaeological Survey   *39*

III   Ballana and Qustol   *52*

IV   Independent Exploration   *92*

V   The Results of the UNESCO Appeal   *98*

PART THREE. Outline of Nubian History

I   The Archaic Period and the Old Kingdom
(*c.* 3100–2160 B.C.)   *169*

II   The First Intermediate Period and the Eleventh
Dynasty (*c.* 2160–1991 B.C.)   *180*   *vii*

Contents

III   The Twelfth Dynasty (*c.* 1991–1786 B.C.)   *189*

IV   The Second Intermediate Period (*c.* 1786–1575 B.C.)   *218*

V   The Eighteenth Dynasty (*c.* 1575–1308 B.C.)   *225*

VI   The Nineteenth Dynasty (*c.* 1308–1194 B.C.)   *248*

VII   The Twentieth Dynasty and the Decadence in
Egypt (*c.* 1184–751 B.C.)   *262*

VIII   The Twenty-fifth Dynasty (*c.* 751–656 B.C.)   *266*

IX   The Ptolemaic-Meroitic Period (*c.* 332 B.C.–A.D. 350) *283*

X   The X-Group Period (*c.* A.D. 200–550)   *294*

APPENDIX   *313*

METRIC TABLE   *315*

BIBLIOGRAPHY   *317*

INDEX   *321*

ILLUSTRATIONS

PLATES

PLATES I–III. Nubia

Natives, the landscape, our headquarters (*pages 126–131*).

PLATES IV–XXI. Ballana and Qustol

The tumuli (*page 132*); embedded skeleton of X-Group King and grave objects (*pages 133–134*); silver horse bridles and trappings (*pages 135 138*); silver crowns (*pages 139–140*); silver jewelry (*pages 141–145*); objects in bronze (*pages 146–149*); weapons (*pages 150–151*); inlaid wooden chest (*page 152*).

PLATES XXII–XXVI. Buhen

Excavation of the fortress (*pages 153–155*); removal of the Temple of Hatshepsut (*pages 156–157*); excavation of the town site (*page 158*).

PLATES XXVII. Kasr Ibrim

General view of the fortress (*page 159*).

PLATES XXVIII–XXIX. Philae and Kalabsha

The "Kiosk" and the outer court at Philae (*pages 160–161*); the Temple of Isis at Philae (*page 162*); the temple at Kalabsha (*page 162*).

PLATES XXX–XXXI. Abu Simbel

The Great Temple and a side view of its colossi (*pages 163–164*); the façade of Queen Nefertari's temple (*page 164*); the reconstruction of the temple (*page 165*).

PLATE XXXII. Soldiers of the Middle Kingdom

Wooden models of an Egyptian infantry company (*page 166*).

ILLUSTRATIONS

FIGURES IN TEXT

1–4 Maps: Nile Valley (*page 5*); Nubia (*page 17*); Area of Philae and the High Dam (*page 19*); Island of Philae (*page 29*).

5 Plan of the dahabeah *Zenit el Nil* (*page 42*).

6 Examples of Tomb Record Cards (*pages 46–47*).

7 X-Group crowns (*pages 79–80*).

8 Ballana: Burial installation Tomb 80 (*page 82*).

9 10 Buhen: West fortifications of the fortress (*page 109*); reconstruction of the West Gate (*page 110*).

11–12 A-Group: Types of burial (*page 171*); types of pottery (*page 172*).

13 Inscription of King Zer at Sheikh Suliman (*page 173*).

14–15 B-Group: Types of burial (*page 175*); types of pottery (*page 176*).

16 Nubian pan grave of the Middle Kingdom and types of Kerma pottery (*page 182*).

17–18 C-Group: Type of early burial (*page 184*); and types of pottery (*page 186*).

19–26 Fortress plans: Semna (*page 193*); Kumma (*page 194*); Uronarti (*page 195*); Shalfak (*page 196*); Mirgissa (*page 197*); Buhen (*page 198*); Aneiba (*page 200*); Kubban (*page 201*).

27–30 C-Group: Type of burial with chapel (*page 211*); with stone-lined grave (*page 212*); with brick-vaulted grave (*page 213*); bed burial (*page 215*).

31 Types of Kerma pottery (*page 216*).

32 C-Group: Type of burial of the Second Intermediate Period (*page 221*).

33–36 New Kingdom: Types of burial (*pages 231, 232, 233*); and types of pottery (*page 235*).

37 Buhen: Plan of the Temple of Hatshepsut (*page 238*).

38 Tribute scene from the tomb of Vizier Huy (*page 246*).

39–40 Abu Simbel: Reconstruction of the façade of the Great Temple (*page 252*); and a plan (*page 255*).

41 Kalabsha: Plan of the Temple (*page 288*).

42–43 Meroitic type of burial (*page 291*); and types of pottery (*page 292*).

44–49 X-Group: Type of royal tomb (*page 304*); types of lesser burial (*pages 306, 307, 308*); and types of pottery (*pages 310, 311*).

LOST LAND EMERGING

1 INTRODUCTION

A Battleground
of the Ancient World

NUBIA, an ancient land, now under a sentence of death, has for thousands of years been one of the most important regions in the whole of the African continent. Although in comparison with other parts of the Nile Valley it is an arid and barren area, on its soil history has written one of its most vital chapters, recording events, some known, and some still to be recalled, which have had an important and even decisive influence on the course of the development of civilization. For Nubia was one of the principal battlegrounds of the ancient world, where was waged the struggle between the black and white peoples for the supremacy of North Africa.

The Egyptians, representing the highest civilization at that time, were pushing south to exploit the gold mines and to trade in ivory, precious woods and the other products of Kush, which was the ancient name of the northern Sudan. The people of the south, whose culture we are beginning to realize through recent excavations and research was by no means negligible, were pushing north to the more fertile parts of the valley of the Nile and the Mediterranean coast.

This highway to battle for the contending armies of the north and south has seen the pendulum of victory swing from one side to the other. Between intermittent warfare and the passage of armies Nubia had periods of peace and comparative prosperity when it came under the colonial rule of one or other of the rival powers; but in general these periods never lasted long and its history is one of constant change. And now the greatest change of all is imminent, for, in the interests of the future prosperity of the northern Nile Valley and delta, Nubia will finally disappear beneath the waters of the great reservoir which will be formed behind the High Dam at Aswan.

Where is Nubia? When this question is asked it is strange, and indeed astonishing, to find how vague the answers of even the best-informed people may be, for its exact boundaries will not be found firmly marked on a map. Such is its history as a highway for contending armies that Nubia never really attained an independent status of its own, and although its present-day inhabitants, the Barabra, are a distinct nationality, very closely knit by blood relationship and a common way of life, their homeland is divided between the north and the south. Lower Nubia on the north, between Shellal and Adindan, is part of Egypt, and Upper Nubia on the south, between Adindan and Dongola, is part of the Sudan (Figure 1).

Even the origin of the name Nubia is obscure. Strabo, quoting Eratosthenes, writes: "On the left of the course of the Nile live Nubae in Libya, a populous nation. They begin from Meroe, and extend as far as the bends [of the river]." It is tempting to see in the name of these people the name of Nubia, but if we are to identify "the bends of the river" as the Dongola Reach of the Nile, they would be occupying a part of the valley wholly south of Nubia as we know it. We must not overlook the fact that the ancient Egyptians called gold *nub,* and that to them the area which we now call Nubia was the land of gold. Although this may be purely coincidence, I cannot help feeling that it is a very plausible theory for the origin of the name of Nubia.

Among the many names by which the ancient Egyptians referred to Nubia the most commonly used was Ta-kens, "The Bend Land" or "The Land of the Bow." But this was only a general term and they distinguished between Lower or Upper Nubia by calling the northern area, between the First and Second Cataracts, Wawat, and south of the Second Cataract, Kush. As far as can be ascertained on the available archaeological evidence, the peoples of Wawat and Kush, although related, were racially distinct. This

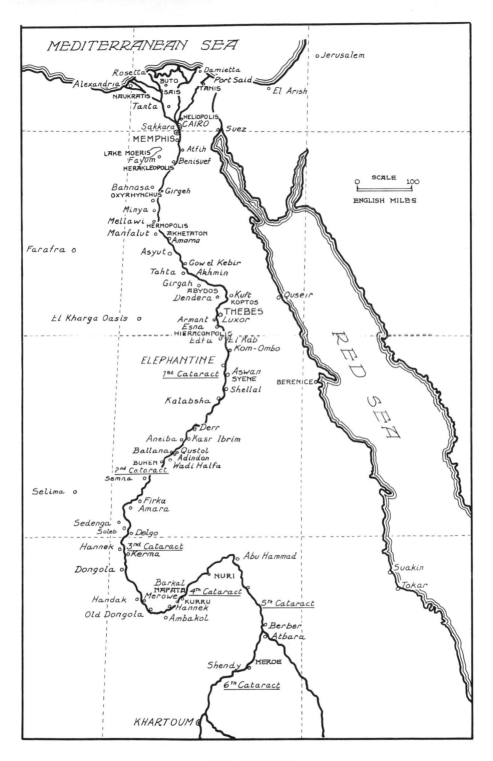

FIGURE I The Nile Valley

evidence suggests that the inhabitants of Wawat were generally an unwarlike people while the people of Kush were of fighting stock, who when Egyptian colonial rule was firmly established in Nubia were eagerly recruited for service in the pharaonic armies of the Empire.

Even in modern times the Barabra are divided by language, although the linguistic boundaries do not correspond with the geographical boundaries of Upper and Lower Nubia. Today these people of Nubia between Aswan and Wadi es Sebua speak a dialect known as Kenûz, and from Korosko to the Third Cataract they speak El-Mahasi; while farther south they speak Dongola, though this latter dialect appears to be only another form of Kenûz. The Nubian language, belonging to a special group of African tongues, is not written, so for writing they depend on Arabic, which is generally used throughout the whole country.

What relationship there is between the modern inhabitants of Nubia and those of ancient times is a matter of considerable uncertainty, for in a land which suffered so much foreign invasion considerable racial mixture is inevitable, and indeed there appears to have been at least one period when Lower Nubia may well have been almost uninhabited. Nevertheless, the undoubted survival of certain burial customs, arts, and crafts goes a long way to support the theory that the modern Nubian is in large part descended from the people who lived in this part of the Nile Valley in the days of the Middle Kingdom pharaohs. As in ancient times, the Nubian of today is racially distinct from the Egyptian, and although a large proportion of the male population live a great part of their lives in Egypt, they remain to a large extent a race apart. Very rarely do they marry Egyptians; home, wife, and family remain in Nubia, which even in its present state, with its beauty largely destroyed by the construction of the Aswan Dam, remains for them the most desirable land in the world. To it they will invariably return at every available opportunity, and in the event of sickness or the onset of old age their one ambition is to get back to the land that gave them birth.

6   It may well be asked why a people so satisfied with their home-

land should leave it for a large part of their lives. There are two reasons: the first is economic, for even before the building of the Aswan Dam Nubia could not support its population; the second is that the Nubian, unlike the Egyptian, is a great traveler, with an insatiable curiosity and wish to see other lands and peoples. I have met Nubians who have lived for a time in America as mechanics, traveled the world as ships' cooks, and even one who had spent some years as an engine driver in India. But I have never heard of one who really settled down in a foreign land by his own choice.

The cultivable areas are limited and cannot supply the food for even their small population, and with no industries it is necessary for all the able-bodied males to find employment in the bigger towns of Egypt and the Sudan. For generations the Nubians have earned their livelihood as domestic servants or as sailors of the Upper Egyptian Nile, in both of which professions I think they may be considered masters. All the best butlers and cooks in Egypt are from Nubia, and certainly the most reliable janitors of Cairo's great apartment houses, offices, and hotels almost invariably come from somewhere south of Aswan.

Long before the idea of organized labor and its care for the interests of the worker came to Egypt, the Nubian servants enjoyed a system which gave them, in a large measure, the protection which in Europe can only be expected from a strong labor union. Nearly every village of any size in Nubia has its representative in Cairo and other large Egyptian cities. In most cases he is employed as a janitor of a block of apartments, an office building, or something similar, and he has the responsibility of looking after the welfare of other members of his village who work in his locality. When a boy of his village is old enough he is sent to Egypt, usually to a relative already employed as a servant, but he will report to his village representative, who will, if necessary, find him employment and generally keep an eye on him. After serving his apprenticeship as a kitchen boy or something similar for perhaps two years, he will finally graduate to the position of an under-butler or cook's assistant, and be in receipt of a living wage. From then on he will   7 pay a small percentage of his salary to his village representative as a sort of unemployment insurance which will secure him food and lodging in hard times. Any resident in Cairo, certainly a foreigner, who is in need of a domestic servant will find it a wise course to ask the janitor of his apartment house for help, for he can always call him to account should the recommended servant prove a failure. The system works well and one frequently finds that a large proportion of the domestics of a block of apartments all come from the same village in Nubia and thus form a united group which helps itself, and in consequence makes life very much easier for the employer.

Apart from making a first-class domestic servant, the Nubian is an excellent sailor, and nearly all the pilots of the large river steamers are natives of Lower Nubia. Although long-distance passenger traffic on the Nile between the Delta and the First Cataract is now a thing of the past, apart from air travel, transport between Shellal and Wadi Halfa is dependent entirely on the Sudan government steamers, for there is no railway connection between Egypt and the Sudan. The crews of all these river steamers are Nubians, but, apart from this, great numbers of them are employed on the cargo traffic by sail or steam which still crowds the Nile between Upper Egypt and Cairo. Nubian families will take to the river as a profession for generations, the son being trained in the lore of the Nile by his father, so that the accumulation of years of experience of the vagaries of the great river which they possess is sometimes almost uncanny. Like the domestic servants, the sailors of Nubia are well organized, and, indeed, when hiring a crew, as I had to do many times when I had my own boat on the Nile, one soon finds that there are special cafés in Cairo where certain types of sailors congregate and wait for their special recruitment; for there are fixed rates of pay for certain classes of sailor. Moreover, an injustice to one is an injustice to all, and the owner of a ship will soon find himself black-listed if he does not conform to the time-honored rules and customs of his crew. It is this independence of spirit and clannishness in the Nubian that I suspect gave him rather a bad reputation among the early travelers in his country; but to those who take the trouble to understand his prejudices and superstitions he can be a very good friend, with a very long memory for past favors.

With the bulk of the able-bodied male population employed abroad, Nubia, with the exception of such areas as Wadi Halfa and Aneiba, is today largely a land inhabited by old men, women, and children, on whose labors the development of its limited agricultural areas must depend. With the exception of dates and fruit from the Wadi Halfa area, Nubia has no exports and retains the scanty products of her soil for her own consumption, and in the northern part of the country even this is inadequate. So that when the waters of the new reservoir cover the remaining cultivated areas, Nubia's remaining population, both human and animal, must be dispersed to other parts of the Nile Valley. But such is the Nubian's love of his homeland that I think many will remain, living on the arid banks of the reservoir and depending on food sent to them by the members of their families employed in Egypt and the Sudan. Also at a later stage, when the Nile silt forms new fertile areas behind Abu Simbel, Seiyala, Dendur, etc., many will return.

The land of Nubia is difficult to describe in a few paragraphs, for although to the casual visitor it may appear from the river as a rather monotonous series of alternate areas of sparse cultivation and patches of arid desert and rock, it is in fact a land of considerable variety. At the First Cataract south of Aswan the geological nature of the Nile Valley changes and a great barrier of granite between latitude 24° and 18°N crosses the valley to form the first frontier between fertile Egypt and the barren lands of the south. Even as far north as Esna the great limestone plateau which flanks the valley has receded, to be replaced by rather formless hills of sandstone, although the land on both sides of the river remains green and productive; but once past the granite rampart, a harsh hint of the character of the African Nile is revealed.

Here at Shellal is the terminus of the Egyptian State Railway, and a point of embarkation for the Sudan government steamers which carry the traveler through Lower Nubia to Wadi Halfa, where he again takes up railway transport to Khartoum. Little remains of Shellal beyond a few huts and the railway station and   *9* wharf buildings, but when I first saw it in 1929 it was still a scattered village of considerable size surrounded by high granite cliffs burnt almost black by the sun. Since then the Nile waters have risen because of the last heightening of the Aswan Dam in 1934 and very few of the inhabitants have remained in this area, which is one of the hottest and most airless in all Nubia, attaining as it does a temperature of frequently over 120°F, for it is denied the cooling desert wind by the high cliffs that surround it. At Shellal, directly south of the First Cataract, the river is wide and dotted with rocky islands, many of which are now visible only as the river subsides to its natural level when the reservoir is emptied in the summer months. On Philae, one of the largest of these islands, stands the famous temple of Isis, whose total destruction, threatened by the new irrigation projects, is one of the principal targets in the UNESCO campaign to preserve the ancient monuments of Nubia. Even now the beauty of this architectural gem can only be admired in late summer, for the rest of the year it is almost totally submerged.

The surrounding cliffs are marked here and there with ancient quarrying and bear inscriptions dating from early pharaonic times down to the Christian era. Just west of Philae is the island of Biga on which stands a small temple built by Ptolemy XIII (80–51 B.C.), little of which remains. Biga was considered a sacred place long before the Ptolemaic period, for relics of the Eighteenth Dynasty have been found there, and there are records of the existence of a fortress on the island at that date. Although most of the island's ancient remains and its natural beauties have been destroyed by the invading waters, it now assumes a new importance, for it is one of the key points in the scheme to preserve and restore Philae, which I will describe later.

With the first raising of the Aswan Dam in 1911, Lower Nubia as far south as Wadi es Sebua was flooded; but, even so, its beauty was not entirely destroyed and cultivated areas above the new waterline were still preserved. When I first saw it in 1929 such typical Nubian villages as that at Debod were still in existence. Seen from the river, such settlements, nestling amid the barren sandstone cliffs, on the edge of narrow strips of green cultivation, were most picturesque; for the Nubian mud-brick house, with its whitewashed walls, barrel-vaulted roof and decorated doorways, is a structure far superior to anything seen in the villages of Egypt. The temples of Debod, Qirtas, Tafa, Kalabsha, and Dakka were still largely visible, even when the waters were high, and although areas, notably round Kalabsha, were arid and barren, the land with its scattered villages, small palm groves, and patches of cultivation was still alive.

Farther south, after Wadi es Sebua and beyond the reach of the destroying reservoir, Nubia was, of course, at that time unchanged, and I was fortunate in seeing it as the early explorers saw it, and as it must have been with little alteration from very early times. Between Wadi es Sebua and the frontier of Lower Nubia at Wadi Halfa the scenery on both banks of the river changed constantly. With the exception of El Malki, where there was a large village surrounded by dense palm groves, the river passed between inhospitable banks of rock and drift as far as Korosko, where the great bend in the Nile starts. Between Korosko and Tumas the west bank was almost entirely barren, with banks of golden sand coming down in places to the river's edge. But on the east bank the edge of the river had an almost continuous strip of narrow but luxuriant cultivation widening out at Derr, which at that time was still the center of government administration, with a police station and a school. At the north end of this town, then the largest in Nubia, was the house of the *Kashif,* who until comparatively recent times was a semi-independent ruler of the whole area. Derr, with the rock-cut temple of Rameses II behind it, partly hidden amid palm groves and sycamores, had a beauty dependent largely on the vivid green of its vegetation. Now that this has been destroyed by the recurrent flooding, even during the period of low water when it is exposed it presents a picture of arid desolation which to those who knew it years ago is a vivid symbol of the tragedy of Nubia.

South of Derr, the arable land was all on the west, while the east bank was barren with low rocks coming down to the river's   *11* edge. At Tumas was a large fertile island and the west side of the Nile was thickly forested with date palms, the produce of which was famous even in Egypt. South of Tumas the arable land again became sparse until Aneiba, which was the site of ancient Ma'am, the viceregal seat and center of government under the pharaohs of the New Kingdom (1570–1085 B.C.). Although a comparatively barren area on the west bank when I first visited it in 1930, after the raising of the dam, in 1934, it soon became thickly populated and cultivated because, being above the new water level, it was selected as the new center of government in succession to Derr, which was destroyed. And now Aneiba must also be sacrificed, for the waters of the new reservoir will cover its fertile plain and wash the foot of the sandstone hills which surround it. A little farther to the south on the east bank are the high cliffs of Kasr Ibrim, on which stands the ancient fortress which we started to excavate in 1963.

South of Aneiba and Kasr Ibrim the vegetation on both banks was scanty and at various points the desert sands reached down to the river, but at Abu Simbel the fertile area widens out and great bays of arable land on both the east and west supported a fairly large population, as they must have done in ancient times. For here on the west bank are the two greatest monuments in Nubia: the rock-cut temples built by Rameses II. In 1931 they were some distance from the Nile, with wide cultivated fields in front of them; but with the completion of the second raising of the Aswan Dam in 1934, the waters of the river were only a few meters from the feet of the great statues which formed the façade of the temple. Now, with the success of the UNESCO appeal, this great rock-cut structure has been carved up into 30-ton blocks and removed piece-meal to higher ground where it will be rebuilt, safe above the threatening waters of the new reservoir.

Between Abu Simbel and the Sudan frontier at Adindan, the country on both banks was flat and uninteresting, with limited cultivation, and cone-shaped mountains in the distant eastern desert. Yet this rather barren area is rich in ancient remains, the most prominent of which were the fortress town of Adda and the tumuli which are the tombs of the late Nubian kings that we discovered at Ballana and Qustol in 1932. It was during our excavations at Ballana that we found fertile soil below the desert sand; with the result that with the aid of modern irrigation methods the Egyptian government was able to turn this barren area into one of the most productive cultivated districts in Nubia in which many dispossessed families from the flooded villages in the north were settled. But today Ballana in its turn has been destroyed by the rising waters of the new reservoir.

Such was Lower Nubia thirty-five years ago: a land of contrasting color, the dark brown of the sandstone cliffs alternating with the yellow sand of the desert and the lush green of the cultivated areas. But all this has been greatly changed by the successive irrigation projects which have destroyed the vegetation. No longer do we see the palm groves of Tumas and Derr; only a great lake when the reservoir is full and a waste of mud flats when the water subsides in late summer. All the picturesque villages with their attractive white houses and their decorated doorways have been abandoned and already many of them have disappeared.

What can be called the Wadi Halfa area, on the east bank from Debeira to the commencement of the Second Cataract was, until 1964, the most fertile part of the country, and even without the merchants, officials, and engineers employed by the Sudan government dockyard and railway workshops, it supported a considerable population. Now all but 2,000 people have left and most of this attractive small town, memorable of the days of Kitchener and Gordon, is flooded and will soon disappear. The few remaining people are congregated on the high ground near the abandoned airport, which is now the northern terminus of the Sudan Government Railways.

South of Wadi Halfa is the second great granite barrier across the Nile. This is the Second Cataract which spreads its rapids over a length of more than ninety miles. This is also the land known as the Batn el Hagar (Belly of Stones), the most arid and desolate part of Nubia. The river here is impassable to the navigation of ships of any size, for it descends over graywacke and   *13* granite rocks which form an archipelago of more than 350 islets. Here in this barren reach of the Nile the ancient Egyptians built a chain of fortresses, for the desolate nature of the region and the difficulties of navigation make it a natural frontier both as a base for defense and as a springboard for attack. The chain of military strongholds starts in the north with Buhen, which was probably the headquarters, and ends at the southernmost point of the cataract with the twin forts of Semna and Kumma. These ancient structures, some built on the banks of the river and others on almost inaccessible islands, have presented a great challenge to the archaeologist, for owing to their great size they had never been completely excavated, and now, when the High Dam is completed, they will be destroyed. Between 1957 and 1964, the Egypt Exploration Society completed the excavation and recording of the fortress of Buhen, opposite Wadi Halfa. This work, which has yielded startling results, will be described later in this book. In reply to the UNESCO appeal, other forts and ancient sites in the Batn el Hagar are being excavated by the Sudan Government Antiquities Service and by various foreign expeditions sent by scientific institutions from Europe and America.

It is this part of Nubia extending as far south as Dongola which is of such potential importance to the archaeologist, for here was the ancient land of Kush, of whose history and culture we know so little. The area is largely unexplored by the archaeologist, and I venture to think that the large-scale excavations being planned because of the threat of the waters of the new reservoir will yield discoveries of great historical importance, perhaps drastically changing our whole conception of the character and power of ancient Egypt's southern enemy.

II

The High Dam

I⊤ is somewhat ironic that the successive irrigation projects which
have in the past destroyed, and in the present are destroying, the
antiquities and monuments of Nubia are to a large extent the
reason for our knowledge of the archaeology and history of this
part of the Nile Valley; for were it not for the periodic threat of
destruction there would not have been the concentration of
archaeological research undertaken at various times since the
Aswan Dam was built between 1899 and 1902. Exploration in
Nubia is difficult, by reason of its isolation, and moreover in comparison with Egypt the results of excavation are not rich in actual
"finds," although productive of valuable scientific information.
Consequently, much of the archaeological exploration was the result of dire necessity and not of choice, and a large part of the
important discoveries was made under a threat of "now or never."

And now the archaeologist had to face the final threat; for the
present cannot be sacrificed for the past, and although some of the
great monuments have been preserved, the ancient sites of town
and necropolis, which hold the secrets and records of past ages,
have been destroyed. Once again the excavators of many nations
have been engaged in a race against time to wrest from Nubia's
barren soil the remaining secrets of her long history.

After the reconquest of the Sudan in 1898 and the final pacification of the Upper Nile Valley, engineers and irrigation experts
turned their attention to the conquest of the river itself, for Egypt's
population was steadily increasing and the necessity of extending
the cultivated areas in the delta was becoming more and more
urgent. All such agricultural development depends on the water
taken from the Nile, for Egypt, even in its northern extremity, is   *15*

a rain-starved land, so the annual flooding of the river was the one and only source of life, and even from the earliest times every effort was made to prevent the too rapid ebbing of the waters by the construction of storage basins, etc. Even so, an immense volume of water was lost to the sea, and to check at least a part of this wastage the construction of a dam across the first cataract south of Aswan was commenced in 1899 and completed in 1902, with the object of controlling the flow of the river by storing water in November and December when there is a surplus, to be discharged in May, June, and July, when the cultivated areas need a supply which the natural flow of the river cannot give.

The Aswan Dam, a masterpiece of engineering science of that time, stretched across the cataract for a distance of more than a mile, was 100 ft. high and could store 980 million cubic meters of water in an artificial lake extending south for a distance of 140 miles. Even so, it was a modification of the original design which was first submitted to the Egyptian government in 1893. This was because it was originally intended to make the water level of the reservoir 27 ft. higher and this would have entailed the partial submersion of the temple of Philae. This gave cause for much criticism and protest, and the authorities, after much discussion, bowed to the storm, so that the original dam was reduced in height, and although some part of the structures on Philae were flooded for a short period of the year, the main buildings remained well above water level. However, because it was feared that the added moisture might weaken the foundations these were strengthened and all weaknesses in the fabric repaired.

But once the dam was built, its benefits became so apparent that the protests of archaeologists and artists were soon forgotten and between 1907 and 1912 it was raised by another 16 ft., which in extending the reservoir another 45 miles south to Wadi es Sebua (Figure 2), gave it a capacity of 2,400 million cubic meters of water. The greatly extended artificial lake, now with a total length of 185 miles, partly submerged Philae and many other temples, as well as destroying many ancient settlements and cemeteries. However, the archaeologist was not inactive, and before the work on the

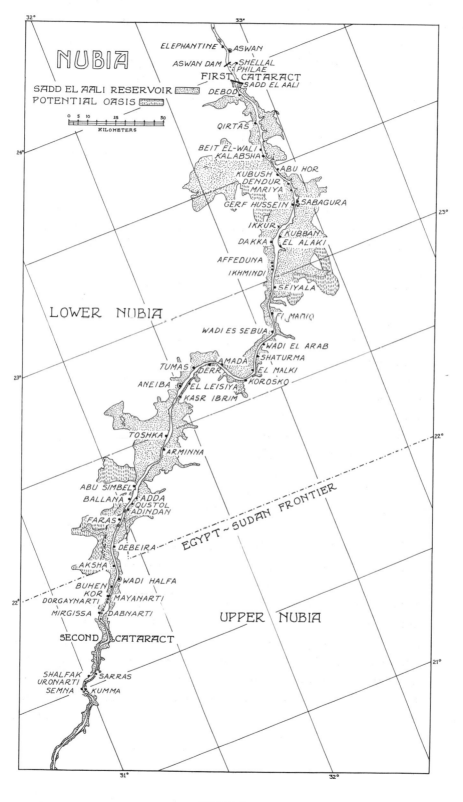

FIGURE 2

dam was completed in 1912 the Egyptian government had organized the First Archaeological Survey, which excavated and recorded all the ancient remains that were to be destroyed by the
waters of the heightened reservoir.

But still the demand of Egypt's thirsty acres was not satisfied and
once more, between 1929 and 1934, the Aswan Dam was heightened
by another 30 ft. and the reservoir extended 225 miles to Wadi
Halfa with a total capacity of 5,000 million cubic meters of water.
The Egyptian government dispatched the Second Archaeological
Survey to the rescue of the threatened antiquities of Nubia, including the priceless treasures of Ballana and Qustol, of which I
will write later.

Today, with a greatly increased population, Egypt can no longer
feed herself, and apart from her need for more food-producing
land, she must turn to industrial production, and with this comes
the demand for power. Only the Nile can satisfy these demands,
so that now one of the world's biggest engineering projects has been
undertaken: the construction of a new dam of gigantic size across
the river at a point some four miles upstream of the original dam.
Known as the High Dam (Sadd el Aali) its purpose is the total
utilization of the Nile waters so that "not a drop of the river will
be lost in the sea." This gigantic structure will be 225 ft. high and
will be more than 3 miles in length (Figure 3). The reservoir behind it will be 300 miles long with a surface area of 1,150 square
miles, holding at its maximum filling nearly 130,000 million cubic
meters of water. It is expected that the High Dam will increase
the arable land surface in Egypt by nearly one half and that even
in sacrificed Nubia new fertile areas will ultimately be created by
the deposits of silt and by the absorption into the atmosphere of
many million cubic meters of water by the intense heat during the
summer months. In addition to this, the water evacuated by the
dam during flood periods will service turbines which will have an
estimated total capacity of two million horsepower and an annual
production of between 10,000 to 12,000 million kilowatt hours a
year. Thus the potential benefits of the undertaking are enormous,
18   and cannot possibly be sacrificed in the interests of historical and

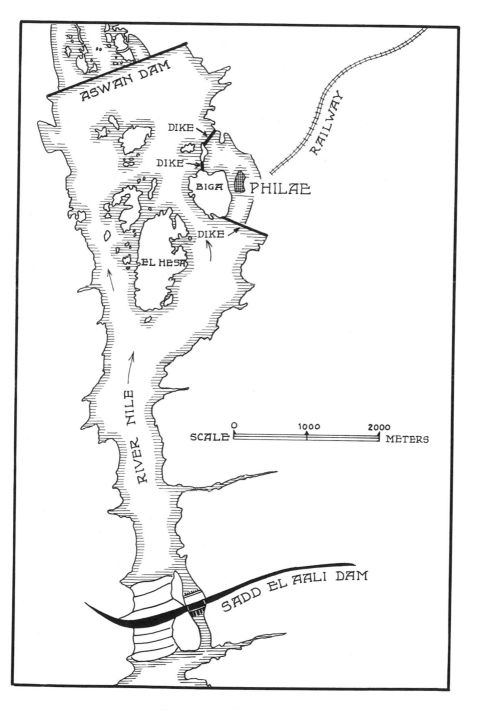

FIGURE 3   The area of Philae and the High Dam

artistic treasures, no matter how valuable. This hard and unpalatable fact is recognized by the archaeologist, but at the same time he also sees his own responsibilities in saving for future generations what he can from the inevitable destruction that must follow the realization of this great project.

The gigantic task of evolving practical schemes to preserve the temples of Abu Simbel and Philae, the dismantling and re-erection of other temples, the recording of their inscribed walls, and, above all, the excavation of hitherto unexplored sites, particularly in Upper Nubia, was beyond the resources, financial and technical, of both Egypt and the Sudan. This being so, the governments of both nations formally appealed to UNESCO for international aid to preserve what are not only their own national treasures but a heritage for all mankind. This appeal was accepted by UNESCO, and at the inauguration of the "International Campaign to save the Monuments of Nubia," which was held in Paris on March 8, 1960, the then director general, M. Vittorino Veronese, said:

> Work has begun on the great Aswan Dam. Within five years, the Middle Valley of the Nile will be turned into a vast lake. Wondrous structures, ranking among the most magnificent on earth, are in danger of disappearing beneath the waters. The dam will bring fertility to huge stretches of desert; but the opening up of new fields to the tractors, the provision of new sources of power to future factories threatens to exact a terrible price.
>
> True, when the welfare of suffering human beings is at stake, then, if need be, images of granite and porphyry must be sacrificed unhesitatingly. But no one forced to make such a choice could contemplate without anguish the necessity for making it. It is not easy to choose between a heritage of the past and the present well-being of a people, living in need in the shadow of one of history's most splendid legacies; it is not easy to choose between temples and crops. I would be sorry for any man called on to make that choice who could do so without a feeling of despair; I would be sorry for any man who, whatever decision he might reach, could bear the responsibility for that decision without a feeling of remorse.

It is not surprising, therefore, that the governments of the United Arab Republic and Sudan have called on an international body, on UNESCO, to try to save the threatened monuments. These monuments, the loss of which may be tragically near, do not belong solely to the countries who hold them on trust. The whole world has the right to see them endure. They are part of a common heritage which comprises Socrates' message and the Ajanta frescoes, the walls of Uxmal and Beethoven's symphonies. Treasures of universal value are entitled to universal protection. When a thing of beauty whose loveliness increases rather than diminishes by being shared, is lost, then all men alike are the losers.

Moreover, it is not merely a question of preserving something which may otherwise be lost; it is a question of bringing to light an as yet undiscovered wealth for the benefit of all. In return for the help the world gives them, the governments of Cairo and Khartoum will open the whole of their countries to archaeological excavation and will allow half of whatever works of art may be unearthed by science or by hazard to go to foreign museums. They will even agree to the transport, stone by stone, of certain monuments of Nubia. A new era of magnificent enrichment is thus opened in the field of Egyptology. Instead of a world deprived of a part of its wonders, mankind may hope for the revelation of hitherto unknown marvels.

So noble a cause deserves a no less generous response. It is, therefore, with every confidence that I invite governments, institutions, public or private foundations and men of goodwill everywhere to contribute to the success of a task without parallel in history. Service, equipment and money, all are needed. There are innumerable ways in which all can help. It is fitting that from a land which throughout the centuries has been the scene of—or the stake in—so many covetous disputes should spring a convincing proof of international solidarity.

"Egypt is a gift of the Nile"; for countless students this was the first Greek phrase which they learnt to translate. May the peoples of the world unite to ensure that the Nile, in becoming a greater source of fertility and power does not bury beneath its waters marvels which we of today have inherited from generations long since vanished.

The reference by the Director General of UNESCO to a new era in the field of Egyptology, coupled with the announcements from both Cairo and Khartoum that the excavator would be entitled to a half share of the results of his work, did not fall on deaf ears, and the response to the appeal was very encouraging. It may seem rather sad that such a response is apparently only forthcoming because of a promised reward, but such is not really the case, as a study of the economics of archaeological research will show. Before the sensational discovery of the tomb of Tutankhamen in 1921 the antiquities law in Egypt provided that the excavator should receive a half share of the objects discovered. This was a vitally important condition in the organization of many foreign missions intending to conduct an extensive campaign of exploration and excavation, for they depended to a considerable extent on subscriptions from the governing bodies of museums and similar institutions who wished to add to their collections of Egyptian antiquities. In fact, foreign museums even organized and dispatched their own expeditions to the Nile Valley with the twofold objective of promoting archaeological and historical knowledge and of gaining additional material for their collections.

One of the most important and most productive excavations in Egypt was started by two officials of a great museum returning from a purchasing tour and persuading their board of trustees that their collections would be more greatly enriched by the products of scientific excavation than by purchase from dealers in antiquities. They pointed out that the value of the finer objects of ancient art was enhanced by the knowledge of their origin, use, and proved authentic date; data not usually forthcoming if they had been brought to light as the result of illegal tomb-plundering by dealers' agents.

Moreover, Egyptologists throughout the world realized that archaeological evidence was year by year being destroyed by the depredations of dealers' agents, who, in ransacking the tombs and other ancient sites, destroyed priceless scientific material. Thus the collector came to depend more on the archaeologist than on the dealer, with the result that ample funds were available for scientific research in the field, and the museums of the world were yearly enriched by the results of widespread excavation in Egypt. But as a result of the hysteria which followed the discovery of the tomb of Tutankhamen, and influenced by the example of several other Mediterranean countries, the Egyptian government of that time revised the antiquities law so that the excavator was no longer entitled to any of his finds and all the antiquities found by him, at his expense, belonged to the state. It is true that in the early years of the new law the excavator was in many cases treated generously, and many duplicate objects were given to him on an *ex gratia* basis. But gradually, perhaps through press criticism and other factors, the conditions were made too onerous and foreign museums found it impossible to give large financial support toward the cost of the excavations of scientific societies and organizations. By degrees, the number of foreign archaeological expeditions in the Nile Valley became fewer, and Egyptology, as far as field work is concerned, declined.

It is true that some foreign archaeological organizations, such as the British Egypt Exploration Society, continued their work of research in the field, but this was only accomplished with great difficulty and many projects had to be abandoned because of limited funds. And the irony of it was that the storerooms in the basement of the great museum at Cairo and big warehouses on the sites of excavations such as those at Sakkara were crammed with duplicate objects, unworthy of a place in the collections of Cairo, but which would have been of great value in foreign museums, where they would have assisted the student in his research and have borne witness to the general public of the greatness and splendor of ancient Egypt.

However, coincident with their appeal to UNESCO, the Egyptian government restored the older ruling that the excavator shall receive half of the objects discovered and he can consequently expect financial assistance from museums. This new and enlightened policy applied not only to foreign excavations in the threatened areas of Nubia but will also be the rule in Egypt itself. In the Sudan the half-and-half law has always applied, so that now there is every inducement for the Egyptologist to return to active field research in both lands of the Nile.

Of recent years, with the growth of nationalism, there has been a tendency among many nations to consider their past as something exclusively their own, and to ignore the fact that although they may indeed be its legal custodians, it is in reality the heritage of all mankind. Through the UNESCO appeal this fact is at last being recognized and a great international effort is gaining impetus on a scale which would never have been dreamed of only few short years ago. So on this score, at least, the death of ancient Nubia will not have been entirely in vain.

2 EXPLORATION

I

The First Archaeological Survey

BEFORE the building of the original Aswan Dam in 1898 Nubia had received scant attention from the archaeologist. This was because, only a short time before, large parts of the country had been the battleground of the Mahdi's army and the British and Egyptian forces, and because then, as now, Egypt offered to the excavator the possibility of more spectacular discoveries and far richer rewards in objects for private collections and museums. In those days the antiquarian and not the archaeological viewpoint was still paramount, and it must be admitted that many excavations were conducted with the primary objective of the discovery of *objets d'art.* Therefore Nubia, with its unknown history, held little attraction for the explorer, and although its great temples were visited and admired, its poverty-stricken cemeteries and ruined town sites, so rich in the secrets of the past, were ignored.

The situation was transformed by the building of the Aswan Dam and the announcement that the foundations of Philae and other temples would be flooded by the waters of the new reservoir, which caused widespread alarm in artistic and scientific circles in Europe and America. Protests against the supposed vandalism were published in letters to the press and from the lecture platform, and although a good deal of this public outcry was little more than mass hysteria it served a good purpose as far as archaeology was concerned. The main interest was centered on the need for preserving the temples. The Ministry of Public Works sent teams of engineers to strengthen the foundations of the temples, particularly Philae, where extensive excavations were also carried out in the surrounding areas. This was particularly necessary because most of the buildings that formed a small town on the sacred island were of mud brick, which obviously would not survive even the light seepage resulting from the preliminary filling of the reservoir. The work of excavation was adequately done, but the publication of the results left much to be desired, being little more than a ground plan of the houses and streets, with little architectural detail and no real record of the pottery and objects found. Consequently much valuable historical information was lost. But the lesson was learned and all subsequent work of this nature in Nubia was placed in the hands of trained archaeologists, and not left to engineers and surveyors whose interest in such work was casual, to say the least. However, the work of consolidation on the island of Philae was thorough, and the stone structures were made so secure that they survive to this day after being alternately submerged and exposed for more than sixty years. It was inevitable that the temple reliefs and painted ceilings, and so on, should suffer damage, but we must be thankful that so much has survived to make it possible for us to give Philae rebirth, so that once again the "Pearl of Egypt" will be seen by future generations in its original setting. The map of Philae on page 29 (Figure 4), based on the original plan made by Captain H. G. Lyons, R.E., in 1893, shows the maze of mud-brick houses, churches, and other buildings excavated at that time and of which we have little or no record. All were destroyed by the water of the reservoir when the Aswan Dam was built, and with them went archaeological evidence of vital importance to the student of Nubia's later history, when the pagan Blemyes and Nobatae came to worship the goddess Isis and to take her statue on its annual visit to their countries in the south. The stone structures on the island remain, but the loss of information which must have existed within the humble brick buildings is, I think, one of the major tragedies in the long record of archaeological research. However, the disaster was confined to Philae, and the districts adjacent to it, for the water level of the reservoir behind the original Aswan Dam fortunately did not reach a very high level, so that valuable sites a few miles south of it still remained safe.

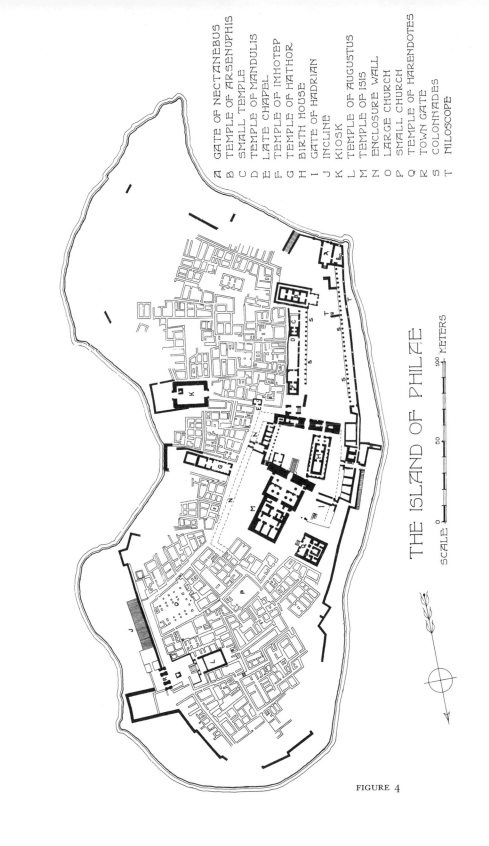

A GATE OF NECTANEBUS
B TEMPLE OF ARSENUPHIS
C SMALL TEMPLE
D TEMPLE OF MANDULIS
E LATE CHAPEL
F TEMPLE OF IMHOTEP
G TEMPLE OF HATHOR
H BIRTH HOUSE
I GATE OF HADRIAN
J INCLINE
K KIOSK
L TEMPLE OF AUGUSTUS
M TEMPLE OF ISIS
N ENCLOSURE WALL
O LARGE CHURCH
P SMALL CHURCH
Q TEMPLE OF HARENDOTES
R TOWN GATE
S COLONNADES
T NILOSCOPE

THE ISLAND OF PHILÆ

SCALE 0   50   100 METERS

FIGURE 4

The publicity and rather hysterical outcry against the supposed destruction of the "Pearl of Egypt" directed the attention of Egyptologists toward Nubia, particularly as, following the success of this great irrigation project, engineers and other experts were soon talking of the necessity of raising the height of the dam and thus enlarging the size of the reservoir. As the months went by, the threat to Nubia's antiquities became more and more obvious, and with this in mind Maspero, then director general of the Egyptian Antiquities Service, visited Nubia in the winter of 1904–1905 and personally inspected the monuments, which he found in a very neglected condition. On his return he instructed Arthur Weigall, who had been recently appointed Chief Inspector of Antiquities for Upper Egypt, to make a short inspection of the antiquities of Nubia as far south as Abu Simbel. By the time Weigall had prepared his preliminary report to the director general the raising of the Aswan Dam had been decided upon. The water level of the reservoir, which would be raised to the level of 113 meters above sea level, would destroy many ancient sites between the First Cataract and Wadi es Sebua. Consequently Weigall was sent back to Nubia in 1906 with instructions to prepare a more detailed report and to make an estimate of the cost of the conservation of existing monuments and of the excavation of sites that he might locate from surface observation. Trained by Petrie, Weigall was at that time considered to be one of the more brilliant of the younger generation of Egyptologists, and his survey of Nubia, published in 1907 under the title *A Report on the Antiquities of Lower Nubia,* amply confirmed the high opinion that his superiors had of him. Using a dahabeah on the Nile as his base, he walked almost the whole length of Lower Nubia, and from surface observation alone he located numerous important sites; in many cases he was able to estimate their chronological position in Nubia's history. Weigall's book was of inestimable value to me twenty-two years later when I directed the Second Archaeological Survey, and even now, fifty-five years after its publication, it remains an essential item in the equipment of an archaeological expedition working in Lower Nubia.

30   With the Egyptian government's final decision to raise the height

of the Aswan Dam the Ministry of Public Works organized the
First Archaeological Survey of Nubia in 1907. There were some
curious features in the launching of this project. First, the name
suggested that its purpose was to survey and mark down ancient
sites for future examination; whereas its true function was to excavate and record in detail every vestige of ancient civilization
that could be traced in the threatened areas behind the dam. This
was what was actually done, and I only mention the point as an
example of how the wrong title of a project can mislead people.
For, when the whole question of the preservation of Nubia's antiquities was revived with the proposed building of the High Dam,
I found that many archaeologists were ignorant of the fact that
the lower levels on each side of the Nile in Lower Nubia had already been exhaustively examined, and that the "survey" had been
carried further than its name implied. The second curious feature
was that the project was not handed over to the Antiquities Service,
as was the case with the Second Archaeological Survey in 1929,
but remained entirely under the control, financial and otherwise,
of the Ministry of Public Works. This arrangement, motivated perhaps by some personal or political reasons, still causes some in-
convenience to the modern archaeologist, who, wishing to obtain
the publications of the first survey, will not find them for sale
among the innumerable works of the Antiquities Service. As it is,
these valuable green-backed books are becoming increasingly difficult to obtain. Although the excavations in Nubia were not controlled by the Antiquities Service, they nevertheless sent missions,
independent of the Ministry of Public Works, to consolidate and
record the existing monuments; of this important work I will write
later.

The organization of the Archaeological Survey was placed in
the capable hands of H. G. Lyons (later Sir Henry Lyons), Director
General of the Survey Department, who wisely appointed the late
Dr. George Reisner as head of the mission to Nubia. Reisner, at
this time forty years of age, has been described as "the greatest
excavator and archaeologist the United States has ever produced
in any field" and certainly his work in Nubia alone shows that *31*

this tribute is not an exaggeration. Reisner outlined the purpose of the Archaeological Survey as follows:

> The Archaeological Survey of Lower Nubia has been undertaken (1) for the purpose of ascertaining the value and extent of the historical material buried under the soil, and (2) for the purpose of making this material available for the construction of the history of Nubia and its relations to Egypt. The questions on which it is hoped to throw light concern the successive races and racial mixtures, the extent of the population in different periods, the economical basis of the existence of these populations, the character of their industrial products and the source and degree of their civilization.

Reisner's organization of the method of excavation and recording in Nubia in order to fulfil this program was a masterpiece of careful planning, and in general is still used by field archaeologists working in this area of the Nile Valley at the present day.

He was indeed fortunate in having as assistants in the initial work, in what at that time was almost an unknown archaeological field, three young men of considerable ability: Cecil Firth, Aylward Blackman, and Oric Bates, all of whom were later to become great figures in the field of Egyptological research. Firth, an Englishman, at that time twenty-nine years of age, had been trained for the bar, but a visit to Egypt was sufficient to make him a keen student of Egyptology, when he received his preparatory training in field work from Sir Flinders Petrie. His greatest achievement, many years after the Nubian Survey, was his discovery of remarkable funerary buildings surrounding the pyramid of King Zoser at Sakkara. Blackman, also an Englishman, joined the Nubian Survey at the age of twenty-four, after a distinguished academic career at Oxford. He became an authority on the language and religion of ancient Egypt, and as Professor of Egyptology at the University of Liverpool he was recognized as a teacher of international reputation, ending his career as a Fellow of the British Academy. Oric Bates, an American, also twenty-four years of age when he joined

Reisner in Nubia, later became Curator of African Archaeology in the Peabody Museum at Harvard. His book *The Eastern Libyans* is still one of the most important works on this subject, so closely connected with the study of Egyptology.

It was, of course, realized that the work of the archaeologist in Nubia had to be supplemented by the studies and recording of the anthropologist. Here again the Egyptian government was singularly fortunate in its selection of the men who were to assist Reisner in this vital section of his work. The School of Medicine in Cairo had at that time on its academic staff an Australian, Grafton Elliot Smith, who held the Chair of Anatomy and who was already a recognized authority on the brain and the evolution of man, and was a Fellow of the Royal Society. Elliot Smith agreed to take over the direction of that portion of the work. Assisted at first by Dr. Wood Jones and later by Dr. Douglas Derry, no archaeological expedition then or since has had so much talent to call on for its study of the human remains uncovered during the excavation of the numerous burial grounds which were to be discovered. Douglas Derry was later to succeed Elliot Smith as Professor of Anatomy at Cairo, and during the years in which he held this post he became the greatest authority on mummification and the anatomical material from the tombs of ancient Egypt. Perhaps the highlight of his career was when he was entrusted with the examination of the mummy of King Tutankhamen in 1923.

These were the men who, under the able direction of George Reisner, laid the foundation of Nubian archaeology, both in its methods and practice and in the successful interpretation of the evidence gathered in the course of the excavations of 1907–1908. Although some of their conclusions have been modified, and even in some cases discarded, the basic result of their research, particularly with regard to the chronology and racial groups of Nubia, has remained unchanged today.

The first season of more than six months' duration in the winter of 1907–1908 must have been far more difficult than any of the succeeding ones because the concentration of ancient sites, towns, and cemeteries was, of course, far more numerous in the area just   *33* south of the First Cataract and adjacent to Philae. More than fifty cemeteries were exhaustively explored, and as these were located on both sides of the river and on the scattered islands of the cataract, the transfer of 190 native workmen from one site to another presented a problem in organization which only a man of Reisner's ability could have handled. Years after, when I was about to embark on the Second Archaeological Survey, Firth, who had been Reisner's chief assistant, described October and November 1907 as a nightmare, with the workmen's camp having to be moved every few days from place to place, and the dahabeahs which housed the staff of archaeologists and anthropologists sailing or being pulled from side to side of the Nile, or from island to island, always having to contend with a strong and erratic current. Remembering some of my own difficulties, which were of a minor character in comparison, I sometimes wonder how they managed to accomplish their task. The following extract from Reisner's day book will give some idea of the scattered activities of this, the first expedition to undertake detailed research in Nubia.

> January 30–31. All gangs on Cemetery 25.
>
> February 13. Five double gangs on east bank; cleared Cemeteries 20, 21 and 29. Six double gangs on west bank cleared Cemeteries 27, 28, 31, 32 and 33.
>
> February 3. Men's camp divided and moved to Birein for the east bank gang, and Khartum for the west bank gang.
>
> February 4–5. East bank gang examining all slopes between Khor Menat and Birein.
>
> February 4–11. West bank gang on Cemeteries 34, 35 and 36.
>
> February 6. Shifted our camp to Wadi Qamar, from which place Cemeteries 30–36 were recorded.
>
> February 6–10. East bank gang on Cemetery 30.
>
> February 10. East bank gang moved south to Siali, examining the ground as they went.

By March 29, 1908 the first season of the Archaeological Survey was finished and the members of the expedition returned to Cairo to analyze and prepare for publication the results of their researches. The whole of the area south of Shellal as far as Ginari had been covered, and cemeteries and settlements of almost every period of Nubian history discovered there, so that a sound foundation for all future research in this part of the Nile Valley had been laid.

With the opening of the second season of the Archaeological Survey on October 1, 1908, there were some changes in the staff of the expedition. Both Professor Elliot Smith and Dr. Wood Jones had other commitments in the anthropological field which forced their retirement, and Dr. Douglas Derry was thenceforth in complete charge of the research on the anatomical material. Reisner himself was compelled to spend the first part of the season in Cairo and for a long period the actual field work was directed by Cecil Firth. Although excavation revealed a considerable number of cemeteries of almost every period, the highlight of the expedition's discoveries was the excavating of the great brick fortress at Ikkur, which was the southernmost point reached by the survey when they closed down at the end of March 1909. The fortress of Ikkur had long been known, for in fact its immense walls could not be missed: its gigantic silhouette dominated the rather arid skyline on the west bank north of Dakka. Nevertheless, although it had been frequently visited by archaeologists, no detailed examination of the structure had ever been attempted. The excavations revealed the existence of two systems of fortification, both rectangular in plan. The inner and older system consisted of a narrow ditch into which protrude round bastions similar to those found at Kubban, Aneiba, and Buhen. The walls of the later structure were high and square, and probably originally had square towers built against their outer face like those of Buhen. Ikkur was the first of the big fortresses to be examined in detail, and, because of the lack of evidence gathered in later excavations, the excavators came to the erroneous conclusion that the older structure with its round bastions must have been built during the A-Group period of Nubian history, while the later building was the work of the Egyptian conquerors of the Twelfth Dynasty. However, excavations   *35* carried out in the Second Nubian Survey at Kubban showed that both structures were probably built during the Middle Kingdom: the first by Senusret I and the second by Senusret III.

The third season of the survey (1909–1910) was to find Cecil Firth in complete charge of both field work and publication, assisted by Oric Bates, for Reisner now had charge of the Palestinian Expedition of the Semitic Department of Harvard University. Elliot Smith had finally left Egypt to take the Chair of Anatomy at Manchester, and Douglas Derry had succeeded him at Cairo University, but still found time to handle the anatomical material from Nubia. The major part of the work of the Archaeological Survey during its third season (1909–1910) was concentrated in the area of Dakka, the ancient Pselchis which throughout history was one of the most thickly populated districts of the Upper Nile Valley. The great burial grounds were as usual largely a repetition of those excavated further north, but the examination of the areas on the west bank of the river north of the temple revealed most interesting material. A huge mass of Roman pottery, including numerous bowls of fine blue glaze, was found near the remains of a small brick building situated a short distance from the temple. It has been suggested that most of the pottery vessels were wine jars, and that the building was a canteen for the use of a military garrison which is known to have been located in the vicinity. Another possibility is that it was a custom house at which cargoes were disembarked.

Around the temple the foundations of an unfinished addition were located, and the remains of the temenos wall of the temple itself were discovered. But from an architectural point of view, the most interesting discovery was that of a fortified encampment housing the Roman garrison which protected the temple on its south and west sides. Evidence showed that this fort was occupied between A.D. 100 and 250; so it was probably built as part of the defense system of this important center against the Meroites and Blemyes in the troubled years before the frontier was withdrawn to the First Cataract by Diocletian in A.D. 297. Indeed, signs of fire on the brickwork and copper sheathing of the wooden door of the west gate suggest that at the end of its history the fort was stormed and carried.

The last season of the First Archaeological Survey (1910–1911) was carried out under considerable difficulty because, for various reasons, the staff had been reduced to Cecil Firth and one Egyptian assistant. How Firth, working virtually alone, succeeded in achieving the tremendous task of exploring both banks of the Nile between Dakka and Wadi es Sebua is indeed hard to understand, and it is no wonder that he was unable to publish the results of his work until 1927. He comments, somewhat dryly, in the preface of his book, that some modification of the original plan was unavoidable; but of this there is no sign in the detailed and final record of this great undertaking, in which, between 1907 and 1911, the whole of the area to be inundated, between Shellal and Wadi es Sebua, was exhaustively explored.

Although, throughout these four seasons of arduous and costly labor, no discovery of a sensational character was made, the sequence of the cultural history of Nubia was established, supported by the evidence of Egyptian intervention in its affairs, these in turn being influenced by events that took place in the northern Nile Valley. The sequence of these periods is shown in the chart on the following page.

While the work of excavation by the First Archaeological Survey was in progress under the direction of the Survey Department, the Antiquities Service had also been active in the threatened part of Nubia, and even in the areas farther to the south. After a general examination of the existing monuments Sir Gaston Maspero, the director general, organized a team of Egyptologists—the Frenchman Henri Gauthier, the German Gunther Roeder, and the Englishman Aylward Blackman—to plan and copy the inscriptions of the temples which were ultimately published in a series of magnificent volumes under the general title of *Les Temples immergés de la Nubie.* Blackman, who retired from the Archaeological Survey after its first season's work in 1909, was allocated the temples of Dendur, Derr, and Biga. He accomplished his task in the record time of five months, ending his work in the great heat of May 1910, and

NUBIA	EGYPT	B.C.
Early Predynastic	Early Predynastic (SD30–39)	*c.* 4000–3600
Middle Predynastic	Middle Predynastic (SD40–52)	*c.* 3600–3400
Late Predynastic	Late Predynastic (SD53–79)	*c.* 3400–3100
A-Group	Early Dynastic: Dyn. I–III	3100–2620
B-Group	Old Kingdom: Dyn. IV–VI	2620–2160
	1st Intermediate: Dyn. VII–XI	2160–1991
C-Group	Middle Kingdom: Dyn. XII	1991–1786
	2nd Intermediate: Dyn. XIII–XVII	1786–1575
D-Group	New Kingdom: Dyn. XVIII–XX	1575–1087
The Gap (Napatan)	Late Period: Dyn. XXI–XXX	1087–343

NUBIA	EGYPT	B.C. A.D.
Meroitic-Ptolemaic	Ptolemaic-Ptolemaic Dynasty	332–30
Meroitic-X		
Group-Roman	Roman-Roman Province	30–324
X-Group-Byzantine	Byzantine-Roman Province	324–565

he published the results of his labors in three volumes: *The Temple of Dendur* (1911), *The Temple of Derr* (1913), and *The Temple of Bigeh* (1915). Gauthier published records of the temple of Kalabsha between 1911 and 1914, of the temple of Wadi es Sebua in 1912, and of the temple of Amada in 1913. The temples of Debod and Dakka were published between 1911 and 1913.

Egyptology owes a great debt to these scholars, who accomplished their task without the facilities and equipment which we have at our disposal today, and although it has been thought expedient to check and re-record some of the monuments on which they worked, this decision has only been made because, with the advance of knowledge and technology, some improvement in the recording of difficult texts may be achieved before these monuments are finally destroyed.

II

The Second Archaeological Survey

A<small>LTHOUGH</small> the new flood level of the reservoir behind the Aswan
Dam did not reach beyond Wadi es Sebua, many Egyptologists
had hoped that this, the first attempt at a systematic excavation
over a large area which had proved so successful, would be continued as far as the Second Cataract. But the fact that the area
south of Wadi es Sebua was safe from the rising waters of the Nile
was sufficient reason for the government in Cairo to refuse all further financial credits. Work on the Aswan Dam was finished, the
demands of archaeology must end too; so the work of the survey
closed in March 1911. It had revealed the value of Nubia's antiquities and had directed the attention of archaeological institutions, mostly foreign, to the historical value of this part of the Nile
Valley; with the result that further work, independent of government support, was undertaken in various localities.

But it was not only the archaeologists' attention which was directed to Nubia at the end of the survey; the dealers in antiquities
of Luxor realized that here was a valuable source of material for
their markets, busy at that time in meeting the ever-increasing
demands of museums, collectors, and tourists. Gangs of illicit diggers were dispatched to the south, where, in contrast to the position in Egypt, they could plunder with little interference from the
inspectors of the Antiquities Service. Adequate supervision of ancient sites situated in areas largely uninhabited was impossible, and,
although many dealers and their men were caught, most of them
escaped the law and were able to return to Luxor with valuable
material lost to history because it had no record. This is a lesson
that each new generation in the field of archaeology must learn:
the excavator must leave no part of his discovery unrecorded and

39

undug. By his discovery he has drawn the attention of the dealers to the area in which it was made, and if he leaves any part of it unexplored there are plenty of illicit diggers who will complete his work for him. I do not want to give the impression that all the area left unexplored by the First Survey was ravaged by illicit excavation; only certain districts that appeared to be specially inviting were plundered. The loss to science is unknown; it may have been negligible, but on the other hand vital evidence in connection with unknown features of Nubia's history may well have been lost, never to be recovered.

With the decision of the Egyptian government in 1929 to raise again the height of the Aswan Dam, which would result in the flooding of the rest of Lower Nubia as far as the Sudan frontier, the Antiquities Service was called upon to organize a second Archaeological Survey. At that time I was directing the Mond Excavations of the University of Liverpool at Luxor and Armant, where, on the latter site, we had discovered the tombs of the sacred bulls in a series of catacombs similar to the well-known Serapeum at Sakkara. This discovery was more than the resources of our expedition could cope with; in consequence it had been taken over by the Egypt Exploration Society and they appointed me as adviser to the late Dr. H. Frankfort, who was their field director. In 1929 Frankfort retired, and the Egypt Exploration Society asked me to take his place. As the original discoverer of the Bucheum, I was naturally very interested in the site and I looked forward to directing the progress of this work. However, before any decision could be made on this matter the Egyptian Antiquities Service offered me the post of Director of the Archaeological Survey of Nubia. After a short period of indecision, and with some trepidation, I said farewell to Armant and prepared for unknown Nubia, a part of the Nile Valley of which I had only book knowledge. This was also the case with the rest of my staff and with most of the 150 Egyptian workmen whom we took with us, so I was indeed fortunate in having Cecil Firth, who had directed a large part of

40   the first survey, to advise and generally act as godfather to the expedition. Firth was, at that time, deeply engaged on his important excavations at Sakkara; nevertheless, he never failed to interrupt his work to attend to our wants and answer my *cri de coeur,* which in the early days of our excavations not infrequently went forth.

I was also very fortunate in my staff who, although as inexperienced as myself, rapidly adjusted themselves to conditions in Nubia. L. P. Kirwan (now Director of the Royal Geographical Society) was appointed subdirector, and in addition I had the able assistance of Neguib Macramallah, Abdel Baki, and Abdel Moneim, who had just taken their diplomas at the University of Cairo. At the end of three years Macramallah had to leave us to take up other duties with the Antiquities Service, and he was replaced by Zaki Yusef Saad, who was with us when the great finds were made at Ballana and Qustol. The rest of the staff consisted of Dr. Ahmed Batrawi as anatomist, Mohammed Husni as surveyor, and Mohammed Hassenein as clerk of works. Another unofficial but very important member of the staff was my wife, who took complete charge of the commissariat, a job of considerable difficulty in the Nubia of thirty-odd years ago; even now Lower Nubia barely supplies enough food for its own sparse population, and its production was even more uncertain in those days. However, we were compensated for the poor quality and monotony of our diet by the comfort of our living quarters. Because all the areas which we were to explore, between Wadi es Sebua and the Sudan frontier were adjacent to the river, and because fairly rapid movement was essential, it was found necessary, as with the previous survey, to make our headquarters on two large sailing dahabeahs. These we hired, with all their equipment, from Thomas Cook & Son. The two vessels, called the *Zenit el Nil* and the *Thames,* gave adequate accommodation for all my staff, as well as space for drawing office, photographic dark room, and facilities for the cleaning and storage of antiquities. The following description of the *Zenit el Nil,* written when we were still living on her, will give some idea of the comfort that such vessels could provide for the exploring archaeologist (Figure 5).   *41*

She has a shallow, flat-bottomed hull of iron, measuring 112 ft. in length and 19 ft. in breadth. The main mast is situated near the prow, and a small mizzen mast right at the stern. The sails are of the lateen type, that on the foremast being 130 ft. in length and that on the mizzen 60 ft. In addition to her sails, the ship can be propelled in calm weather by great 30 ft. sweeps, which are worked from rowing pits in the foredeck. These rowing pits have lockers, etc., on each side of them which provide storage accommodation for the crew, who number in all fourteen men. The passenger accommodation occupies the after part of the vessel and consists of a large saloon, one big double cabin, four single cabins, two WCs, bathroom, servants' cabin and pantry. On each side of the entrance door to the passengers' quarters are two stairways leading to an upper deck. The galley is situated in front of the foremast and is thus entirely separated from the living quarters. Each cabin is equipped with running water, which is pumped up from the river, and passing through an elaborate filter system, is stored in tanks on the upper deck.

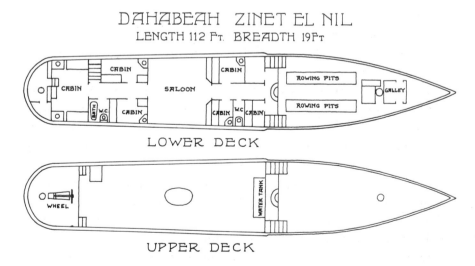

DAHABEAH ZINET EL NIL
LENGTH 112 Ft. BREADTH 19 Ft

LOWER DECK

UPPER DECK

FIGURE 5   A plan of our floating headquarters. See also Plate III

And so, early in October 1929, we set sail in these comfortable ships up the Nile on the Second Archaeological Survey to Wadi es Sebua, the limit of the previous survey which Firth had completed in 1911. With the two dahabeahs we had a number of smaller boats which included a motor launch for the use of the Surveyor and his assistants, and a *gyassa*, a cargo-carrying sailing boat for all the tentage and baggage of our workmen, who were to follow us on a river steamer which would then land them at the starting point of our work.

These men, most of them highly skilled in excavation, were all Egyptians, for there is no local labor available in Lower Nubia. In addition to the workers we had also to transport their bread, the main part of their food, and it is astonishing how much 150 men will eat in six months. This bread is made by the workmen's wives in Egypt, and after it has been dried in the sun until it is as hard as a brick it is packed in sacks for transport. As the consumer requires it, he soaks it in water to make it edible.

Finally, after many mistakes and what we considered miracles of organization on our part, we all arrived at Wadi es Sebua ready to start work. Three distinct seasons of excavation were planned for the six winter months of 1929, 1930, and 1931, in which it was considered possible to explore the whole of the remaining part of Lower Nubia as far south as the Sudan frontier at Adindan. Work of this description cannot usually be carried out during the summer because of the intense heat which sometimes reaches 120°F, and in any case a large part of the summer had to be spent at the museum in Cairo, cleaning and examining the discovered antiquities and preparing the material for publication. For the whole of this work, covering a period of three years, the Egyptian government gave us a grant of $165,000 out of which all expenses were to be defrayed, including the cost of publication. This seems a paltry sum in comparison with that being spent in the present campaign of excavation in Nubia, but the cost of everything was very different in those days, and though I had a certain amount of financial worry, the sum proved sufficient.

But to return to the start of our work. We were soon engaged   *43* on a large cemetery of both New Kingdom and Meroitic graves, the results of which gave us some encouragement badly needed at that time; for work on the Nubian Survey was very different from my previous experience in Egypt, where one could sit down on a site with no worries about the time factor. Here on the survey I had to make rapid decisions on how much of the site must be cleared in order to obtain the full scientific value from it; how long it would take to clear so many graves of each period; when to send out the exploring parties to find the next site; how long the photography and survey would take; and whether the party could catch up with us at the next location, and so on. To the beginner in work of this sort Nubia can be a nightmare, for all the time one's thought was "what I miss now will never be recovered, and I have so little time to make sure."

Fortunately, before we left Cairo, Cecil Firth gave us a few type-written sheets of what he called "The Nubian Body Snatchers' Vade Mecum," containing a detailed account of Reisner's method of recording during the First Nubian Survey. We, of course, fol-lowed this method, and I have found through long experience that, with certain modifications and additions, it is the only prac-tical way in which cemetery digging can be done when the expedi-tion is constantly on the move and no time is to be lost. At the request of UNESCO, at the commencement of the present cam-paign I submitted an outline of this procedure with the modifica-tions which we had found practical during 1929–1934. It may be of interest to some of my readers if I reproduce it here. To simplify the description I have taken as an example a cemetery of the Mid-dle C-Group; the same procedures, with the necessary variations, can be applied to cemeteries of other periods in Nubia.

RECORDING IN THE FIELD (Figure 6)

1. When the cemetery site is discovered the area is cleared down to the original ground level, disclosing the grave superstructure, if any, or the top of the grave pits. During this operation, notes will

be taken of stratification (a rare feature in the Nubian desert) and the position of pottery offerings outside the superstructures (a common feature in the C-group period).

2. Each grave or superstructure is numbered with the numerals painted in black on a flat stone.

3. General photographs are taken of the cemetery before any further excavation is undertaken.

4. Photographs are taken of individual superstructures with scale stick and number plainly visible.

5. The recorder then draws a plan and section on his tomb card to a scale of 1:25.

6. The recorder draws each offering pot on the tomb card to a scale of 1:5, noting the following points:

(a) Ware, slip, painted, or incised decorations, etc.

(b) Position of offering in relation to the superstructure.

7. The offering pots are marked (in chinagraph) as follows: 350 (Cemetery no.); 5 (Grave no.); 1 (Cat. no.) = 350/5—1.

8. The pottery is removed.

9. After all such surface recording is completed the workmen remove the superstructures, disclosing the mouths of the grave pits. The numbered stone marking each burial is placed at the top right-hand corner of the grave pit.

10. General photographs are taken of the cemetery when all the superstructures are removed.

11. The skilled workmen then clear the grave under the direct supervision of individual recorders, who note on the tomb card such details as type of filling, etc.

12. When the grave is cleared and its contents disclosed it is photographed with scale stick and number plainly showing.

13. The recorder draws the plan of the grave and the contents to a scale of 1:25, inserting it in relation to the superstructure already drawn on the tomb card.

14. The recorder removes the objects, one by one, but does not disturb the skeleton. As each object is removed he numbers it (with chinagraph) and marks his tomb card drawing with the same number, showing its position in the grave.

45

15. As each object is removed from the grave the recorder draws it to scale on the tomb card: pottery at 1:5, beads and smaller objects at 1:2 or 1:1.

16. When all objects are removed the skeleton is examined, and general information, such as sex, age, etc., marked on the tomb card. The skull is removed for measurement, and if it or other

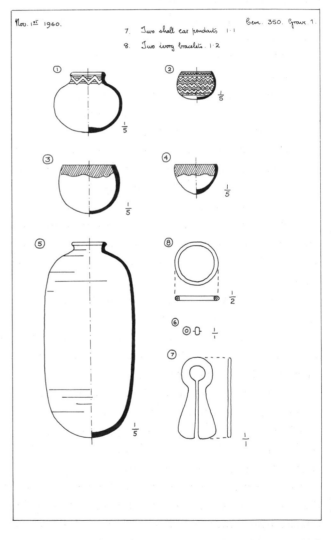

46

FIGURE 6

parts of the skeleton show features of anatomical importance they are preserved. Otherwise they are left.

Note: Information of anatomical detail is not recorded on the tomb card, only sex, age, and general observations.

17. After the removal of the skeleton, and any remaining objects which may be found below it, the sand deposit is sieved.

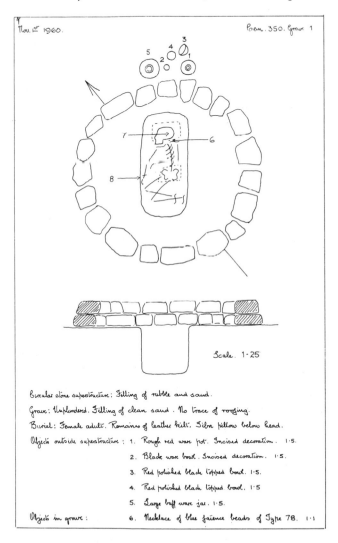

Nov. 2ᵈ 1960.

Prem. 350. Grave 1

Scale. 1·25

Circular stone superstructure: Filling of rubble and sand.

Grave: Unplundered. Filling of clean sand. No trace of roofing.

Burial: Female adult. Remains of leather kilt. Silex pillow below head.

Objects outside superstructure : 1. Rough red ware pot. Incised decoration. 1·5.

2. Black ware bowl. Incised decoration. 1·5.

3. Red polished black topped bowl. 1·5.

4. Red polished black topped bowl. 1·5

5. Large buff ware jar. 1·5.

Objects in grave : 6. Necklace of blue faience beads of Type 78. 1·1

Examples of tomb record cards

18. The orientation of the grave is taken by compass and the plan on the tomb card is marked by a large arrow drawn straight through it.

19. When all graves have been recorded the surveyor makes a map of the position of each number stone which has been placed at the top right-hand corner of each grave.

20. When this work is completed he will present a map, on tracing paper *or* linen (Scale 1:25), consisting of numbered dots. Then, placing each individual tomb card plan under its corresponding number, the card can be twisted to its correct orientation and the plan traced on to the map. Only the tomb plan and the skeleton are shown on this general map of the cemetery.

RECORDING AT THE BASE CAMP

The four essential records which must be kept on a day-to-day basis are:

1. The diary, which must be written up at the end of each day of excavation by the director. For this purpose each member of the expedition will give him the tomb cards and field notes that he has made during the day. From this material he will compile a short account of the progress of the work, and his observations and conclusions.

2. Pottery register (in duplicate), with each pot typed according to the Corpus. A Corpus is already in existence from the previous Archaeological Survey (1929–1934) and it is the duty of the archaeologist in charge of this section to keep it up to date by adding any new type which may occur. The pottery of the Corpus is drawn to a scale of 1:5.

3. Object register (in duplicate). With this is included a bead Corpus, which again can be based on the existing Corpus of the Archaeological Survey of 1929–1934.

4. Photograph register and the attachment of the relevant photographs (when printed) to the back of the tomb cards.

Following this method of recording, our expedition moved slowly south, excavating every ancient site we discovered on both banks of the river which were below the projected water line of the enlarged reservoir. Time was such an important factor that we were compelled to follow to a large extent the strict instructions we had been given to leave undisturbed all ancient sites on the higher ground not threatened by the new flood level. Fortunately, most of the ancient remains were situated in the threatened area close to the river's edge and we were able to excavate them with a clear conscience; but there were others that we felt compelled to investigate which were, I must confess, beyond our charter. However, there were some for which no excuse could be found and these we had to pass by with only a cursory examination; such a one was the big necropolis of Kasr Ibrim, a tragedy of which I will write later. (See p. 119.)

Cemeteries and settlements of almost every period of Nubian history were discovered, ranging in date from about 3500 B.C. to A.D. 500, but the results, although producing much museum material, yielded comparatively few additions to our knowledge and were largely a repetition of the results obtained by Reisner and Firth farther north. We had been encouraged in the belief that a large part of our second season's work would be concentrated on the district of Aneiba, the site of ancient Ma'am, which was the capital of Nubia during the New Kingdom. Here was the seat of the Egyptian viceroys, and here we knew were the remains of a great fortress town. However, we were to be disappointed in this, because just before we reached the frontiers of this important area I received instructions from Cairo that we were to bypass the whole district, as it was to be reserved for the German Archaeological Institute so that they could continue the work of Ernst Sieglin, who had held this concession in 1912–1914. We were bitterly disappointed at the time, but, looking back, I realize that this was a wise decision, for our German colleagues had both the equipment and, above all, the time, which was not at our disposal; for work on such a site demanded the concentrated attention of a   *49* stationary expedition. Above all, this work was placed under the direction of Dr. Georg Steindorff, a veteran in the Nubian field, and one of the greatest Egyptologists of his generation.

Disappointed as we were, we received some compensation, for Firth asked me to reopen our second season in the autumn of 1930 by excavating the fortress of Kubban, which during the First Archaeological Survey had been bypassed because it was above the water-level of that time. Now it would be submerged and its great mud-brick walls destroyed in a few weeks. Nearly two months were spent in the excavation of this gigantic structure, which in ancient times was called Bakit and formed a unit with a contemporary fortress at Ikkur, on the opposite side of the Nile, which had been excavated by Firth in 1910.

The complete excavation of Kubban resulted in the discovery of an earlier fortress beneath the foundations of the main structure of exactly the same design as that found by Firth at Ikkur, which he believed to be of Old Kingdom date. However, evidence revealed by our excavations showed that this earlier building was not earlier than the beginning of Egyptian colonization in the Twelfth Dynasty under Senusret I, and that the later fortress was probably built not many years afterward when the Egyptian power expanded in the south under Senusret III.

The fortress of Kubban was notable for the extraordinary state of preservation of the barrack buildings, with the enclosure of its great defense walls which were still standing to a height of 8 meters. Beneath great mounds of rubble we found many of the interior buildings with their original brick-vaulted roofing intact, while others even had their upper stories intact. To walk up stairways and to stand on the upper flooring of buildings constructed more than 3,800 years ago was an unforgettable experience, curiously different from, and in some ways more thrilling than, entering the sealed entrance of a tomb of perhaps a greater age. In some ways it was like entering an empty house only recently vacated, particularly when one stood before a small fireplace still containing the remains of charcoal and burnt wood.

I think that Kubban was certainly the highlight of our discoveries during the first two seasons of the survey, and we left the site with some regret on December 28, 1930, to continue the seemingly endless series of plundered cemeteries south of Aneiba, reaching Abu Simbel on March 14, 1931. Here we closed down, with the prospect of one more rather dull season ahead of us when we would complete our project with the exploration of the remaining areas north of Adindan. Little did we anticipate then that three more years were to be spent in Nubia in excavating tombs of the X-Group kings, which we were to discover at the start of our next season at Ballana and Qustol.

Independently of the Archaeological Survey, the Antiquities Service sent the Italian Professor Monneret de Villard to study and record the Christian antiquities of Nubia, on which he was a recognized authority of international repute. Curiously enough, he was not given facilities for actual excavation and he had to content himself with the planning and general recording of churches and other sites as he found them, partly buried. Even so, he was able to publish a splendid record of these remains which up to date must be considered the most important work yet done on the Christian period in Nubia. But, through the lack of systematic excavation, Monneret de Villard's recording was of necessity incomplete, and much research remains to be carried out on the monuments of this, one of the most interesting periods of Nubia's history.

III

Ballana and Qustol

It is usually difficult to recapture the thrill and excitement of an experience after an interval of thirty years, but as unforeseen circumstances have brought me back to Nubia I find little difficulty in reliving the exciting days of the discovery of the tombs of the X-Group kings at Ballana and Qustol. There is perhaps a form of inverted snobbery among archaeologists that encourages them to decry the thrills which the layman believes we must get if we are fortunate enough to discover objects of gold and silver and precious stones. Certainly it is true that frequently we find more interest in unearthing new facts from humble objects such as pottery and town rubbish, which build up the history of nations long dead and forgotten, than in finding material of great intrinsic value that tells us little or nothing. But when the archaeologist finds, as we did at Ballana and Qustol, a great treasure, together with other material which revealed the culture and religious customs of an unknown people, the thrill is complete and the experience never likely to be forgotten.

The discovery came as something in the nature of a great compensation, for the results of our previous two seasons' exploration in the area between Wadi es Sebua and Abu Simbel had revealed little that was new or of great scientific importance. Our previous work had achieved little beyond confirming the conclusions reached by our predecessors of the first Archaeological Survey, and here at the beginning of our final season's excavations, within a few miles of the southern limit of the threatened area, we saw little prospect of our research adding much to Nubia's long and varied history. Nevertheless, the record had to be made complete and we arrived at Abu Simbel, to start what we then thought was to be our last season's work, on November 2, 1931.

We had arrived, as usual, on our two dahabeahs accompanied by a survey launch, and we moored our ships just south of the great temple of Rameses II to await the arrival of our 150 workmen who were being brought up the Nile from Shellal on a Sudan government steamer. While waiting for the arrival of the workmen I decided to occupy our time with exploring the area on the west side of the river, south of Abu Simbel. This district, known as Ballana, was then very sparsely populated and the village itself consisted of a few rather poor houses scattered among scanty palm groves on the river's edge. The surrounding desert was covered with blown sand and with scrub relieved only by small groups of sunt trees and tamarisks eking out a precarious existence on the river bank. Not a very inviting part of the country—but today Ballana is a large and prosperous village of well-built houses surrounded by large areas of fertile ground under cultivation. This great change in the fortunes of Ballana came as a direct result of our discovery, as I shall explain later. (See page 89.)

Following our usual practice of exploration we picked our way in extended formation among the dunes and scrub of this rather unattractive country looking for an indication of ancient remains. I myself was exploring the area nearest the river and wandering about in the area just south of the village, and I soon came within sight of a confused jumble of small hills partly covered in scrub. As I approached nearer to them, they took on a more circular and regular form, but it was not until I had climbed to the top of one of them, in order to get a better view of the surrounding desert, that I appreciated the regularity of their shape and considered the possibility of their being man-made tumuli.

In this age, when the archaeologist is assisted by air photography, the artificial character of the Ballana mounds would have at once been apparent; but viewing them, as we did, from a very broken and uneven ground level, this was by no means obvious. In fact a geological expedition which had preceded us two years before had pronounced the mounds to be natural deposits of river *53* silt, blown and weathered to their circular formations. It is perhaps fortunate that at that time I was ignorant of their verdict, which, had I known it, might have influenced me toward an acceptance of their views and caused me to ignore the mounds as potential subjects for archaeological research. As it was, being ignorant of what curious forms wind and weather can create, the mound on which I sat appeared to me to be decidedly artificial and man-made, and a view of the others from this more elevated position confirmed me in my opinion. If I had any lingering doubts of the value of my judgment these were soon dispelled by the arrival of Kirwan, who joined me on the top of the mound after exploring the desert side of the area. One look round from our elevated position and he immediately agreed that these were indeed man-made tumuli which must at all costs be investigated.

We returned that evening to our dahabeah at Abu Simbel with our minds full of the mystery of this unexpected discovery, for we had no prior knowledge of these great earthworks. On an archaeological expedition such as ours we were not in a position to bring with us a lot of reference books, and we had hitherto depended, with generally satisfactory results, on Weigall's published account of his preliminary exploration of Lower Nubia (*A Report on the Antiquities of Lower Nubia*) which he made on behalf of the Antiquities Service in 1906, prior to the launching of the first Archaeological Survey in 1907. We examined his valuable book, but were left even more puzzled by his statement that "To the archaeologist, the country here is uninteresting, and the writer found no traces of any ancient sites, except where a few Roman and mediaeval fragments of pottery indicated the existence of villages of that time." We could only conclude that Weigall, exhausted at the end of his long exploration, mostly on foot, did not look very hard, but I must admit that his flat denial of the existence of anything of archaeological importance in the area rather shook my confidence.

Had I but known it, written encouragement was lying almost at my elbow, for in our small library we had a copy of the Tauchnitz edition of Amelia Edwards' classic travel book *A Thousand Miles up the Nile,* which was an account by this very gifted woman of a journey she made on a dahabeah through Upper Egypt and Nubia in 1874. But I had read her book in my student days and had long forgotten her description of the country south of Abu Simbel, and it just did not occur to me that any relevant information might be obtained from this rather battered volume. It was only some years after the discovery that in rereading her book in an idle hour I was astounded to find the following account, which shows the almost uncanny insight she had into the archaeological value of the tumuli and of the objects we were later to find in them. "Some way beyond Kalat Adda," she wrote, "when the Abou Simbel range and the palm island have all but vanished in the distance, and the lonely peak called the Mountain of the Sun (Gebel esh-Shems) has been left far behind, we come upon a new wonder—namely, upon two groups of scattered tumuli, one on the eastern, one on the western bank. Not volcanic forms these; not even accidental forms, if one may venture to form an opinion from so far off. They are of various sizes: some little, some big; all perfectly round and smooth, and covered with a rich greenish-brown alluvial soil. How did they come there? Who made them? What did they contain? The Roman ruins close by—the 240,000 deserters who must have passed this way—the Egyptian and Ethiopian armies that certainly poured their thousands along these very banks, and might have fought many a battle on this open plain, suggest all kinds of possibilities, and fill one's head with visions of buried arms, and jewels, and cinerary urns. We are more than half-minded to stop the boat and land that very moment; but are content on second thought with promising ourselves that we will at least excavate one of the smaller hillocks on our way back." Miss Edwards never found the opportunity to investigate the tumuli, but her guess regarding their contents was, as you will see, not very wide of the mark.

Other travelers, such as Burckhardt in 1813 and Golenisheff in 1883, had noted the possibility of the mounds being artificial, but, as I say, at the time of our discovery of those on the west bank we were ignorant of this and had only Weigall's negative statement, which was by no means encouraging. However, after much *55* discussion we decided that the tumuli were certainly worthy of further investigation, and with the arrival of our workmen we moved the dahabeah nearer to Ballana.

At that time we had confined our attention entirely to the west bank of the river and were only aware of the existence of the tumuli at Ballana. Before we had time to organize test excavations at Ballana we were visited by a local guard of the Antiquities Service who told us that only two weeks before our arrival he had caught three of the local inhabitants digging some graves at Qustol on the opposite side of the river. Although not very much interested in what was obviously a minor case of illicit excavation, we crossed the Nile to inspect the scene of the crime. To our astonishment, we found that the tomb robbers had been plundering some small graves of the X-Group period which were situated in the flat ground between a series of earthern tumuli like those at Ballana. Unobscured by drift sand and scrub, their artificial character was apparent, and all remaining doubts we might have had with regard to the Ballana earthworks were finally dispelled. The only question now was: How were we to tackle the problem of their excavation and which group, Ballana or Qustol, should we investigate first?

My principal worry was financial, for 1931–1932 was the final year of the credit granted by the Ministry of Finance for the work of the Archaeological Survey of Nubia, and with this last allocation of $55,000 we had still to explore the area between Abu Simbel and the frontier, as well as the whole of the east bank of the Nile back to Wadi es Sebua. Moreover, time was also a factor to be taken into consideration, for, as I have already mentioned, we had been given a total period of three years for the completion of our work, by which time the heightening of the Aswan Dam was expected to be finished. No one, least of all ourselves, had contemplated the removal of vast earthworks of the character of the Ballana and Qustol tumuli. It was a gamble, for if, after the costly removal of part of one of the mounds, the results were barren, I knew we would receive little sympathy, particularly as most of the tumuli were above the areas threatened by the new reservoir.

56 However, Ballana and Qustol was the only occasion in my career

when I found myself very pleased to discover that ancient tomb robbers had been there before me. A preliminary examination of the base of one of the large Qustol mounds revealed the existence of a slight depression at ground level on its west side, and further exploration showed that this was a feature common to all of them. At first we thought that these depressions marked the true entrance to whatever was buried beneath, but a little scratching soon revealed scattered fragments of broken X-Group pottery and it was obvious that they marked the mouths of robbers' tunnels. Here was our opportunity to establish the character and value of the tumuli without great expenditure of time and money, and our workmen commenced the excavation of the entrance of the robbers' passage on Tomb 3, which was the largest of the Qustol group. Soon we were working our way along a level passage about 2 ft. wide and 3 ft. high, which had been roughly cut in the hard alluvium on which the tumulus was built. The work of clearance was difficult and sometimes a little dangerous, for in parts the sides of the passage had crumbled away, leaving a rather uncertain roof above us. However, with our highly skilled laborers we made good progress and after some hours the passage was open and we crawled down it for a distance of about 50 ft. to a point where it broke through a brick wall and we found ourselves in one of the vaulted chambers of a large subterranean structure.

The light of our flickering candles revealed a scene of almost indescribable confusion and it was obvious that our predecessors had done a very thorough job. The floor was covered with masses of broken pottery, moldering pieces of wood, and scattered human bones. Examination of the other rooms showed a similar state of affairs: masses of broken human bones and broken pottery. My first impression was that I must abandon all ideas of removing the tumuli and must content myself with examining these strange burial installations by entry from the robbers' passage and of rescuing what little archaeological evidence they had left us. It was all very discouraging, and sitting there amidst the scattered debris of what had once been an archaeological treasure I felt it also represented the debris of our hopes which had been slowly building up since *57* we had first seen the mounds of Ballana a few days before. But soon, having got over our initial disappointment, we started a more balanced and less excited appraisal of our discovery.

The room into which we had entered from the robbers' passage was certainly the burial chamber, and beyond it was the antechamber, on the east side of which was the door of the tomb. We had, as it were, entered this house of the dead by the back door and we faced the inner side of the front door, which was still closed. The doorway, with a heavy stone lintel, had been blocked with brick and part of this barrier had been removed by our predecessors under the impression that they would find more rooms behind it. But they must soon have realized their mistake when sand started to pour in through the opening they had made and it became obvious that behind the blocked door was an open space in front of the actual entrance of the tomb. This open space must be filled with sand and earth, and above it was, of course, the mass of the tumulus.

When this fact was appreciated I was faced once more with the difficult decision as to whether we should remove the tumulus or rest content with the information we could gain from a clearance of the interior of the tomb through the robbers' passage. The facts were plain: the tombs themselves were thoroughly plundered but the open area, which perhaps consisted of a forecourt and stairway, was certainly intact. Was the expenditure of time and labor in removing the tumulus justified, in the hope of finding objects and offerings at the entrance of the tomb? It was obvious that these tombs belonged to people of considerable importance and that these people might well have been the rulers of the mysterious X-Group, about whom we knew so little. Even though they had been plundered, exhaustive clearance of the tombs might well provide us with archaeological material of the utmost importance; but such a clearance would be difficult, working through the rather dangerous robbers' passages. Above all was the tantalizing thought that, by confining our attention to the plundered tombs, we might be leaving in the untouched entrance priceless material of artistic and historical value.

Finally we decided to take the risk, and on November 10, 1931, we commenced the removal of part of the west side of Tomb 2 in our search for the entrance. Tomb 2, although one of the larger tumuli in the Qustol group, was smaller than Tomb 3 and I felt that in the circumstances it presented a rather more reasonable proposition, in view of a very natural impatience to ascertain as soon as possible the value of what we knew would be the only untouched part of the burial structure.

The strength of our working party at that time did not exceed 150 men and boys and our progress seemed very slow. However, by the end of November we had completed a large V-shaped cut in the mound and on its east side were down to ground level. The head of a ramp sloping downward toward the west was soon revealed and we commenced the gradual descent to the entrance of the tomb. The first objects which came to light were two iron axheads, so perfectly preserved that they still retained the dark blue colour of iron that has just left the smith's anvil, and I must confess that had I found them in other circumstances I would never have guessed their antiquity. Our next find, at the head of the ramp, was a heavy metal object that at the time of its discovery completely puzzled us, and although we laughed at the suggestion we could think of no modern article it resembled more than police handcuffs! Whatever it was, it was, like the axheads, in mint condition and we took it back to the dahabeah in triumph, where it was soon cleaned by my wife. Polishing revealed that it was made of solid silver, but its true character was not recognized until we had found similar objects later in the course of our work. It was in reality a horse's bit which would have proved a brutal curb to the most fractious animal. The bit is composed of two separate parts in the form of a semicircular curve at one end and a straight rod at the other. The curved ends are hinged together at the top and thus form a circular hole through which the lower jaw of the animal is passed. The two straight rods are joined at the end by a wide ring to which are attached the reins, and side rings are placed for attachment to the cheekpieces of the headstall. One pull on the reins will bring the straight rods together and

59

close the circular mouthpiece right around the lower jaw of the horse.

However, as I say, at the time we had no idea of the purpose of this strange contraption, but the discovery next day of the skeleton of a horse from which the bit must have come showed us what it was. I cannot say which astonished us more: the revelation of the true purpose of this curious object or the horse itself, and it was not until we had descended farther down the ramp and uncovered more skeletons of horses, donkeys, and camels that we realized the significance of this jumble of animal remains. The owner of the tomb took his camels with him for service in the afterlife and as in life they would be kept waiting or stabled outside his residence. Soon we reached a small courtyard at the bottom of the ramp in front of the doorway of the tomb. Here we found the remains of what were obviously the favorite horses of the owner, for some of them had silver-mounted wooden saddles and silver trappings consisting of chains of flat or slightly convex disks from which were suspended drop pendants and disks. Although the silverwork was perfectly preserved, the woodwork of the saddles and their leather seats and aprons were much decayed; in fact, the leather was reduced to the consistency of burnt paper. So at the time of their discovery little could be done, after photography and drawing, except embedding them in paraffin wax for future examination. With the remains of the horses we found the skeletons of the grooms who were to attend to them in the next world. The animals had all been pole-axed, but we found no signs of violence on the human remains, and we can only conclude that they were drugged or poisoned before the entrance of the tomb was filled in.

With these discoveries we gained a fair appreciation of the value of our find. It was obvious that the exterior of the tombs would always be found intact as long as the tumulus above had not been removed, and it was almost certain that objects of a unique character would be found there. Furthermore, detailed examination of the plundered interior of the tomb showed us that valuable archaeological material had in many cases been overlooked by the plunderers. Here we found more evidence of human sacrifice, for the scattered bones of men and women were identified amid broken pottery vessels which had contained food and drink. As always in excavations of any period, the pottery gave us conclusive evidence of the identity of the people who had made these barbaric tombs. We were now quite certain that they were that mysterious race which we call the X-Group who occupied Nubia between the third and sixth centuries after Christ.

I was also certain that a great archaeological treasure lay within our grasp, but the magnitude of the task of removing thousands of tons of earth in order to obtain it was still a formidable problem. Time and money were needed, and I felt that more concrete evidence of the wealth and importance of the discovery must be obtained before I approached my superiors in the Antiquities Service in Cairo. So I decided that before sending back news of the find I would uncover the largest tomb in the Qustol group: No. 3, the interior of which we had cursorily examined through the robbers' passage in the initial stages of our investigations.

So, at the beginning of December, we started the removal of the east side of this great tumulus which measured 53.40 meters in diameter and 9.70 meters in height. At first, even with 150 men hard at work, our progress seemed slow, and we fully expected a very dull and unexciting time until we reached ground level and found the head of the entrance ramp. But the tumuli of Qustol had another surprise for us: this was the custom of the X-Group people of burying miscellaneous objects in the mound itself, rather like currants in a cake, or coins in a Christmas pudding. When we first found these objects we believed that they were just things that had been lost or forgotten by members of the work party who had raised the tumulus. But frequent recurrence of these finds showed that they were funerary offerings that had been deliberately buried after the burial had taken place. Our first find was a large circular shield of leather in a state of almost perfect preservation. Its resemblance to the shield still used by the Bega tribes in the Sudan at first made us almost doubtful of its antiquity, for it *61* was found very near the surface of the mound. It was elaborately decorated with embossed spiral patterns, and the only part which had decayed was the wooden hand grip at the back.

The next object that turned up in the debris of the tumulus was the iron blade of a spear of the "shovel" type usually associated with the Masai of Kenya. Here again the object was almost perfectly preserved, with only the faintest traces of rust; but of the wooden haft to which the blade had been attached nothing remained but a line of brown powder. Nearby was an iron spike butt; as this had been misplaced, however, the exact length of the weapon could not be ascertained. Our next find was a group of three domestic knives with hollow-ground blades of iron. Two of them had flat handles of horn and the third had a handle of ivory carved in the form of the ancient Egyptian god Bes. This was the first object of pharaonic character we had found in the excavations, and to me it seemed strange to meet with the conventional figures of old Egypt at a time when Christianity was perhaps 500 years old; for at this preliminary stage of our work we did not realize that we were digging up what I call the last chapter of the long record of ancient Egypt. In contrast to the Bes knife, we found nearby an ivory comb of almost Mongolian design, with a high rounded back decorated with floral designs in red and brown paint.

Our next example of offerings buried in the tumulus was found at its base almost on ground level, and was of an even more unusual and unexpected character than those already discovered. This was a wooden gaming board of a most unusual type in the form of a flat tray with a framed border with corner brackets of silver. The "places" were marked with ivory fretwork inlay and consisted of three rows of twelve squares, in conventional floral design. Each line of "places" was divided into a group of six by centerpieces, which in the top and bottom rows took the form of a half circle and in the middle a full circle. For carrying purposes the board has a silver handle attached to one side.

When we lifted the gaming board we found beneath it the remains of a leather bag which contained fifteen ivory and fifteen ebony pieces. With them were five ivory dice and the fragments of what appeared to be a small wooden box mounted with silver. The character of the dice was obvious, for they were marked in the same way as the modern variety, from one to six; but the fragments of the wooden box were indeed a puzzle and it was not until many months later, after much trial and error, that the pieces were fitted together in the laboratory of the Cairo Museum. It was foolish of us not to have realized at once that to play with dice one must have a dicebox, and here was a dicebox of a most strange design. Known as the pyrgus, it was largely used by gamesters of the Graeco-Roman world; its popularity no doubt being enhanced by the fact that with it, it is impossible to cheat. The contraption was not shaken at play; the dice were dropped through the open top, where they fell onto a series of grooved boards which turned them over before they were discharged through an opening at the bottom. As far as I am aware, this is the only specimen of a pyrgus that has yet been found, although its appearance and general design have been known from Roman pictures. Later, this ancient dicebox so interested friends in Cairo that we had a replica made which was presented to the Turf Club, where it was frequently used by members when they diced for drinks. However, its popularity waned, and after a time members returned to the use of the leather dicecup, so I reclaimed it and now have it as a souvenir of the first discovery at Qustol. All these objects—board, pieces, dice, and box—were undoubtedly used for one game, probably very similar to the so-called draughts of the Egyptians. The exact method of play is unknown, but I think it is probable that the dice were thrown to determine the moves on the board, as in the game of backgammon.

Although it appeared probable that more objects might be buried in other parts of the tumulus, as our V-shaped cut into its east side was down to ground level with the edges of the entrance ramp disclosed, I felt that further clearance was unnecessary and unjustified. It was a tantalizing thought that other fine objects might be lying only a few feet from us, buried in the debris of the mound, but such a search would entail the removal of the whole structure at a vast cost of time and money. We therefore concen-   *63* trated our whole attention on the excavation of the ramp which descended from east to west, as with Tomb 2. As we descended the ramp, we uncovered the skeletons of horses, camels, donkeys, dogs, and sheep. Some of the horses had silver-mounted saddles, silver chain trappings, and plaited leather bridles with bronze fittings, and across the saddles we found the remains of embroidered saddle cloths and blue-dyed sheepskins. The confusion of the remains of the sacrificed animals with their trappings and equipment, piled one on top of the other, was beyond description and might be said, without exaggeration, to be an archaeologist's nightmare. Adding to the confusion was the fact that the bodies of the animals had not been laid out after slaughter on the floor of the entrance ramp and courtyard, but had been left where they fell, probably plunging about before they expired; with the result that one body was found on top of another. Nothing of the tissue remained, and the difficulty of distinguishing one skeleton from another was immense. However, we had among our Gufti workmen some who had specialized in the cleaning of anatomical materials, and gradually the skeletons were cleaned of dust and debris so that the remains of each animal were so exposed that they could not be confused with each other. But the equipment of the horses was even more difficult to deal with, for although the leatherwork of the saddles was plainly visible when first exposed, it rapidly disintegrated, leaving only the congealed chopped straw, with which the seats were stuffed, exposed to view. Furthermore, the leather thongs which bound the wooden saddle frames together soon fell apart at the slightest touch. With a view to the ultimate reconstruction of the saddles, every detail of their manufacture had to be studied, and hours were spent in drawing and photography and in the application of boiling paraffin wax which we poured over them so that they could be removed in one piece—which usually consisted of a confused mass of wooden framework, straw stuffing, remains of leather, saddle cloth, earth and sand, welded together with paraffin wax. I must confess that the appearance of these precious objects when they were removed after such first-aid treatment was rather depressing; but later, when the wax was reheated and removed, it took with it all the congealed earth and sand, so that the wooden frames of the saddles were revealed in their entirety, although little of the leatherwork could be preserved. The removal of each individual animal skeleton was another arduous task, but fortunately the bones were well preserved and not fragile, so that chemical treatment was not necessary.

Working under these conditions, it was some time before the courtyard in front of the entrance to the tomb was revealed, but when it was we were delighted to find two perfectly preserved flagons, one of silver and the other of bronze, which had been left on the floor in front of the doorway. With them was another silver vessel of very strange design, so strange, in fact, that we thought at first that it represented a large fat pig. It was in a very bad condition, so that it had to be covered with paraffin wax before we dared to remove it. When it was cleaned its original design became apparent—it represented a water skin, with the neck forming a detachable lid and a ring handle attached to the four legs by chains.

At each end of the narrow courtyard were the blocked doors of two rock-cut rooms, and after the area in front of the tomb had been cleared we turned our attention to the door at the south end. The removal of the brick blocking was the work of only a few minutes and very soon we were able to enter the room, and by the light of flickering candles pick our way among the skeletons which covered the floor. Near the entrance was the skeleton of a man with an iron sword and curiously enough a barrel-shaped drum of wood. Behind him were the skeletons of six horses and at a first glance we could see that they had been adorned with jeweled silver bridles and trappings.

In our excitement at the discovery we had failed to note the precarious condition of the rock above the door, but it was soon brought to our attention when we heard the rumble of falling debris and turned around to see the entrance fill up with broken rubble and brickwork. It was a nasty moment, but workmen outside soon dug us out. However, it was an experience I am not likely to forget, sitting there in the semidarkness, with mixed feelings of elation at the discovery of a treasure and of a vague fear   *65* that I might be buried with it. Still, the scare was soon over and we turned our attention to the discovery.

It was obvious that these six horses were the favorite chargers of the owner of the tomb, and the sacrificed man buried with them must have been their groom. It is possible that the sword, which had no scabbard, was the weapon used in dispatching him, although no traces of sword cuts were apparent on the skeleton. For the presence of the drum I have simply no explanation, for a more incongruous object to find in such a charnel house would be difficult to imagine. The bridles on three of the horses were of a most elaborate type, composed of headstall, reins, and bit. The headstall was formed by heavy silver ribbon chains joined by medallions in the form of lions' heads, at points behind the ears, on the forehead, and in the middle of the nose. The medallions, of beaten silver, had eyes inlaid with lapis lazuli, and the protruding tongue was of carved ivory. The bits, made of solid silver, were of the same cruel type as the one found in Tomb 2, although a little more elaborate in their decoration. They were attached to the headstall by hinged brackets in the form of seated lions which were riveted on each side of the mouthpiece. The reins were made of silver rope chains measuring 78 cm. in length. The three bridles, which were identical in design, showed a perfection of craftsmanship which could not be bettered by silversmiths today and the puzzle of their origin is still unsolved. The general character of the X-Group remains does not suggest that they were a people with a high standard of culture, and, as I will explain later, we know that many of the finer objects found in their tombs were of Byzantine manufacture and had come into their hands as plunder of war or by barter in trade. We might be tempted to explain these beautiful bridles in this way, save for their design which does not suggest a European origin. Furthermore, the form of the bit is, as far as I am aware, unique and has not been found in Egypt or other parts of the East Roman Empire. I think it is much more probable that this magnificent horse harness was an heirloom inherited from ancient Meroe.

66   But these questions did not bother us at the time of the discovery;

we were too astonished at the remarkable state of their preservation, with the beautiful chainwork as flexible as if it had been made of soft leather. All six horses had bronze bells attached to their necks with tasseled cords, and some had necklaces of cowrie shells; but the most sensational find of the lot was the decayed remains of a horse collar of red leather, attached to which was a series of silver medallions set with precious stones. Five of the medallions were in the form of lions' heads with the eyes set with garnets, and the rest were open fretwork of silver, with large oval onyx set in the center. The largest of the medallions which was placed in the center of the collar had a frame set with garnets; beryls, and moonstones, which surrounded a large blue faïence Egyptian scarab held in place by a claw setting. Another medallion was set with a fine onyx cameo of a Roman emperor. This astonishing mixture of Byzantine jewelwork, ancient Egyptian scarab, and Roman cameo was a foretaste of the extraordinary mixed character of the treasures we were to discover later, when silver spoons, the same as those found in the great burial at Sutton Hoo in England, were found side by side with objects that belonged to the Saite period of pharaonic Egypt.

When the bridles and other objects had been removed the skeletons, both animal and human, were examined by our anatomist, Dr. Ahmed Batrawi, and later packed for transport to Cairo and further examination at the School of Anatomy. Then we turned our attention to the other sealed room at the north end of the courtyard in the expectation of more treasure; but in this we were a little disappointed, for although it contained two more horses, they were unadorned by bridles or trappings. With them were the skeletons of two men and fifty large dogs, many of which had small bronze bells suspended from their necks, and leashes of plaited hair. We can only suppose that these were a pack of hunting dogs and that the sacrificed men were their keepers, who went with them to continue their service in the afterlife.

With the clearance of this room, our examination of the outside ramp and courtyard was completed and we turned our attention to the tomb itself. It was formed by a series of six rooms built of   *67*

burnt brick and stone, with barrel-vaulted roofing. The whole structure was built within a large pit measuring 9.80 by 9.28 meters,
cut to a depth of 5.30 meters from the natural ground level. We
had, of course, during our preliminary examination already been
inside the tomb when we entered it from the robbers' passage, and
so we had no expectation of finding any part of it unplundered.
The entrance was situated in the center of the west wall of the
open courtyard and when we first cleared it we saw that it was
heavily blocked with bricks. These were removed and behind them
was the rectangular doorway with double lintels of roughly dressed
stone with a wide step of the same material. It had originally had
a heavy wooden door, reinforced by a series of circular bronze
plates fastened to its exterior side. But the woodwork had decayed
and the bronze plates had fallen in a jumbled mass onto the stone
step. Sufficient remained of the decayed woodwork of the door
with the bronze-plated hinges still in position to enable us to ascertain all the details of its original design and construction, but
we failed to get any evidence of the decorative design for which
the circular bronze plates must have been employed.

Just over the threshold of the tomb we found the scattered bones
of oxen which had probably been slaughtered and placed there as
food for the deceased. Entering the sepulcher, we found each of its
six rooms had been thoroughly ransacked by our predecessors, who
had left a confused mass of human bones, male and female, pottery
wine jars, cups, and bowls mixed up with the remains of leather
bags, fragments of decayed woodwork, and beads of blue, green,
and red faïence. Only one object of intrinsic value had been overlooked by the plunderers: a bronze hand lamp in the form of a
male human head, with the oil hole at the top of the forehead and
the burner at the base of the neck. The eyes were represented by
garnets set in silver.

After an exhaustive examination of this mass of wreckage, when
the pottery vessels were typed and catalogued and the anatomic
material studied by Dr. Batrawi, we decided to re-examine the
robbers' passage by which we had first entered the tomb. This was
68 because, from previous experience, we have found that in their

hurried work by poor lamplight, tomb robbers frequently dropped objects or parts of objects as they scrambled away from the scene of their sacrilege. In this case our precaution was justified, for in clearing away debris which had fallen on the floor of the passage we found part of a leather breastplate and a leather arrow quiver which had probably been part of the dress of the owner of the tomb. It was a common practice of ancient plunderers to drag the body of the owner out into the daylight so that it could be stripped of its jewelry with greater facility. This, I think, had been done in the present case, for leather garments and equipment would hardly be considered worthwhile plunder. However, we found no trace of the body, although a careful search was made in the sand and debris at the mouth of the passage. But at least even here we were rewarded for our trouble, for we found the remains of a circular casket of inlaid wood and ivory which had been broken up by the plunderers when they rifled it of its contents. Although only a part of it remained, and that in fragments, it was an interesting discovery, for it was possible to make a reconstruction of its original appearance and to appreciate the beauty of its design.

With the successful conclusion of our work on Tomb 3, I felt that the time had come to announce our discovery and I sent a short and fairly guarded report to the Department of Antiquities in Cairo. I say "guarded," for I knew the financial credits for the Archaeological Survey were running rather low and we were expected to finish our work at the end of that season. I knew that my superiors would not welcome demands on my part for more money and time, for it must be admitted that the present results of the survey were not particularly interesting, although it was realized that in spite of the fact that the discoveries were largely a repetition of what had been achieved in the 1901–1911 survey, it was work that had to be done. They also knew that I wanted to continue the survey into the northern Sudan in order to establish if possible the limits of the C-Group culture, and with this idea they were by no means in sympathy. In fact, the Archaeological Survey was viewed in Cairo as a necessary duty which they would be glad to see over and done with. Therefore, I was afraid that any report of a sensa- 69

tional find would at that juncture be viewed with suspicion. To
see the antiquities we had found at the museum in Cairo without
seeing the mounds themselves would give no idea of the potential
value of the discovery, and I felt that at all costs I must get the
director general to come to Qustol and see for himself. In this my
report was successful, and on January 15 the director general with
other officials arrived at Qustol. In the saloon of our boat we dis-
played the silver bridles, jeweled horse collar, and the other objects, and he appreciated at once their unique character and historical importance. I then showed him over the site, pointing out
that under each mound the entrance area of the tomb was certainly
intact, and that even the plundered burials might well retain vital
historical evidence. Moreover, we had established the fact that in
the mounds themselves offerings might well be discovered; then
there were the vast possibilities of the other group of mounds on
the west bank of the river at Ballana. However, the director general needed no persuasion. He immediately arranged for a small
subsidiary credit to be placed at our disposal for the work at Qustol,
and he undertook to approach the Ministry of Education for sufficient funds to meet the cost of an increased labor force and two
more seasons' excavations. His application was successful and with
the knowledge that fresh funds were available, arrangements were
made to increase the number of our workmen from 150 to 400 and
to transfer from Sakkara a light railway which would certainly be
necessary when we came to tackle the great tumuli at Ballana.

In the meantime, before the arrival of our new labor force and
the light railway, we set to work on the other tumuli at Qustol.
Tomb after tomb was examined and all without exception had been
plundered, but in every case the entrance area was found intact
with its sacrificed horses, donkeys, and camels. Although none was
as rich as Tomb 3, they nevertheless yielded a great collection of
silver horse trappings, silver- and bronze-mounted saddles—one I
recollect with a splendid figure of the goddess Isis embossed on
the pommel. There were also iron spears, lamps, jewelry and a
variety of other objects which easily compensated us for the great
70   labor involved in the removal of large parts of the tumulus. Then,

of course, there were the objects buried in the actual tumuli. This strange custom did not apply to every burial, and some of the mounds, though carefully sifted, yielded no objects of any sort; others produced only offerings of a rather humble character, such as weapons and cooking pots. But the most extraordinary discovery of this character was made in the tumulus of Tomb 14.

At a fairly high level in the mound we uncovered what at first appeared to be a bundle of gaily colored cloth, but as we cleared away the sand and rubble we were faced with a very gruesome discovery: the bundle of cloth was the linen garment of a young girl who had obviously been murdered. The body was naturally preserved, a phenomenon not uncommon in Nubia when the remains have been buried in dry sand and rubble. The girl's body was so little decayed that it was plain to see how she had met her death: her throat had been cut, and the brown bloodstains were still plainly visible on the wound and on her dress. Whatever the reason for her murder, it was certainly not robbery, for by her side was a bundle of linen and the remains of a leather satchel, both of which contained valuable jewelry as well as other objects. One can let one's imagination run riot in seeking for an explanation of this discovery. Was the girl originally destined for sacrifice with other women in the tomb and had she escaped, only to be captured when the burial ceremony was over and the mound above it partly raised? Or was she sacrificed and placed in the mound as an offering of the same character as such inanimate objects as the gaming board? Or had she suffered death as a penalty for robbing a treasure chest which had been placed in the mound as an offering? (For we found a rifled chest at no great distance from her body.)

The satchel at her side, very modern in design, had been made of thick leather with iron handles and a hasp lock. It appeared to be in perfect condition, but examination soon showed that even the application of paraffin wax could not preserve it, and after measured drawings and the usual photographs had been taken it crumbled away at the first touch, disclosing its contents. These consisted of a small iron knife with a horn handle and two small *71* brass bowls, probably used in the mixing of cosmetics. Other toilet articles were two carved wooden kohl flasks with the iron implements for applying the gray-black powder, so essential for an Eastern beauty's eyes. The flasks were of great interest, both being of ancient Egyptian design; one was in the form of a seated sphinx resting on a pedestal. The human head was framed in the conventional heavy wig with fillet and the eyes were inlaid in ivory. The other flask represented a seated mummiform figure of the god Ra. On the hawk head was the usual heavy wig, surmounted by a cone which was detachable and acted as a stopper for the flask. Both these objects, beautifully carved, were quite small, being little more than 4 in. in height.

The remainder of the contents of the satchel consisted entirely of jewelry, the most outstanding example of which was a pair of silver earrings set in filigree work with two beryls and two carnelians. Next came four heavy silver signet rings, one engraved with a representation of the Egyptian lotus and another with the figure of a standing lion, the remaining two being quite plain. A fifth ring of beaten silver was studded with five beryls and five garnets. At the bottom of the satchel was a very fine necklace of silver and coral beads, a bracelet of silverware, and numerous small studs of alabaster, silver, and carnelian.

Then came an examination of the linen bundle which, when unwrapped, revealed more jewelry, principally necklaces of silver, carnelian, coral, glass, and faïence beads of almost every variety of shape and design. The most valuable pieces, however, were two pairs of large silver earrings, both of similar design, but with different settings. The design took the form of a silver plaque, in the center of which was set a large oval amethyst. Suspended from the base of the plaque were two pendants of silver filigree work set with coral. Another interesting find in the linen bundle was a small bracelet of silver set with five amethysts, four garnets, and two beryls, perhaps worn by the murdered girl when she had been a child.

As I have already mentioned, only a short distance from the body of the murdered girl we found a large wooden chest which had been broken open and emptied of its contents. The chest, which is now one of the treasures of the Cairo Museum, was found lying on its side with the lid torn off. Rectangular in shape, it originally stood about 3 ft. high on four legs, which when we found it had largely crumbled away. The back, sides, and top had plain wooden paneling, but the front was elaborately decorated with inlaid ivory and ebony bosses, set between a series of ivory panels engraved with erotic mythological figures painted in red and green. The lid of the chest had been secured by brass hinges and two hasps fitting into a rectangular lock. This lock was a masterpiece of workmanship, with the plate elaborately engraved and the ends of the hasps molded in the form of two crouching lions. It was of the trick variety, and just as it had defied the robber, so it defied us, for owing to the fragile state of the woodwork we were unable to remove it in order to examine its mechanism. The people who had rifled the chest had obviously come prepared, for the hasps had been cleanly cut through by blows from a cold chisel. It is perhaps idle to speculate on the connection, if any, of the rifled chest and the murdered girl, but I must confess that the jewelry in her possession inclines me to think that there is some link between them. If, as I suggested above, the girl had escaped from the general sacrifice during the burial ceremonies in the tomb, it would appear unlikely that she would handicap her flight by being laden with the satchel and the bundle of jewelry. On the other hand, the bundle of jewelry certainly suggests the "swag" from a robbery. But, again, if she had been caught robbing the chest, surely after dealing out punishment her captors would have replaced the contents of the chest. Carrying one's imagination a little further, is it possible that the murdered girl was an accomplice of a group of thieves who killed her because they mistrusted her and thought she knew too much? Even this suggestion is rather weak, for after her elimination it is unlikely that such desperate men would have left the jewelry behind. Anyway, here we have a murder mystery of 1,500 years ago and there we must leave it.

The finding of miscellaneous objects buried in haphazard fashion   *73* in the mounds presented us with a question to which, even today, we have found no satisfactory answer. As far as we could ascertain, not every mound at Qustol contained objects; at least we did not find any. Others yielded only the odd spearhead or cooking pot. The question, therefore, was whether it was justifiable to spend very large sums of money in leveling all the mounds in the hope of finding such objects—bearing in mind that to examine thoroughly the tomb and substructure, it was only necessary to remove about one-third of the mound. It is possible that even today the systematic clearance of the tumuli would yield some objects, perhaps of great archaeological and intrinsic value; but would it be worth it? Nearly two years after, at the end of our work in Nubia, we returned for a few days to Qustol and removed a further part of the mound of Tomb 2. We were rewarded with two magnificent ewers of beaten silver in perfect preservation, both standing 25 centimeters in height. But this was all, and small test digs in other mounds revealed nothing. At the end of January 1932, therefore, with all the tombs of Qustol examined, I felt that further clearance of the tumuli could not be justified, and early in February we moved across the river to undertake the major part of our task: the excavation of the tumuli of Ballana.

It must be understood that the Ballana mounds presented a very different appearance from those at Qustol, their artificial character being by no means as apparent. In fact, partly buried in drift sand and overgrown with scrub, their appearance sometimes weakened my confidence in their man-made origin and I felt compelled to look at the Qustol tumuli to restore my faith. We had intended to postpone our excavation of the Ballana group until the following season, when we would have many more workmen and the services of a light railway; but with unexpected time at our disposal, the temptation to put our theories to the test was too great to be resisted, and so we commenced the clearance of the tumulus above Tomb 3. Before we actually attacked the mound, we searched for the entrance of a robbers' tunnel, such as we had discovered at Qustol, but an exhaustive search failed to produce results and further added to my recurrent attacks of doubt. Tumulus No. 3 was of vast size, far bigger than any of the Qustol group, measuring 12 meters in height and 77 meters in diameter. Day after day we attacked the great pile of earth and our progress appeared to be painfully slow and, in the early stages at any rate, we seemed to make little impression on it. All through what was one of Nubia's coldest Februarys our men struggled to make a wide V-shaped cut reaching down to ground level, only to find as they neared their objective that the sides of the cutting must be widened because the soft nature of the earth made the steep sides dangerous. No objects were found in the mound to encourage us and for me at any rate those four weeks with nothing to do but watch the slow progress of the work were the most boring and uncertain that I have ever experienced. But everything must come to an end, and in the late afternoon of March 6 we reached the natural ground level, having removed nearly half the mound. We cleared a wide area below the center of the tumulus and confidently expected soon to trace the edge of the pit in which the tomb structure would be situated, as in the mounds at Qustol. But instead of this all we saw was a flat expanse of hard rocklike alluvium which our workmen pronounced with certainty as being *gebel,* in other words natural ground. To say I was disappointed is to put it far too mildly; I was horrified, and all my suppressed fears that the Ballana mounds were natural deposits came crowding back with a vengeance. But while we stood around arguing, one of our most skilled workers set to work chipping away at the hard ground until he had cut out a small pit, and only about 2 ft. below the surface he uncovered three small fragments of pottery. As he held up these objects for inspection I realized with almost hysterical joy that our fears were misplaced and that the ground on which we stood was indeed artificial; moisture probably caused by floods, or the seepage of high Niles, had welded the mud bricks of the tomb structure and the natural alluvium into a solid mass.

Nothing more could be done that evening and we returned to our boat with high hopes for the morrow; in fact our hopes were even higher than they had been after the discovery at Qustol, for we realized that if the tombs had been welded into a solid mass   *75* by the action of water it was probable that we might find them intact, since in these circumstances entry by tunneling would have been impossible for even the most determined plunderer. Later we were to find that our hopes in this direction were to be partly fulfilled, for although some of the tombs had been plundered by tunneling—perhaps before the flood—others were intact. Thus the destruction of the tomb structures by water was a blessing as far as we were concerned, but, I must add, not an entirely unmixed one, for the moisture destroyed many objects which would other-wise have been perfectly preserved, as at Qustol. Moreover, the difficulties of excavation were greatly increased, for each object had to be cut out by knifework from the hard congealed mud in which it was embedded. In addition, the walls of the tomb structures had to be traced, a very difficult task when the whole edifice had been welded into a solid mass of dried mud.

Next day the work of excavation started in earnest, and as our workmen became more experienced in the strange kind of ground they were digging it was not long before we were able to delineate the outline of the pit in which the tomb was built. Soon we were able to recognize the remains of the mud-brick-vaulted roof of one of the rooms, which was filled almost solid with stacks of large wine jars. When these were removed we found at the south end of the room a small treasure of silver objects consisting of large em-bossed plates, bowls and cups, a casket, incense-burner, and spoons. One of the large plates was particularly fine. It had been cast and engraved, and had a shallow foot ring which was attached with solder. The surface was embossed with a classical representation of the god Hermes, who is represented in the seminude, seated on a globe.

Working our way into another and larger room we discovered the scattered bones of what must have been the burial, obviously plundered by tomb robbers who had entered the tomb by the usual method, as at Qustol. But they must have been disturbed, for we found great bronze standard lamps and vessels, more objects of silver and a magnificent gold necklace of beads and pendants of ancient Egyptian design.

With the completion of our work in Tomb 3 we closed down and returned to Cairo, eager to spend a few months of research on the objects that we had found. It is one of the most tantalizing things about archaeological field work that most expeditions in such desolate countries as Lower Nubia can only carry with them a bare minimum of reference books; so that sometimes when the excavator finds an unusual object of whose character and date he is ignorant, he must contain himself with patience until he can return to civilization and the world of libraries and reference books. This was particularly so with regard to our discoveries at Ballana and Qustol, for they belonged to a period of which I, for one, was largely ignorant, and I was all the more eager to compare them with similar material that had been previously found. So that the three months spent in Cairo, before our annual leave in England, was a period almost as exciting as the months when the discoveries were being made. The identification of such mysterious objects as the dicebox from Qustol, and, above all, the cleaning of the jeweled bridles, etc., in the laboratory of the museum, provided us continuously with new and unexpected discoveries. But, of course, it was not all excitement; laborious hours had to be spent in sorting, cataloguing, and typing the pottery and like material; by the end of June we were ready for a period of rest in a cooler climate.

During the interval the Egyptian Ministry of Education granted the supplementary credits asked for by the Department of Antiquities and early in October 1932 we returned to Nubia with a company of 400 workmen and the added equipment of a light railway. We naturally expected that the larger tumuli would cover the richer tombs and in this belief the whole season was devoted to the biggest mounds, with results which were, on the whole, rather disappointing. Many of these tombs were intact, but most of them were small and far less rich than the Qustol burials. As we gained in knowledge and experience, we realized that they were of a slightly later date and perhaps belonged to a period when the power and wealth of the X-Group people were declining. However, very many fine and valuable objects were found in the tombs, the most notable of which was a silver crown on the head of the owner   *77* of Tomb 6. This crown, a deep circlet without a crest, was embossed with a series of busts of the goddess Isis, and between each figure were oval and round carnelians set in beaded silver settings, a curious mixture of ancient Egyptian and Byzantine art (Figure 7). Other objects of great interest were great silver-mounted iron spears, and silver archer's bracer and arrow looses. A considerable amount of jewelry was also recovered, but, as I say, we were rather disappointed. I suppose we had come to expect too much from the startling results of the previous season's work. But the hard fact remained that we returned to Cairo in February 1933, having spent nearly three times as much money as in the previous year, and having found considerably less. Yet our finds, particularly the crown, evoked great interest at the museum in Cairo, and to my relief there was no suggestion that the work should be abandoned, or its scope curtailed; for I was determined that every mound, even the smallest, should be thoroughly examined.

We had been in Cairo for only a little more than a month, and were developing that pleasant "on leave" feeling, when the director general sent for me in a hurry and told me that the Irrigation Department had announced that the work on the Aswan Dam would be finished at a much earlier date than had been anticipated. This meant that all our excavations in Nubia, not only those at Ballana and Qustol, would have to be completed by the end of March 1934. There was no alternative: we had to return to Nubia forthwith, and any question of early leave in England was out of the question. We had a wide experience of winter in Nubia, and at times had found it uncomfortably hot, and I must admit that the prospect of April, May, and June was not a very inviting one. However, our morale had been to a large extent restored by the interest shown at the museum in what we had considered the rather disappointing results of our last season's work, so we left for the south and the anticipated heat in a fairly contented, if not enthusiastic, state of mind. Had we known what awaited us we would certainly have needed little persuasion, for it was during this short and uncomfortable season that we made our biggest and richest discoveries.

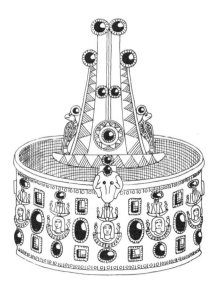

B.95-22

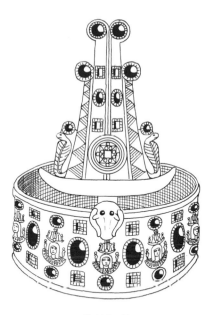

B.114-11

B.80-48

B.47-13

FIGURE 7*a* Reconstruction of Nubian X-Group crowns

Soon after our arrival at Ballana in early April we started the excavation of Tomb 80, which was covered by one of the small tumuli at the north end of the necropolis, and here for the first time we found a royal burial completely undisturbed, so that at last we could see the whole system and order of the funerary customs of the rulers of the X-Group people (Figure 8). The interment in Tomb 80 cannot have been as rich or elaborate as those of an earlier date at Qustol, but it was intact and as such gave us the answers to many unsolved problems which we had encountered in the rifled burials on the other side of the Nile. The progress of

B.118-29

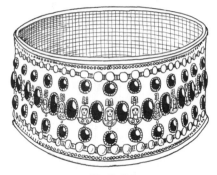

B.6-20

B.80-3

B.95-18

FIGURE 7*b*   Reconstruction of Nubian X-Group crowns

excavation was laboriously slow, for the four vaulted rooms of the tomb, built of mud brick, had been welded by the action of water into a mass of congealed mud, and if the foundations of the walls had not had lower courses of stone I doubt if we would have been able to trace them. As it was, from the natural ground level below the base of the tumulus there was no indication of the plan of the tomb or of the edges of the series of pits in which it was built. So we had to sink a test pit in the hope that it would strike some point near the ramp entrance to the substructure; but in this we miscalculated and in fact we landed right in the middle of the burial chamber. However, it was some time before we realized this, for, as I have explained, the Ballana tombs were just solid masses of congealed mud, and it was only after every wall and object had been individually carved out by careful knifework, from the dried mud in which it was embedded, that the room and its contents could be identified and their arrangement appreciated. In fact, one of the first objects that the knives of our workmen laid bare was a massive silver crown which rested on the head of the king; but at the time we certainly did not recognize it as a crown, nor could we know that it rested on a human skull—all we could see was some strangely shaped silverwork encrusted with precious stones. In clearing an object under such conditions it is necessary to remove a small part of the damp earth covering it and then wait for the cut section to dry, so that the exposed surface can be cleaned with the aid of brush and bellows. All this takes considerable time, so that the excavator may be working for hours before he can recognize the object of his attention. So it was when we found the crown; the crest in the form of the Atef plumes was first disclosed and finally the circlet revealing to us for the first time the typical royal headgear of a Meroitic king (Figure 7), the design of which archaeologists had only known from representation of it on the reliefs on the walls of ancient monuments. Hours of painstaking work with knife, brush, and bellows revealed first the crushed skull with the crown and finally the whole skeleton of the king, who lay in an extended position on his back with the right arm outflung. Around his neck were necklaces of carnelian, quartz, *81*

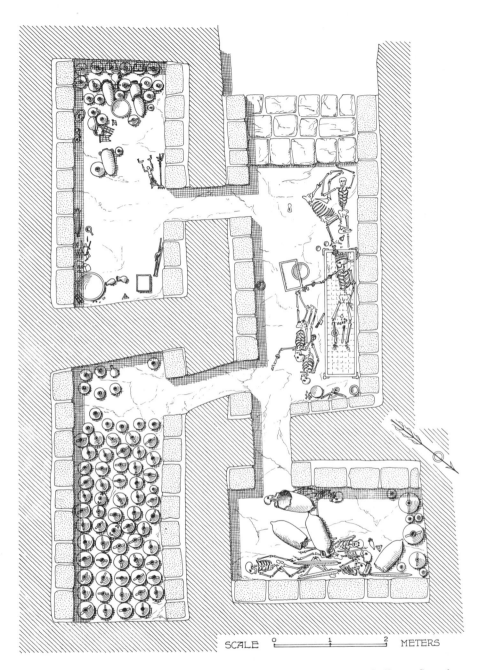

FIGURE 8 Position of the burial installation in Tomb 80 at Ballana. See also Figure 44 (p. 304)

crystal, and jasper beadwork, and on the arms were bracelets of silver. On the right hand was an archer's silver arrow loose, and on his left a bracer of silver beautifully engraved with ancient Egyptian designs. Between his knees was a short iron sword with a jeweled silver hilt and an embossed silver scabbard. Further clearance explained the curious position of the skeleton, for it had originally lain on a wooden bier with a mattress of interlaced ropework, which had given way under the weight of the fallen roof of the burial chamber. The wood of this bier had long since disintegrated, but the bronze brackets which strengthened its frame were still preserved in their original position, so that the dimensions of the bier were still ascertainable. The ropework of the mattress had, of course, also disappeared, but the impression of it was plainly visible on the congealed mud of the floor. The fact that the bones of the skeleton were not scattered indicates that the collapse of the tomb, which could only have been caused by flood water, must have happened not long after the interment, when the tissue of the body was still preserved.

Below the head of the bier was the skeleton of a large dog and between the bier and the blocked entrance of the tomb were the remains of a camel and a man who lay on his back with arms upraised as if to protect his head from the blows of the executioner. The fragmentary bones of two more humans were found on the south side of the bier, but their sex was unascertainable. One had bracelets of silver and inlaid stone, and the other an iron sword with silver hilt and scabbard. More swords and massive silver-mounted spears, with blades more than 3 ft. long, were found in a heap in the north corner of the room, and from their position it was obvious that some of the spears had been placed in an upright position, leaning against the foot of the bier. With them were bronze vessels and a group of archers' arrow looses made of semiprecious stones. In the center of the burial chamber we found more bronze vessels and an iron folding chair similar in every respect to the modern camp stool. The seat had been made of leather or cloth which had, of course, long since decayed. As the contents of the burial chamber were slowly revealed, our photographer was *83* at work and detailed drawings were made, showing the position of each object. Then came the difficult task of their removal, and the examination of the human remains by our anatomist; the fragments of the skull of the king were taken from the inside of the crown, and this delicate operation had to be achieved without moving the crown itself, for it was obviously in a very fragile condition. To remove it safely we had recourse to that valuable ally of the field archaeologist in an emergency—paraffin wax, without the aid of which I doubt if we could have preserved many of our most important finds at Ballana. A floorless box of small wooden boards was formed around the crown, the delicate outer jeweled surfaces of the circlet and crest were painted with salad oil and finally boiling wax was poured into the box, embedding the crown in a mass of wax and soil. When it had cooled and solidified it was lifted and carried to our boat where the wax was gently reheated so that it could be easily peeled from the outer surfaces of the crown which had been smeared with the coating of oil. The wax in the interior of the circlet and the back of the crest was left intact until it reached the museum laboratories in Cairo, where it was finally removed.

When all the contents of the burial chamber had been removed we turned our attention to the ramp entrance of the tomb, and here we found the remains of the usual sacrificed horses and camels, but no signs of saddles or trappings. Apart from the smaller size of the tomb, this showed that, rich as these burials were, they were far poorer than those at Qustol. We can only guess at the vast wealth which must have been hidden in these earlier interments, which, as I have already pointed out, were probably older in date than those at Ballana. At the other end of the burial chamber, facing the main entrance, was a small low door leading into another room in which we found the skeleton of the queen surrounded by her female slaves, all of whom had obviously been sacrificed at the burial of her royal consort. On the queen's head was a silver crown without a crest; the circlet, with three magnificent carnelians set in the front, was embossed with conventional figures of an Egyptian king. In addition to the human remains, this room contained more silver-mounted spears and masses of large pottery vessels.

The two remaining rooms were then examined and found to contain funerary equipment of almost every kind and variety: massive bronze standard lamps, bronze tables and tripods, innumerable bronze vessels, bronze incense burners, of a design that showed marked Chinese characteristics, bronze balances with a set of weights, and a gold ring set with a fine garnet, which undoubtedly was placed with the weighing instruments, with which it had some ceremonial connection. With all these objects was a vast quantity of pottery vessels, some of which must have originally contained food and drink for the sustenance of the king in the afterlife. Some of this X-Group pottery is very attractive, with its painted decoration reminiscent of the fine Meroitic biscuit ware from which it was undoubtedly descended.

Another group of objects of particular interest was a large quantity of iron spear blades, axheads, iron ingots, and iron tools, most of the latter being made for metalworking. Here we had evidence of the continuation of an Egyptian funerary custom which we know was in existence in the tombs of the kings of the First Dynasty, nearly 4,000 years before this unknown Nubian king died. The ancient Egyptian believed that when you died "you could take it with you" and consequently food and drink, furniture, clothing, games, weapons, etc., were buried with him for his use in the afterlife. Always far-thinking, he realized that essential articles such as weapons would, over a period, get broken or wear out, and to insure against this the dead man was left with materials with which he could make more. For example, in the royal tombs of the First Dynasty at Sakkara I found magnificent flint knives and, with them, natural nodules of flint from which the deceased could manufacture more, should the need arise. Here in Nubia, at a period when the old beliefs were long forgotten in Christian Egypt, the X-Group kings still adhered to them and with their swords and spears they were given the iron and the metalworking tools to make more when the weapons became broken and useless. The iron tools were surprisingly modern in design, and had they been found in mint condition in other circumstances would hardly have caused comment in

85

a present-day workshop. Apart from these tools, which consisted of hammers, chisels, saws, pincers, tongs, and metal cutters, the king was supplied with hoes, so that he might be fully equipped to cultivate the fields of the next world.

Throughout the period of the excavation of Tomb 80 the April weather in Nubia was kind to us, and although it was hot, the nights brought relief, and living as we were on the river we had the advantage of the prevailing breeze from the north. In fact, we were agreeably surprised with a temperature very little higher than we were accustomed to at the end of March. But with the commencement of May there came a rapid change, and within twenty-four hours we were faced with the almost unbearable heat of a Nubian summer. We had a thermometer in the companionway of our boat; it registered up to 120°F and it reached that figure at ten o'clock in the morning. Certainly it was not always as bad as that, but from the beginning of May, until we left, our thermometer never went below 110°F during the day, and there was little relief at night.

However, after the exciting discoveries in Tomb 80 we were all prepared to put up with a good deal of discomfort, and one by one other tombs in the northern group were examined, with equally successful results. Most of them had escaped the attention of ancient plunderers and although difficult to excavate they were most rewarding.

Although the tombs differed to a certain extent in size and design, the general scheme of the interment was the same, and we gradually obtained a clear view of the barbaric burial customs of these strange people who in the fourth to sixth centuries A.D. were still following the religious beliefs of old Egypt. But the humanity of the Egyptians was forgotten and human sacrifice was prevalent. The ancient Egyptian believed that servants and slaves were as necessary for the comfort of their great dead as was the use of furniture, food and drink, etc., but only in the earliest period did this belief entail human sacrifice at a funeral. Realizing the barbarity of such procedure, the Egyptians solved the problem with the aid of magic. Models of servants were placed in the tomb and these were confidently believed to come to life in the hereafter to give service to the owner of the tomb. Not so the X-Group people, who believed in having the real thing, and we found in the tombs of their kings and nobility the ghastly evidence of wholesale human sacrifice. Apparently the death of one of these ancient monarchs entailed the sacrifice of all those nearest to him, even his queen, who, wearing her crown and jewelry, was compelled to accompany her lord into the afterlife. He took everything with him: his slaves, male and female, his guards, grooms, horses, and even his dogs. We found many of the human skeletons lying face downward, as if they had been struck with ax blows from behind, and others who had probably met their death by strangulation. As we cleared these charnel houses with their mixture of human pomp and human suffering it was not difficult to visualize that scene of horror as the body of the king was laid on the bed in his tomb, followed by terror-stricken men and women, dragged down into the darkness by their slayers.

As tomb after tomb was excavated in the stifling heat, more jewel-encrusted silver crowns were discovered, some of them far finer than the one recovered from Tomb 80, and all had to be treated with paraffin wax before they could be safely removed (Figure 7). This work at the bottom of a deep pit, in close proximity to a roaring primus stove and buckets of boiling wax, in a temperature of more than 110°F in the shade, was indeed difficult to endure and if we had not been in the midst of such extraordinary discoveries I do not think we should have had the spirit to continue. But there it was; each tomb had some new and exciting feature which spurred us on. As I have mentioned above, the plan of the tombs, while following a general design, frequently varied in detail and there were some where quite drastic changes in plan were made, obviously in an effort to deceive tomb robbers. Such a one was Tomb 47, which housed the burial of a queen whom for obvious reasons we nicknamed "Jingling Millie." The main part of the tomb had been robbed, but the architects of the structure had through their ingenuity saved the actual burial from violation. In many of the Ballana tombs attempts had been made to deceive possible robbers by concealing the burial below the floor level. In every case, if the plunderers had succeeded in entering the tomb, this subterfuge had failed and the concealed burial had been found. But the designer of this queen's tomb had succeeded by placing the burial high above the floor level and we ourselves only discovered it when we were cutting back parts of the tumulus that overhung the edges of the pit in which the tomb was built. The burial chamber was very small and only connected with the main part of the tomb by a small arched doorway high in the west wall of the main chamber. After interment this door had been bricked up and plastered over. I must say it gave us considerable satisfaction to think of our predecessors' frustration, particularly when we found how rich "Jingling Millie" was. To have succeeded in penetrating a royal tomb by arduous tunneling and then to fail in locating the burial of the owner must have been very galling. However, their misfortune was our gain, and after the usual gradual clearance of the fallen vaulted roofing of the burial chamber there lay the skeleton of the queen covered, I might say overloaded, with jewelry, for it was obvious that she could not possibly have worn it all at the same time. Unfortunately, because of the moisture, the skeleton had decayed and very little remained, although it was possible to ascertain that the body had lain in an extended position on its back. On the head was a silver crown with three crests in the form of the horns and plumes of Isis, set with precious stones. On the arms we found twenty silver bracelets, some plain circlets, and others of most elaborate design encrusted with onyx, beryls, amethysts, and garnets. Around the neck was a heavy silver torque of design identical to those worn by unmarried girls in the oasis of Siwa today. With this torque were fourteen necklaces, made up of beads of silver, carnelian, quartz, jasper, olivine, obsidian, glazed steatite, faïence, and glass. On each side of the head were nine pairs of silver earrings set with coral and faïence and on the hands were eleven silver rings, some plain and others set with precious stones. Three silver and four coral anklets were found

on the legs, and the feet were adorned with a variety of silver rings. This was the largest collective find of jewelry, though other tombs yielded material of an equally sensational character.

' But by the end of May the intense heat was beginning to tell on both staff and workmen, and even though we tried the expedients of working only in the early morning and at night, it became obvious that we could not continue much longer. Our workmen finally announced that they could not carry on; I think they reached their limit when they found themselves compelled to wear their shoes while working, because the ground was too hot for their feet. So at the beginning of June we spent a nightmare week in packing our precious finds and closed down, returning to Cairo in triumph, but in a rather exhausted state.

After a short leave in England we returned to Nubia in October and excavated the remaining tombs at Ballana and also re-examined some of the burials at Qustol. Before finally leaving the district we made an exhaustive search for any traces of a settlement or town which we felt sure must have existed in the vicinity of such a great necropolis. But, although we discovered traces of a buried town, this proved on investigation to belong to a later period and was in no way connected with the X-Group tombs—unless it was to supply the men who plundered them! However, in this search we made one valuable discovery, for we noted in the desert near the river edge small irrigation channels which had been used for ancient cultivation and which had been sanded over. Further tests showed that the whole area had originally been fertile and that below a foot or two of sand was black alluvial soil. With the advent of the new reservoir level, the Egyptian government was looking for areas above the new water level on which they could settle some of the dispossessed inhabitants of Nubia. I reported the discovery to the Ministry of Agriculture, who sent experts down to examine its possibilities, and after they had delivered a favorable verdict the Ministry of Public Works dug canals and installed an elaborate pumping system, with the result that the land we found as desert is now one of Nubia's most valuable cultivated areas. I revisited Ballana in October 1960, after an interval of twenty-six years, and I was astonished to see the change in its appearance, with its great palm groves and lush vegetation—alas, soon to be finally and utterly destroyed by yet another raising of the water level of the reservoir.

The discoveries at Ballana and Qustol marked the end of the work of the Second Archaeological Survey of Nubia, but another year was spent at the museum in Cairo, preparing the material for publication, which was finally accomplished in 1935. It was an astonishing discovery, but satisfactory as it was, it left many questions unanswered. Who were the X-Group people? How far south did their culture extend? We knew of the existence of similar, if smaller, tumuli tombs at Firka and Sai and other places in the northern Sudan. In addition to this, other problems raised by the work of the Archaeological Survey, such as the southern limits of the C-Group culture, could only be solved by carrying its work farther south into the Sudan. With this in view I tried to arrange for a continuation of our work; but although at first my suggestions received favorable consideration, they were finally turned down on the grounds that the antiquities of Upper Nubia in the Sudan were not threatened by the waters of the heightened reservoir, nor were they likely to be in the foreseeable future. I was at the time so confident that my project would be approved that I had even prepared maps, etc., for the expedition. It was a grievous disappointment; but now, after more than twenty-five years, these maps are proving useful, as Egyptology is faced with the problem of the third Archaeological Survey of Nubia whose work must extend far into the northern Sudan.

Even with the completion of the publication there was still much work to be done in Cairo in the arrangement of the exhibition of the objects in the museum. Only a part of the finds could be shown, for there were many duplicates and even as it was, two galleries were necessary for the exhibition. One of the big problems was to find the best way to show the silver bridles, trappings, and saddles, and our first thought was to exhibit them on stuffed horses; but these were not procurable in Cairo at that time. Finally the chief curator of the museum remembered that a certain saddler's shop

had a life-size wooden horse on which horsemen could try their saddles. The owner of the business was kind enough to lend the horse to us, and plaster casts were made of it in the museum workshops. The only disadvantage was that the wooden horse had been made on the measurements of an Australian hunter, whereas our bridles, trappings, and saddles had belonged to small African horses of not more than fourteen hands. However, it was possible to adjust the bridles and trappings, though I think the small saddles look rather absurd on the back of so large an animal. But I have never heard any adverse comment on this score, and there the plaster horses stand today in the museum, decked out in the ancient equipment; on the whole I think they are a most impressive sight.

From the archaeological point of view the work on the discoveries at Ballana and Qustol is unfinished. The excavation and the collection of the treasure below the tumuli is complete, but the degree of our knowledge of the X-Group people is extremely limited, and, as I have already said, we are still uncertain of their origin and even of who they were. The contents of their royal tombs show an extraordinary mixture of ancient Egyptian, Byzantine Christian, and pure African culture—if such it could be called—but the connecting links are still uncertain. It is partly with this fact in mind that the Egypt Exploration Society selected the site of Kasr Ibrim as one of its undertakings in the general campaign to salvage the antiquities of Nubia. The excavations at Kasr Ibrim, now directed by Professor J. M. Plumley, may well produce evidence which perhaps will solve the problem of the X-Group culture.

IV

Independent Exploration

Apart from the major work undertaken by the Egyptian government in connection with the successive raisings of the Aswan Dam, various archaeological institutions and organizations have sponsored excavations and recording expeditions, the results of whose discoveries have in a greater or lesser degree contributed to the building up of the history of Nubia. Although before the building of the dam and the threatened destruction of the evidence of Nubia's past little or no actual excavation had been undertaken on the banks of the Nile between the First and Second Cataracts, the recording of the monuments and rock inscriptions of the area received considerable attention and even in the earliest days of Egyptology scholars labored in this rich field of historical research.

The founder of Egyptology, Jean-François Champollion, visited Nubia with Niccolo Rossellini in 1828–1829 and made many important records of both the inscriptions and architecture of the monuments. Even before this, in 1819, the famous French architect Huyot, who designed the Arc de Triomphe, planned many of the temples, and placed many of his drawings at the disposal of Champollion, who used them in correcting details of the illustrations in his *Description de l'Égypte.*

Archaeological research in Nubia in those days must have been by no means easy; slow travel by sailing boat, coupled with a precarious state of public security, made the life of the explorer very difficult. This is shown by the records that they have left us, which, by their inaccuracy, bear all the marks of hurried work carried out under constant threat of interruption.

It was not until the middle of the last century that really scientific documentation of Nubia's monuments was undertaken and successfully achieved. Between 1842 and 1845 Karl Richard Lepsius led the Prussian Expedition to Egypt and Nubia, and with the aid of a highly qualified staff of epigraphists he collected a vast amount of material which in 1859 he published in the twelve great volumes of *Denkmäler,* which remains to this day one of the most important works of reference in any Egyptological library. A proportionately large part of this great work was devoted to the monuments of Nubia, and it is astonishing to see the quality of the epigraphic work and the general accuracy of the architectural drawings when one considers the limited time at the disposal of the expedition; it must indeed have been a miracle of organization. Even with all this labor and responsibility Lepsius found time to make a study of the Nubian dialects, and he published the results of this research as *Nubische Grammatik* in 1880.

Although by the beginning of the century photography had come to the aid of the archaeological recorder, it was not until 1907 that its full value was utilized in Nubia. In that year the famous American Egyptologist and historian J. H. Breasted visited the country in the course of an extensive tour which carried him down into the Sudan. Apart from making hand copies of important inscriptions, Breasted made good use of photography and much of his recording by this medium cannot be excelled at the present day. His work was also particularly valuable because some of the material he studied has since disappeared. He also examined the frontier fortresses of the Second Cataract, leaving records which were of great value to Reisner when he excavated some of these sites in later years. Reisner was also indebted to Somers Clarke, who was at one time Surveyor of the Fabric of St. Paul's Cathedral and who was always interested in the architecture of ancient Egypt. Clarke published a study of the Egyptian fortresses of Nubia in 1916, which, although of a very general character, laid the foundation for the study of this class of Egyptian architecture.

Of the numerous excavations that were conducted in Nubia, independent of the two archaeological surveys, during the last half century, we may list the following:

The German Ernst von Seiglin Expedition, which under the di-   *93* rection of Professor Georg Steindorff between 1912 and 1914 excavated in the district of Aneiba which was the site of Ma'am, the ancient capital of Lower Nubia in the Eighteenth Dynasty. Here Steindorff found many important burial grounds of the C-Group period and here he also located the site of the great walled fortress which, like other military strongholds, was built in the Twelfth Dynasty and later enlarged in the days of the Empire so that it became, at that time, the largest fortified town in all Nubia. The outbreak of the First World War prevented Steindorff making any detailed examination of his discovery and it was not until the time of the Second Archaeological Survey, between 1929 and 1933, that he was able to return and excavate this important site on behalf of the Egyptian Antiquities Service. Although the condition of the ruins of this vast fortress was somewhat disappointing because of wind erosion, Steindorff was rewarded with valuable information regarding the military architecture of the period, which amply repaid all the years of research and large sums of money expended on this project.

Then there was the Eckley B. Coxe Expedition of the University of Pennsylvania, which, under the direction of Dr. David Randall-MacIver, explored various sites between the First and Second Cataracts between 1907 and 1911. Randall-MacIver was assisted by Leonard Woolley, who was later to become famous as the discoverer of the tombs of the Sumerian kings at Ur, and to be knighted for his services to Middle Eastern archaeology. These two men, both at the beginning of their careers, contributed in a major degree to the advance of our knowledge of Nubian history, with excavations at Areika, Karanog, and Buhen, the results of which they published in considerable detail. At that time our knowledge of Nubian archaeology was elementary and consequently some of the dating and identification of their discoveries was mistaken, but because of the detailed manner of their recording these inevitable errors were easily rectified in later years when the over-all picture of Nubian history was clarified.

Between 1910 and 1912 the Oxford Expedition to Nubia, directed by Professor F. Ll. Griffith, conducted extensive excavations

94

at Faras, the ancient Pakhoras, which is situated on the border-line between Egypt and the Sudan, 25 miles north of the Second Cataract. Here on this valuable site Griffith discovered remains of almost every period ranging from Proto-Dynastic or Nubian A-Group to Christian times. Griffith's excavations at Faras were carried out on a large scale, but even so much was left unexplored; the site has since been explored by a Polish expedition, and has yielded most interesting results, particularly important with regard to the early days of Christianity in the Nile Valley.

Dr. George Reisner retired from the First Archaeological Survey in 1909, but the problems of Nubian archaeology were not easily forgotten, and in 1912 he commenced the excavation of Kerma near the Third Cataract. His discoveries on this site were among the most sensational made in Nubia, and although some of the historical conclusions he drew from them have been brought into question in the light of evidence revealed by later discoveries, they were made doubly important because of the meticulous recording which was always a feature of Reisner's work. Here at Kerma were the remains of two great structures of mud brick and in the vicinity were burials covered by big earthen tumuli, the largest of which had a floor area of nearly 500 square meters. Reisner identified one of the brick structures as a fortified trading station built by the Egyptians of the Middle Kingdom, and in this he was probably correct, but the identity of the other structure is still open to doubt, although it certainly was also of Egyptian origin. But the great tumuli tombs are certainly Nubian and may well have been the burial places of the kings of ancient Kush at the time of her struggle with Egypt in the Middle Kingdom and the Second Intermediate Period. Barbaric interments, in which human sacrifice was a most important feature, they were totally un-Egyptian in character, and although many Egyptian objects were found in them, these were probably the products of trade and the plunder of war, and not, as Reisner believed, evidence which showed that their owners were Egyptians who ruled Kerma as a colony and dying there had been buried according to native custom. Although Kerma is not threatened by the waters of the new reservoirs, I think there

95

is no site in Nubia which merits re-excavation more than this, and I hope it will soon receive the attention it deserves.

Between 1924 and 1932 Reisner was again in Nubia when he directed the Harvard University-Boston Museum of Fine Arts Expedition in the excavations of some of the Egyptian forts situated in the Second Cataract area, and here again we are indebted to this great archaeologist for his very detailed recording, which has made possible the sumptuous publications of his work that have appeared so many years after his death in 1942.

Other excavations that yielded results of historical value were conducted by British expeditions on sites located south of the areas to be flooded by the waters of the new reservoir. In the years 1930, 1934, 1935, and 1936 the Oxford Expedition explored the sites of Kawa and Firka under the direction of F. Ll. Griffith and L. P. Kirwan, and the records of their work have been published in considerable detail. At Kawa, in 1930, Griffith excavated the temple of Taharka and the remains of religious structures of Amenhotep III, Akhenaton, and Tutankhamen. He was able finally to establish that Kawa was to be identified with Gematon, the town founded in Upper Nubia by Akhenaton for the propagation of his new religion in his southern dominions. No further exploration of Kawa was attempted until 1935 when the Oxford Expedition returned under the direction of Kirwan, whose researches gave ample evidence of the long occupation of the town which was occupied at least down to the Late Meroitic period. The date of the foundation of the town is not known, but it has been suggested that it may go back as far as the Middle Kingdom. Much remains to be done at Kawa which may be regarded as potentially one of the most valuable sites in Upper Nubia.

The Oxford Expedition under the direction of Kirwan also carried out extensive excavations at Firka in 1934, where interesting discoveries were made in the X-Group necropolis which, although badly plundered, yielded valuable material contributing to our knowledge of the last years of paganism in Nubia.

The New Kingdom towns at Sesebi and Amara West were partly explored by the Egypt Exploration Society, under the direction of

Professors Blackman and Fairman. Sesebi, which Fairman excavated in 1937, proved to be another Nubian town founded by Akhenaton, where he built a temple to the Aton, of which unfortunately little remains beyond three columns, for the site is much denuded by wind erosion. The site of Amara West has also suffered from erosion, but even so, excavations carried out in 1939 and 1947 yielded important results which are to be published very shortly. The denuded ruins of the walled town deserve further exploration, for there is little doubt that the town, built by Seti I, was the administrative center of Upper Nubia during the Nineteenth Dynasty.

At the time of the Second Archaeological Survey J. H. Dunbar, then an official of the Sudan government, taking advantage of his duties in Nubia, spent his spare time in detailed hand-copying and photographing the innumerable inscriptions and drawings he found on the rocks on both sides of the Nile. He recorded his invaluable discoveries in an Egyptian Antiquities Service publication that remains the standard work on this subject, and although much more of this material has since been discovered, and is likely to be in the future, Dunbar's work is a monument to one man's achievement and it is the framework on which future research in this branch of Nubian archaeology must be built.

V

The Results of the
UNESCO Appeal

BECAUSE of what might be considered the overemphasis in the
publicity given to the undecided fate of the great monuments at
Abu Simbel many people are inclined, through ignorance, to believe that the UNESCO appeal to international archaeology is a
failure. This is not so, for although certain monuments may, through
lack of financial aid, have to be sacrificed, we can now be confident that before the waters of the reservoir destroy Nubia every
ancient site will have been systematically explored and recorded.
In fact, no large area of the world has been so thoroughly investigated by the archaeologist. Apart from the financial contributions
of various nations, the following summary of field work—excavations, documentation and preservation—will give some idea of the
vast international effort which has already been made in response
to UNESCO's appeal:

Argentina. The University of La Plata, in cooperation with the
French National Excavations Commission, started excavation on
the site of Aksha early in 1961, work which was completed in 1962.

Austria. Starting in December 1961, an expedition from the University of Vienna has been excavating and recording prehistoric
sites in the district of Sayala. They have also recorded rock inscriptions of many periods in this area and in doing so have established the fact that representations of giraffes were contemporary
with the A-Group culture in Nubia.

Belgium. An expedition sponsored by the Belgian government has
made photogrammetric records of the temples of Semna and

Kumma and in agreement with the Egypt Exploration Society, has also made a survey, by the same method, of part of the Middle Kingdom fortifications at Buhen.

Canada. The National Museum of Canada, in cooperation with Harvard University, has conducted a prehistoric survey in Lower Nubia.

Czechoslovakia. The Czechoslovak Institute of Egyptology of Charles University has conducted excavations in the late period fortress at Qirtas, on sites at Tafa, and in the region between Wadi es Sebua and Amada.

Denmark. See Scandinavia.

Finland. See Scandinavia.

France. In cooperation with the Swiss Institute for Archaeological Research in Ancient Egypt, the French Institute for Oriental Archaeology has excavated at Wadi es Sebua and has made epigraphic surveys of the temple of Rameses II situated there, prior to its removal by the Egyptian Antiquities Service. A mission sent by the French National Geographic Institute made a complete photogrammetric survey of the whole of Lower Nubia, from which line maps were produced. These maps, supplied to all the various expeditions working in this part of the Nile Valley, have proved to be of very great value and have been the foundation on which most of the recording has been based.

In Sudanese Nubia, in cooperation with the University of La Plata, the French National Excavations Commission completed the excavation and recording of the small temple of Aksha prior to its removal to the Museum at Khartoum (*see Argentina*). Since 1962 they have been excavating the great Middle Kingdom fortress of Mirgissa, where discoveries of great importance are being made in connection with the study of ancient military architecture. France also undertook the salvage of the small temple of Amada, an architectural gem. After the front of the sanctuary had been dismantled by the Egyptian Antiquities Service, French engineers and archaeologists transported the main structure in one piece, with the aid of rails and hydraulic jacks, a distance of more than a mile to higher ground above flood level.

99

Germany (F.R.). The German Archaeological Institute of Cairo has completed the excavation of an area in the vicinity of the temple of Amada. The great temple of Kalabsha has been dismantled and re-erected on high ground in the vicinity of its original location by a mission paid for by the German government and directed by the German Archaeological Institute.

Ghana. In the district of Debeira West on the west bank of the Nile, the University of Ghana discovered a large town of the early Christian period which has produced considerable material of architectural importance.

India. An expedition sponsored by the Indian Government has carried out excavations in the district of Afyeh in Lower Nubia, where they discovered valuable material of the A-Group and C-Group periods.

Italy. The Turin Museum of Egyptology has carried out excavations between Debod in the north and Khor Dehmit in the south of Lower Nubia, in which latter place they have recorded many rock drawings and inscriptions. The University of Milan has also conducted excavations in the regions of Sabagura, Kubban, Tamit, and on the bank of the Nile at Abu Simbel. This expedition has also completed exploration at Maharraga and at Ikhmindi.

Holland. A well preserved town site of the Meroitic, X-Group, and Christian periods was discovered on the west bank of the Nile north of Abu Simbel by the expedition of Leiden Museum. Christian frescoes of considerable merit were discovered, as well as other material of architectural importance.

Norway. See Scandinavia.

Poland. In Egyptian Nubia the Polish Center of Mediterranean Archaeology of the University of Warsaw has completed excavations in the area adjacent to the temple of Debod and has then become engaged in the exploration of the big site at Faras in Sudanese Nubia where sensational discoveries were made at the end of the first season's work. Beneath a great mound the excavators found a large church, certainly as old as the seventh century A.D. On the walls of the church and associated buildings of the same period were revealed brilliantly colored religious frescoes as fine in their design and preservation as any yet discovered in the Nile Valley. This magnificent find has presented many problems, for on a single wall many frescoes were found painted one over the other and all had to be removed layer by layer. But modern technology has triumphed and experts from Warsaw have achieved results that only a few years ago would have been impossible. Before the Polish expedition finally closed down its work at Faras, 169 beautiful frescoes of the finest early Christian art had been safely removed from the stone and brick walls of the church, for future exhibition in museums. The Polish expedition has also discovered the tombs of the early Christian bishops of Faras, and with them many fine objects of unique character.

Scandinavia. The Scandinavian Joint Expedition, organized by Norway, Denmark, Sweden, and Finland, undertook a general archaeological survey on the east bank of the Nile between Debeira and Gamai in Sudanese Nubia. Cemeteries and settlements of almost every period have been cleared and recorded, and these large-scale excavations have revealed a rich collection of objects, particularly of the C-Group. One of the most important achievements of the expedition was the discovery of the rock-cut tomb of Prince Amenemhat, an Egyptianized Nubian ruler of the sixteenth century B.C.

Spain. The expedition of the Spanish National Committee for Nubia has completed excavation at Masmas and Tumas in Egyptian Nubia and Argin, Kasr Ico and Abkanarti in Sudanese Nubia.

Sudan. The Sudan Antiquities Service, with the assistance of archaeologists supplied by UNESCO, completed a detailed survey of all ancient sites on both banks of the Nile and on the islands of the Second Cataract. The information thus gained has enabled the Service to advise foreign expeditions on the relative importance of sites available for excavation. They are now engaged in survey and excavation in the area between Semna and the Dal cataract. Apart from this routine exploration the Antiquities Service carved out a full-scale excavation of the Christian town on the island of Mayanarti, work which has yielded most valuable information relative to the history of this period in Nubia.

Sweden. See Scandinavia.

Switzerland. A mission of the Swiss Institute for Archaeological Research on Ancient Egypt co-operated with the French Institute of Oriental Archaeology in making an epigraphic survey of the temple of Wadi es Sebua prior to its removal. They also cooperated with the Oriental Institute of the University of Chicago in excavations between Khor Dehmit and Kalabsha in Egyptian Nubia. Here the joint expedition examined more than five hundred graves of the X-Group period, and the discovery of pottery vessels of a new type may supply us with fresh evidence relative to the problem of the nationality of the X-Group people.

United Arab Republic. Even before the UNESCO appeal, an expedition of the University of Cairo had been excavating at Aneiba, where cemeteries of almost every period of Nubian history were examined. By reason of the continuity over a long period of years of this research, its results have been of very great value.

The principal activities of the Egyptian Antiquities Service have been devoted to the saving of the threatened monuments and in this they have indeed a proud record. Between 1960 and 1965 the temples of Debod, Tafa, Kertassi, Dendur, Dakka, Maharraga, Derr, Gerf Hussein and many smaller monuments have been dismantled and now await re-erection on sites above the waterline of the new reservoir.

United Kingdom. The expedition of the Egypt Exploration Society has completed its large-scale excavation of the fortress of Buhen in Sudanese Nubia. The temple of Hatshepsut, situated within the fortress walls, has been recorded and dismantled stone by stone and transported to Khartoum, where it is now being re-erected in the grounds of the new museum by the Sudan Antiquities Service. A little to the north of the fortress the expedition discovered the much denuded remains of a town dated to the Fourth and Fifth Dynasties which gave proof of Egyptian occupation of Nubia at a much earlier date than had been hitherto supposed. The excavation of this site showed that copper was mined and worked in the area at this early period. The fortified settlement of Kor, at the head of the Second Cataract, was also excavated by the Society's expeditions; dated to the Middle and New Kingdom period, this site has proved to be of great interest.

In Egyptian Nubia, the Egypt Exploration Society undertook and completed the archaeological survey of both banks of the Nile between Shellal and Adindan with the exception of areas conceded to other missions. More than 500 miles were traversed on foot and over 80 sites were examined by trial excavation and recorded. At Kasr Ibrim the Society's expedition completely excavated the vast necropolis of the Meroitic and X-Group periods, with most rewarding results. Following the end of these excavations, the expedition turned its attention to the town site of Kasr Ibrim; work on this great rock-fortress continues at the present time with discoveries of major importance on the Christian periods of Nubian history (see p. 120). Queen's College, Oxford, sent an epigraphic expert to assist in the recording of rock graffiti in the Abu Simbel area.

United States. In Egyptian Nubia the Oriental Institute of the University of Chicago completed an epigraphic record of the temple of Beit el-Wali before it was dismantled in 1964. In collaboration with the Swiss Institute of Archaeology, they completed excavation of areas between Dehmit and Kalabsha (see *Switzerland*). The Oriental Institute also conducted large-scale excavations at Ballana and Qustol and in the Middle Kingdom fortresses at Serra East and Dorganarti, the latter site yielding valuable information on ancient military architecture.

The American Research Center in Cairo has recently completed large-scale excavations in the town and necropolis of Gebel Adda, where material relative to the Meroitic, X-Group and Christian periods has been recovered. A joint expedition sent out by the University of New Mexico and Columbia University has completed a prehistoric survey through which much has been learned in this branch of archaeological research which was hitherto unknown in this part of Africa.

A mission from Brown University has made a complete epigraphic survey of the temples of Semna and Kumma prior to their removal to Khartoum. The two Middle Kingdom forts at *103*

Askut and Dabnarti have been excavated by the expedition of the University of California; and the expedition of the University of Colorado has explored and recorded X-Group and Christian settlements at Dabarosa. The joint expedition of the University of Pennsylvania and Yale University, after having excavated the rock-tomb of Hekanefer, Prince of Ma'am, at Toshka, turned their attention to the surrounding area and cleared a number of interesting cemeteries of Meroitic and X-Group date. But their most striking discovery was an inscribed clay jar sealing of the early First Dynasty—a further indication of early Egyptian penetration of Nubia at the dawn of written history.

Union of Soviet Socialist Republics. The Institute of Archaeology of the Leningrad section of the Academy of Sciences has carried out excavations in the area between Kubban and the Wadi el Alaki in Egyptian Nubia.

Yugoslavia. The Yugoslav government has sent an architectural mission to assist in the survey and recording of the Gerf Hussein temple prior to its dismantling.

Apart from the work in progress in the threatened areas of Egyptian and Sudanese Nubia, two other foreign expeditions carried out extensive excavations in the Sudan: the East German mission of the Institute of Egyptology of the Humboldt University of Berlin at Musawwarat es Sufra, and the Italian Schiff Giorgini Expedition of the University of Pisa at Sulb.

Never before has so much archaeological research been concentrated in so comparatively limited an area, and so far the results have been, at least in my opinion, far beyond our expectations. It is yet too early to make a final assessment of the value of the work, for much of it is unfinished, and publication of the results is still a matter of the future.

Of my own work as Field Director of the Egypt Exploration Society, I can, of course, write with more authority and in more detail. However, it must be appreciated that the foregoing account of the British participation in the salvage work in Nubia is only the barest outline culled from my own preliminary reports which have been published in *Kush,* the journal of the Sudan Government Antiquities Service, and in the *Annales du Service des Antiquités de l'Égypte.*

The Egypt Exploration Society anticipated the appeal of UNESCO, and in fact our excavations at Buhen had been in progress for some three years before the international campaign to save Nubia's antiquities was started. I like to think, perhaps wrongly, that the success of the response to UNESCO's appeal was in part attributable to the publicity that followed our rather sensational discoveries made in the first season of our excavations at Buhen.

Early in 1956, on the instructions of the society, I visited Wadi Halfa, and on my return I recommended that we should apply to the Sudan Antiquities Service for a concession to explore Buhen and the adjacent areas as far south as Kor, near the head of the Second Cataract. The committee accepted the proposal and, following the granting of the concession, I started excavation on November 12, 1956.

Ours was not the first excavation of Buhen. The garrison temple had been cleared of debris early in this century and had been scientifically investigated by many of the early Egyptologists, including Champollion (see page 92). Large-scale excavation had been made there in 1910–1911 by the late Randall-MacIver and Leonard Woolley on behalf of the University of Pennsylvania (see page 94). However, I was certain that much remained undiscovered, and in view of the future destruction of all archaeological material in Nubia we felt that a careful re-examination was justified. Moreover, Egyptology's knowledge of ancient Egyptian military architecture was very limited because no fortress site had ever been completely excavated, and it was felt that before it was too late this gap in our knowledge should be filled. It was at the same time realized that such a project would cost a great deal both in time and money and might well be the largest single excavation that the Egypt Exploration Society had ever undertaken. This indeed proved to be the case; in 1963 we completed our sixth season and three more months' work was necessary in 1964 before our undertaking was   *105* completed. But it was well worth it, for the great fortress buried beneath tons of drift sand proved to be wonderfully preserved, and almost every detail of Egyptian military architecture was revealed, so that reliable reconstruction such as that shown in Figures 9 and 10 could be made, material not only of great value to the Egyptologist but also to the military historian. Features of defense which were thought to have been invented in medieval Europe are now known to have been used by the Egyptians of the Middle Kingdom 4,000 years ago, and a totally new perspective of Egyptian military purpose in Nubia has been revealed. It is obvious that in the limited amount of time left to us it will be impossible to excavate completely all the strongholds in the great chain of fortifications which stretch through the Second Cataract area. Thus the detailed record of at least one of them is especially valuable, for it can act as a guide and explain many features which might remain an unsolved puzzle in a similar structure only partly explored.

Before describing the course of events leading to the various discoveries at Buhen I must first summarize the history of the fortress as revealed so far by the excavations. Built with other strongholds by the great pharaohs of the Twelfth Dynasty (1991–1786 B.C.) to guard the frontier of their newly acquired empire in the south, Buhen was probably the administrative center for the whole of the fortified region of the Second Cataract. As far as can be ascertained, it remained unscathed during the period of Egypt's military supremacy of more than 200 years. But, in the troubled days following the Hyksos invasion of the homeland, the armies of Kush took the stronghold by storm and parts of the structure were destroyed by fire. It was probably occupied by its conquerors at certain times, but no attempt was made to rebuild the damaged structure, and Buhen remained a more or less gigantic ruin until the reconquest of Nubia by the Egyptian pharaohs of the Eighteenth Dynasty (1575–1308 B.C.). The fortress was then reoccupied and its walls were restored and strengthened. Within, the original town was restored, but with comparatively little alteration in its general design, except that the large houses of the officials were divided up into smaller dwellings. The only radical changes made

were the erection of Queen Hatshepsut's temple over the foundations of a large Middle Kingdom building which may also have
been a temple, and the addition of a new stone-built quay on the
river's edge in front of it. Thus the fortress continued to serve its
purpose until the final collapse of Egyptian power in Nubia, at the
close of the Twentieth Dynasty. It may have been peacefully evacuated, but there are indications that it was taken by storm a second
time, for some of the New Kingdom buildings show signs of fire.
And so it remained a crumbling mass, until in modern times the
desert sands had covered up all of it except a single tower of brickwork, originally part of the east defense wall, which by some trick
of the wind had been spared. Parts of Hatshepsut's temple were
also exposed above the layers of drift sand, and the remains of a
small Meroitic and of Christian settlements were still visible above
the south end of the New Kingdom town.

After preliminary test excavations it was decided to concentrate
our work on the inner fortress or citadel, and this, of course, entailed the detailed investigation of a structure made up of the work
of two periods: the original belonging to the Middle Kingdom with
subsequent additions and alterations when it was rebuilt during
the early Eighteenth Dynasty. This structure, rectangular in shape,
covers an area of 170 by 150 meters, which was enclosed by the
main walls of the fortifications, lower ramparts, and dry ditch,
broken only by two gates on the river side and the main gate facing the desert. The excavation of the walls and dry ditch was an
immense task entailing the labor of large numbers of men over a
very long period, but it was most rewarding, for sufficient remained
for us to ascertain full details of the design of the defense system of
both periods. From the existing remains we are able to reconstruct
with a considerable degree of accuracy the original appearance of
this fine example of Egyptian military architecture, which bears
so striking a resemblance to that of medieval Europe (Figure 9).

This elaborate defense system consists of a massive brick wall
4.85 meters thick and at least 10 meters high, relieved on its outer
face at regular intervals with projecting towers. The top of the
wall is nowhere preserved, but on the basis of ancient Egyptian   *107*

representations of both Middle and New Kingdom date, and of existing fortifications of Medinet Habu at Thebes, we can assume that the parapet had rounded battlements, and that the projecting towers were raised to a higher level than the wall. At the foot of the wall we found a brick-paved rampart, protected by a loopholed parapet overhanging the scarp of the dry ditch, which is 8.40 meters wide and 6.50 meters deep. The counterscarp on the other side of the ditch was originally surmounted by a narrow covered way of brickwork, beyond which we found traces of a glacis rising from the natural ground level. Projecting into the ditch from the scarp at intervals are round bastions, some of which are almost perfectly preserved. Both the parapet and the round bastions, which have rows of loopholes arranged in groups of three, center on a single shooting embrasure from which the defending archers could direct their arrows from three different angles downward onto the attackers in the ditch and level onto targets coming over the counterscarp. Some conception of the immense strength of these defenses is apparent when, standing at the bottom of the ditch, we realize that an attacking force must first storm the glacis, destroying any outposts concealed in the covered way, while under fire from slingshots and arrows from the main wall above. They would then have to descend the steep counterscarp to the bottom of the ditch, under an intense cross-fire from the loopholed ramparts and bastions, behind which the defenders would be completely concealed. Should they survive this ordeal, they would then have to storm the scarp and rampart above it, only to find themselves in a narrow corridor at the foot of the main walls, from the top of which would come a shower of stones and other missiles. The most strongly fortified part of the fortress was the great gate built into the center of the west wall. Although the upper part had been largely destroyed by the alterations of the New Kingdom, the foundations were found well preserved, and full information was obtained regarding its defense system. We have evidence of great double doors in the gateway through the main wall, and of a wooden drawbridge which was pulled back and forth on rollers. The gate and bridge were flanked by two spur walls that extended over the dry ditch, forming a

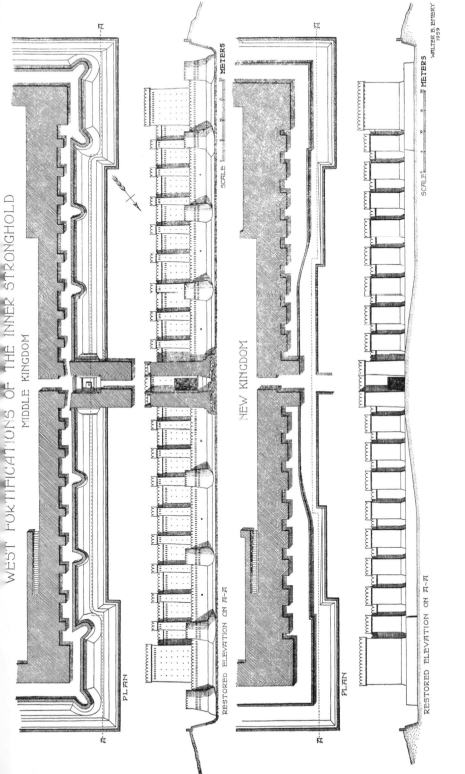

FIGURE 9 The fortress at Buhen

corridor of considerable length, through which an attacking force would have to battle its way, exposed to a rain of missiles from the battlements on three sides (Figure 10).

RECONSTRUCTION OF THE
WEST GATE OF BUHEN

AXONOMETRIC PROJECTION

SCALE ⊢⊢⊢⊢⊢⊢⊢⊢⊢⊢⊣ METERS

WALTER B EMERY
1959

110

FIGURE 10

Nevertheless, we know that these apparently impregnable defenses were breached and the fortress captured by the forces of Kush at the end of the Middle Kingdom. But looking at them even in their present ruined state we cannot help wondering if some form of treachery was not responsible for their capture. There can be little doubt that the garrison of Buhen feared attack only from the north, south, and west sides of the fortress, which were protected by the system of defenses I have described. On the east side facing the Nile, two gates gave direct access to the town, and no lower ramparts existed, only a series of terraces and quays to accommodate the war fleets and merchant shipping of the pharaohs.

When the ruined fortress was reoccupied by the Egyptians in the New Kingdom the west gateway was itself rebuilt, but the spur walls that protected it were cut down to make way for a road which was built over the filled-in ditch and the lower defenses. Obviously the latter were considered as no longer necessary, in view of the new defenses which had been built on a much wider perimeter. The walls and towers of the Middle Kingdom were also greatly altered by the New Kingdom reconstruction, and in order to ascertain the original design we found it necessary to remove the whole of the later additions. This demolition revealed that the walls and towers had been strengthened by the addition of skin walls by the restorers, which altered the whole appearance of the façade (Figure 9). It was not a very thorough job, and the New Kingdom builders did not trouble to remove the heavy deposit of rubble which had accumulated at the base of the ruined walls of the Middle Kingdom. They were well content to build their thick skin walls on this deposit, and it is indeed astonishing that their handiwork survived.

It was during the removal of these New Kingdom skin walls that we made one of our most interesting discoveries. In the recess between the third and fourth towers of the west wall we found the burial of a horse, the skeleton lying directly on the brick pavement of the Middle Kingdom rampart. There can be no doubt of its date, for it was covered with a stratified deposit 1.15 meters deep, on which the brickwork of the New Kingdom was laid. More- *111* over, the bones lay about 0.50 meters beneath a layer of cinders and charred wood, remains of the burning of the fortress when it was stormed at a date approximating to 1675 B.C. Preliminary radio-carbon tests on charcoal from the deposit above the burial have yielded the figure of 3630 $\pm$ 150 years. Although the horse was known in Mesopotamia as early as 2000 B.C., there is no evidence of its presence in the Nile Valley until the Eighteenth Dynasty, and it was generally believed to have been introduced into Egypt by the Hyksos invaders. It is therefore of considerable interest to find remains of this animal, which on sound archaeological evidence can be antedated by probably 200 years. The skeleton has been examined at the British Museum (Natural History), where it has been identified as probably male and aged about nineteen years. But it is impossible to ascertain its breed.

Within the fortress little remained of the New Kingdom town, which, being at a higher level, had been largely destroyed; but the remains of the original Middle Kingdom settlement were found surprisingly well preserved; so much so that, with the exception of the southeast corner, a complete plan of the layout of streets and buildings was ascertainable.

The most prominent building in the town was naturally the governor's residence, which was situated in the northwest corner of the enclosed area, it being a double-story house built against the interior walls of the fortress with direct access to a long stairway leading to the ramparts and battlements. The structure remained substantially unaltered in design throughout the whole period of the occupation of the fortress, and even when we excavated it, nearly 4,000 years after it was built, and with only the ground floor preserved, sufficient evidence remained for us to ascertain its original design. Although partly destroyed by fire when the fortress was sacked at the end of the Middle Kingdom, the building was apparently restored in its entirety when the Egyptians reoccupied the stronghold on their return to Nubia during the New Kingdom, some 200 years later. With its pillared audience hall surrounded by administrative quarters and the domestic rooms for the governor and his family, it reflects the high standard of living maintained in this outpost of pharaonic power, 2,000 years before the Christian era. The ceilings of this luxurious building were originally supported by wooden octagonal pillars, painted red, the half-burnt remains of which we found in position resting on circular stone plinths. Sufficient remained to show that the door-ways to the main rooms had inscribed wooden jambs, and even the painted wall decorations were preserved in many parts. The flooring of all the rooms was of brick, laid in tile fashion and faced with white gypsum plaster which had been cleaned and patched during the rebuilding of the town when it was reoccupied in the New Kingdom. But in some of the smaller rooms and passages of the governor's house, adjoining the great halls, the deposits of ash and charred wood on the original Middle Kingdom foundations had not been removed during the reconstruction of the building; the debris was merely leveled and new flooring brickwork and gypsum plaster was laid over it. It was in some deposits below this later flooring that some of the most interesting objects were found, the most notable of which were small inscribed clay sealings which had been placed over the knots of the strings binding rolls of papyrus documents. From the impressions on these sealings, mostly of Thirteenth Dynasty date, we were encouraged by the possibility of discovering documentary material relating to military activity at this most interesting period of Nubia's history. One small room below the stone stairway leading to the upper story of the building looked particularly promising, so the later floor level was broken up and the debris below it was carefully sieved. Our efforts were rewarded, for in it we found quantities of papyrus which had, alas, been deliberately torn up into small fragments; perhaps the handiwork of some security-minded military clerk of this bygone age. With the permission of the Sudan Antiquities Service these fragments of papyrus inscribed in Middle Kingdom hieratic are being examined in the British Museum, and although it is as yet too early to estimate their value, preliminary research suggests that they are the remains of dispatches from Egypt.

Block by block, the buildings were excavated and the symmetrical plan of the fortress town revealed, probably the most com- *113* plete plan of a small Middle Kingdom urban area yet discovered in the Nile Valley. Divided by two arterial roads running from east to west, it shows that districts were allocated to the different types of buildings necessary to a fortress community. There was a district for the villas of the families of officers and officials, a district for the big barrack buildings of the garrison, another for workshops, stores, and perhaps traders' quarters, and, above all, the site of the temple of Horus of Buhen, the patron deity of the fortress. The two arterial roads, which were paved with stone and burnt brick tiles, each had a drain runnel down the center, which suggests that Nubia must have had a greater rainfall at that time than it has now; for such a feature would be unnecessary today. The arterial roads were crossed at intervals by narrow streets that divided the town into regular squares.

The preservation of these remains varied considerably, but except in limited areas the whole plan of the Middle Kingdom structures was ascertainable; however, since they were located at a higher level, the rebuilding and reconstruction of the New Kingdom had been destroyed. Examination of the exterior of the east wall of the fortress, which had to a large extent been destroyed by the erosion of the Nile, revealed two tower gates at the end of the two arterial roads. Outside the gates were stone-built quays which projected into the river, and it was here that the warships, military transports, and cargo vessels of the Egyptians must have been moored during the Middle Kingdom period, only to be replaced, when the site was reoccupied during the New Kingdom, by a single large quay built directly in front of Hatshepsut's temple. Apart from the gates, excavation on the river bank has shown that the fortress on this side followed the usual pattern with projecting towers and recesses, but with no lower ramparts and ditch. Instead, at the foot of the wall, between it and the river, were two stone-paved terraces supported by a stone-built revetment. Here also, under one of the quays, we found the secret water gate, which in time of siege would also give members of the garrison access to the river through a subterranean passage, the entrance of which was within the fortress enclosure.

At the close of our season in April 1962 the whole town area of the fortress had been excavated and the outer fortifications explored. Only the area below the New Kingdom temple of Queen Hatshepsut remained untouched, and test pits confirmed here the existence of a large structure beneath it, which is certainly of Middle Kingdom date and may well be the fortress sanctuary of that period. This area was certainly the most valuable part of the site, for here we found remains which have assuredly not seen the light of day for more than 3,400 years.

With further financial aid from the British government we were able to join with the Sudan Antiquities Service in the transfer of Hatshepsut's temple to Khartoum, where it will be re-erected on the grounds of the new museum. The temple, one of the finest in Nubia, had to be moved, for otherwise it would be destroyed by the waters of the new reservoir, which will cover all Buhen when the High Dam is completed. The British share of this combined operation was the dismantling of the building and the transfer of the packed stone blocks, some weighing as much as four tons, to the banks of the Nile, where they were loaded on to barges which took them downriver to the railhead at Wadi Halfa.

But before this work of rescue could be started there were certain preliminary tasks to be undertaken, the most important being the epigraphic recording of the temple's reliefs and inscriptions. During our 1960–1961 season Dr. Ricardo Caminos joined our expedition for this purpose and within four and a half months he completed this arduous task. Then came the question of the chemical preparations necessary for strengthening the fragile stone and preserving the painted frescoes on the walls of the sanctuary. With the aid and advice of Dr. Plenderleith, of the Rome Center for the Preservation of Ancient Monuments, this essential work was soon accomplished and the dismantling of the structure was commenced on January 20, 1963 and successfully completed eighty days later. The heavy stone blocks of the temple are now at rest in the new museum at Khartoum, having been transported without damage a distance of 700 miles. The credit for the whole of this most successful operation must go to Dr. Hinkel of the Hum- *115* boldt University, Berlin, whose services have been generously given to the Sudan Antiquities Service and who on their behalf will re-erect the temple on its new site outside the museum.

With the New Kingdom temple removed, we commenced the excavation of the last remaining part of the fortress early in October 1963. This proved to be a much greater undertaking than we had anticipated, because of the very deep foundations of the structure which had been dismantled. The foundation stone blocks below both walls and pillars weighed on average 1½ tons and were sunk to a considerable depth in the mud-brick ruins of the original Middle Kingdom buildings lying below them.

Although these deep foundations made our task difficult, there were nevertheless compensations, the principal one being the gathering of complete evidence of the method, step by step, of the construction of an Egyptian temple. Moreover, the earlier buildings of brick which lay beneath were found in such a good state of preservation that their character was at once apparent. The area was divided into two parts; one devoted to living quarters and storerooms for the use of the priesthood of an adjacent temple, which was certainly the original place of worship for the garrison of the fortress when it was first built about 4,000 years ago.

Our exploration at Buhen was not confined to the great fortress; adjacent areas were examined, one of them with the most startling results. This was a site about half a mile north of the fortress on the sandy banks of the river. It had long been listed for investigation because in 1960 my wife, during a casual walk exercising her dogs, had picked up small fragments of copper ore which she brought back to camp for examination. These interested us, and later we noted pottery sherds of an unusual type of red ware in the drift sand that covered the whole area. Test trenches soon revealed brick and rough stone walls so denuded that they rarely exceeded 0.40 meter in height. This was not very promising, but we were intrigued by the quantities of copper ore and the sherds of red-ware pottery, the character of which we did not at that time recognize. The preliminary tests showed that the site stretched along the river bank for a distance of more than 300 meters, so it was squared off and detailed excavation started on January 3, 1962.

More and more fragments of the carinated red-ware pottery were discovered, until sherds sufficiently large were found showing them to belong to a well-known type of vessel known to the archaeologist as the Meydum bowl, dated to the Fourth and Fifth Dynasties (2620–2340 B.C.). Confirming this date was the presence of unmistakable Nubian B-Group pottery, which, of course, we know to have been contemporary with the period of the Old Kingdom in Egypt. Other types of Fourth and Fifth Dynasty pottery were found, and we were at last certain of the date of this town. Finally, at a fairly high level, we recovered an ostracon inscribed with the cartouche of Kakai (Neferirkara), third king of the Fifth Dynasty. This was followed by clay jar sealings (from papyrus, bags, and jars) bearing the names of a number of kings of the Old Kingdom.

Although greatly denuded, the remains of the town showed definite evidence of an uninterrupted occupation for a considerable period, but no pottery of a date later than the Old Kingdom was found. Shallow stratified areas showed various periods of rebuilding and development, but with no intervals between these changes. Excavation revealed big defense walls of rough stone, 2 meters wide, which we were able to trace to the river's edge some 150 meters north of the perimeter of the fortress, while on the river side we located a deep stone-lined ditch. We had at first thought that the southern area with the defense wall was denuded, because trenching to more than one meter in depth revealed only clean drift sand. However the discoveries near the river's edge caused us to reconsider this conclusion and deep digging revealed brick walls partly below the rough stone lining of the riverside ditch. Here, under one meter of drift sand, we uncovered a well-built structure with walls standing 1.15 meters high (Plate XXVI). On each side of it, at a still lower level, we discovered three well-preserved furnaces in which copper ore had been smelted.

The building was made of bricks of unusually large size, similar to the large variety common in the Second Dynasty. An indication of its early date is shown by the fact that parts of it were   *117*

overbuilt by walls of the small bricks which, from the evidence of
clay sealings and ostraca, we may date to the Fifth Dynasty. The
question of an archaic date for the foundation of the town must
therefore be considered, although conclusive evidence is lacking.
Although this site was so denuded, months of detailed examination produced evidence showing that these remains were not simply those of an isolated trading post but were of a settlement with
a long and uninterrupted occupation. From this discovery, we have
conclusive evidence that the actual Egyptian colonization of Nubia
started at an earlier date than hitherto supposed, perhaps immediately following the campaign of Sneferu. Some conception of the
site's importance to Nubian history can be gained by considering
the following facts established by this discovery.

1. The town was a purely Egyptian colony, for although Nubian
B-Group is present, at least 95 per cent of the pottery sherds are
Egyptian.
2. Copper working was one of its industries, and so we may
conclude that deposits of this metal are to be found somewhere in
the northern Sudan.
3. A well-organized dispatch service was maintained with Egypt
throughout the Fourth and Fifth Dynasties, to judge from the
mass of papyrus and jar sealings.
4. Already the names of the following kings have been identified on sealings and ostraca: Khafra, Menkaura, Userkaf, Sahura,
Neferirkara, Neuserra.

The British contribution to the UNESCO Campaign to Save
the Monuments of Nubia was not confined to our work in the
Sudan; the Egypt Exploration Society also undertook two separate
projects in Egypt. First, under the leadership of Mr. H. S. Smith,
a general archaeological survey was organized to explore all areas
between the Sudan frontier and Shellal which had not been already allocated to the various expeditions who had answered the
UNESCO appeal. This entailed a light mobile expedition which
had to traverse both banks of the Nile for a distance of more than

300 kilometers. Nearly 200 ancient sites were discovered, and although most of them were unworthy of large-scale excavation, their period and character were established and marked on maps supplied by the Egyptian Antiquities Service. As a result of these trial excavations a number of these sites which appeared to be of potential value have been given as concessions to various foreign expeditions, with profitable results. This arduous undertaking was started in January 1961 and continued to the end of March in the first season and in October and November of the same year—a total of nearly five months of foot-slogging under the most difficult conditions.

Our second and major work in Egyptian Nubia was the complete excavation of the necropolis of Kasr Ibrim (see Plate XXVII). The fortress, built on the high cliffs overhanging the east bank of the Nile, would not be affected by the rising water for some time; but the vast necropolis which surrounds it, being on low ground, was obviously in danger. Consequently, when we started our work on October 15, 1961 we concentrated all our efforts on the necropolis, with a view to completing its excavation in one season.

Cemeteries of both Meroitic and X-Group origin were explored. All, with very few exceptions, had been plundered in ancient times and in the case of the later mounds of the X-Group period, they had been reused in the Christian period. Nevertheless, they repaid excavation, and yielded a very fine collection of pottery vessels of almost every variety, ranging from large amphorae to the small painted cups of Meroitic type. Unfortunately many of the large tombs had been plundered in recent times, and these on examination proved to be worthless, for in almost every case they were entirely empty. Consequently, our attention was almost entirely devoted to the burials, which showed unmistakable signs of being undisturbed since early Christian times. In two of the largest tombs of the northern necropolis, discoveries of considerable value were made, for in both cases the plunderers had overlooked, or were ignorant of, the fact that the substructure had two rooms: one for the burial and the other for the funerary equipment. The rooms containing the burial had been ransacked in the usual man-   *119* ner, but we found the storerooms intact. These contained a variety of fine bronze vessels, bronze lamps, glassware, the remains of ivory inlaid wooden boxes, toilet implements, painted pottery, etc. In other tombs, tools and weapons were discovered, so that in general our finds give a fair representation in miniature of the great collection of X-Group material found in the royal tombs of Qustol and Ballana in 1931 (see page 52). The tombs are all minor varieties of the same Ballana and Qustol plan: a rubble or earthen tumulus erected above a rectangular pit cut below ground level. This pit, in which the burial is installed, is roofed by a mud-brick leaning barrel vault, or by large flat stones supported by ledges cut in the walls.

Three Meroitic sites were examined, but all had been thoroughly ransacked by both ancient and modern plunderers. However, sufficient remained to show that the burial installations belonged to a rich and important community. The remains of three *ba* statues, representations of human-headed birds, were recovered; but by far the most important discovery of this period was that of two stelae bearing Meroitic texts of considerable length, one of fourteen, the other of nineteen lines of close writing.

While the work of excavation was in progress, our epigrapher, Dr. Ricardo Caminos, concentrated his attention on the four rock-cut chapels of Thotmose III, Amenhotep II and Rameses II, situated at the base of the rock of Ibrim. These monuments have now been completely recorded on full-scale drawings based on rubbings and tracings. He has also copied, by the same method, the great rock inscription of Seti I, which is situated at the south end of the concession.

When we closed down the excavations of the Ibrim necropolis, more than 300 tombs had been examined, yielding a fine collection of objects. More than half of these came to London, and after a public exhibition were divided among museums in both Britain and the Commonwealth.

After a general survey, made in 1963, had shown that the site of the fortress town of Kasr Ibrim merited a large-scale excavation, this was undertaken by Professor J. Martin Plumley on behalf of the Egypt Exploration Society in 1964. Work was mainly concentrated on the excavation of the magnificent early Christian church which dominates the citadel of the town. Here in the crypt was found the untouched burial of a bishop and with it were two perfectly preserved illuminated paper scrolls dated to A.D. 1372, one in Coptic and the other in Arabic. More than 15 ft. in length, these unique documents are deeds of authority from the patriarch for the consecration of the bishop. Further excavation in the church resulted in the discovery of more documents of the period, written in Greek, Coptic, and Old Nubian, on paper, papyrus, and leather, a veritable treasure trove for the philologist.

The excavation of the remaining parts of the town of Ibrim continue at the present time and probably two more seasons' work will be necessary before this important research is complete. When this is done the commitments of the United Kingdom undertaken in response to the UNESCO appeal will have been fulfilled.

More than six years have passed since the Director General of UNESCO made his appeal to international archaeology to save the relics of Nubia's past, and the response, particularly with regard to excavation, has been such that many of the most important aspects of this part of the campaign have already been accomplished.

Nearly all the temples in both Egyptian and Sudanese Nubia have been recorded in detail, the inscriptions and reliefs on their walls having been copied by photography and line drawings. A great part of this work has been done by the Documentation Center for the History of Art and Civilization of Ancient Egypt, which was established in Cairo by the United Arab Republic government with the assistance of UNESCO in 1955. Apart from the work of the Center, large-scale documentation has also been done by British, French, German, Polish, Belgian, and American expeditions. Many of the temples have been dismantled and removed from the danger zone, preparatory to their being erected on new sites, and arrangements are in hand for the removal of others before the waters of the reservoir reach their maximum level in 1968.

So far, so good. But there remained the greatest problem of all: how to preserve the three great gems of ancient Egyptian ar- *121* chitecture—the temples of Philae and Abu Simbel. With regard to Philae, fears for its future have now been allayed by an undertaking of the United States government, which has approved the allocation of funds more than sufficient to cover the cost of its preservation—a matter of more than $6,000,000. But for the moment let us put the question of money aside and examine the schemes put forward by the engineers for the preservation of both Philae and Abu Simbel.

To begin with Philae. The island on which the great temple of Isis stands is situated in the Nile about 8 kilometers south of Aswan, and is thus located in the reservoir behind the old Aswan Dam. Before the dam was built, early in this century, the island with the group of temple buildings, surrounded by palm trees and lush vegetation, was undoubtedly one of the most beautiful sights in the world.

Now the temple is only fully visible during the few summer months when the reservoir is emptied, and even then its beauty is largely destroyed, situated as it is on a sort of mud bank in the middle of the river. However, the slow lowering and raising of the Nile waters has done comparatively little damage to the structure, and at least at certain times of the year it could be examined and studied by the artist, the architect and the archaeologist.

But now all this would be changed. With the advent of the High Dam its total destruction in a very short time would be inevitable, since the island of Philae will be situated in a reservoir almost midway between the new dam and the old. The water level of this reservoir will be lower than the present high-water level and the upper part of the temple will be permanently exposed during the daytime, but the lower part of the structure will always be under water at night and the level will rise and fall 13 ft. as the water drives the turbines at the old dam for the generation of electricity. The result of this constant fluctuation will be the rapid erosion of the stonework of the building, which will be very soon totally destroyed.

Although situated at the head of the First Cataract, the island
of Philae lies east of the main stream and is flanked on its west

side by the islands of Biga and Agilkia. The engineers of the Egyptian Antiquities Service conceived the idea of joining these islands by dikes so that they would form a barrier attached to the east bank of the river and enclose a lake separate from the reservoir that will be formed between the Aswan Dam and the High Dam. In response to the UNESCO appeal the Dutch government offered to send experts from Holland to study the feasibility of this suggestion and their offer was gratefully accepted by the government of the United Arab Republic (Figure 3).

After exhaustive investigation, these experts pronounced the scheme entirely practical, and detailed plans have now been made which, if carried out, will create a separate island around Philae with a controlled low water level resulting in its restoration to its original setting as it was before the building of the Aswan Dam. Once more "The Pearl of Egypt" will be accessible to visitors all the year round, and very soon it will be surrounded by the lush vegetation which made it one of the world's beauty spots. Above all, this masterpiece of ancient architecture will be finally preserved for the admiration and inspiration of future generations.

The preservation of the two temples of Abu Simbel was a much more difficult problem. The great temple of Rameses II is undoubtedly one of the greatest examples of architectural design and engineering skill, and still in our modern age, it is one of the largest specimens of sculpture cut out of the living rock. Some conception of its immense size will be appreciated when we consider the fact that the seated colossi which form its façade are 65 ft. high. The smaller temple of Queen Nefertari is also entirely rock-cut and it, too, is a superb architectural conception that must somehow be preserved.

Archaeologists and engineers at first decided that the only way to preserve these two splendid monuments was to build a dam around them, and with this solution in view a renowned firm of French consulting engineers was commissioned to examine the practicability of the scheme and if possible to design the form in which such a dam would be constructed. After some months of study, the engineers submitted the design of an earth- and rock-   *123* filled dam semicircular in form, with gradually sloping inner sides, which would abut on the cliff face at two points 758 yards apart. This dam would provide protection for both temples, and with the trees and stretch of water in front of them would preserve to a very large extent the present environment of the area. In every way this appeared to be the most satisfactory way in which the monuments could be preserved, but apart from the great cost of building such a structure, it was apparent that there remained several technical difficulties, most important of which was the question of seepage and capillary attraction, which could not be entirely eliminated.

With regard to seepage, the engineers recommended the installation of a pumping station which would have to work unceasingly to keep the water in front of the temples and behind the dam at a fixed level. The cost of working such an installation would be considerable and there would always be the danger of breakdown from one cause or another which would result in the flooding of the temples, with perhaps disastrous consequences. Therefore, after serious consideration by experts, the project of preserving the temples behind a dam was abandoned, and an alternative scheme, put forward by Italian engineers, was carefully considered.

This alternative solution would appear at first glance, especially to the layman, as fantastic; but an international committee of famous engineers examined its possibilities and pronounced it to be entirely feasible. Briefly, it was this: to carve both monuments free of the living rock and then lift them vertically to a height above the water level of the new reservoir. When we consider that in the case of the great temple alone the weight to be lifted would be approximately 300,000 tons we can only sit back astounded at the wonders of modern engineering. In brief, the method proposed was that the whole temple structure, its sculptured façade, excavated halls and galleries, would be cut away from the parent rock as one great block. This block would then be encased in a concrete cage and raised by ranks of electronically controlled hydraulic jacks situated below it in galleries which would have been driven below the structure. Each lift would be about 30 centimeters and precast concrete blocks would be built below the structure as the lift progressed. By this method the temples would ultimately be raised to a height of 190 ft. above their present level, and their natural setting of rock would be re-created. However, this scheme in its turn was abandoned, because of the prohibitive cost of the operation, which would have amounted to nearly $85,000,000.

Finally, after consideration of various alternative suggestions, such as lifting the temples on "floating foundations" which would rise with the Nile waters as the reservoir filled, or of moth-balling them for preservation under water, it was decided to adopt a plan submitted by Swedish engineers. This scheme called for the cutting up and reconstruction of the temples on high ground in the vicinity of their original location. The total cost of this will be less than half that estimated for the first schemes of building a dam round the temple area or of lifting the monument in one block. Work on the Swedish scheme, which was started in 1964, has met with every success, and by the end of March 1965 the carved up blocks of both temples had been elevated to the site, 211 ft. above, on which they will be reassembled. The reconstruction of the great temple has started after the ceremony of laying the first of the 30-ton blocks, which took place on January 26, 1966, and it is expected that this great undertaking will be completed by the end of 1967.

At work—rowing the *Zenit el Nil* upstream

At play—a band and dancer entertain us at Ballana

A Nubian mother and her son

The ancient island of Elephantine opposite Aswan

Bathers in a backwater of the First Cataract

Below: a distant view of Philae (left center) cradled between palm-fringed banks before the building of the First Aswan Dam

On the *Zenit el Nil* from 1929 to 1934

From 1956 at the Egypt Exploration Society house at Buhen

The tumuli at Qustol before excavation began and
the half-way stage in our removal of one of the tumuli at Ballana

The skeleton of an X-Group king, still wearing his crown, and the ornamental doorway to a burial chamber

Piled bronze and pottery vessels, partly cleared
of the congealed mud in which we found them,
and two close-ups of silver and bronze objects

Model horses in Cairo Museum, as
we equipped them with the bridles and
trappings from the Qustol tombs

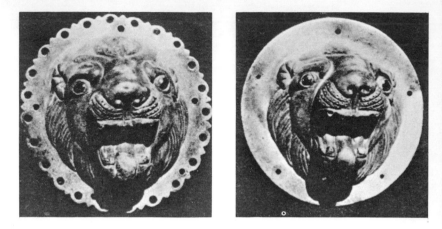

A series of jewelled silver medallions from a horse collar

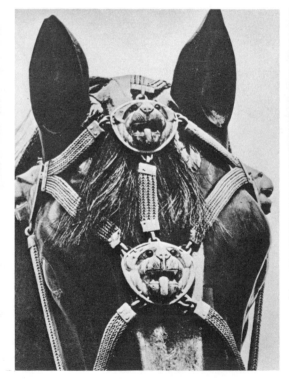

Detail of one of the bridles and the fitting of the

 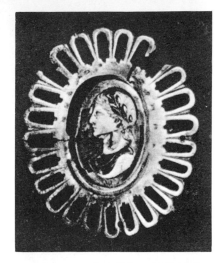

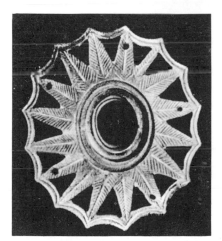 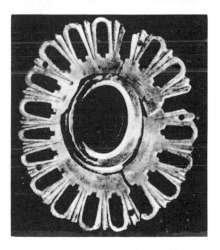

 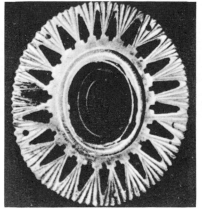 

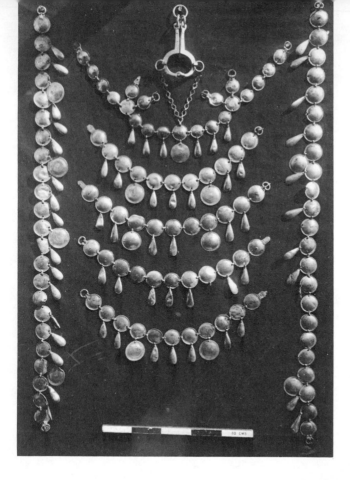

A complete set of silver horse trappings
from Tomb 2 at Qustol and a close-up of
the bit seen on the model on page 136

The silver crowns of X-Group queens, set with carnelians

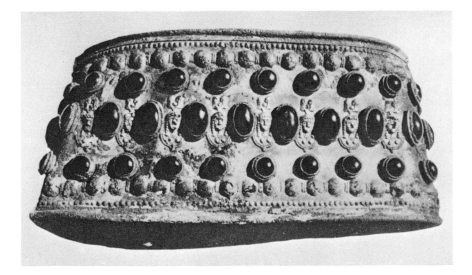

A close-up of the crown of the X-Group king seen in Plate V, of silver set with carnelians

Heavy silver bracelets set with onyx,
beryls, amethysts, and garnets

A necklace of gold beads and pendants

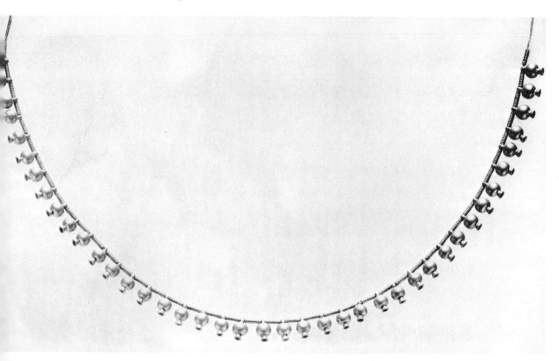

Two necklaces of silver pendants and carnelian beads

A silver chain necklace
and silver torque

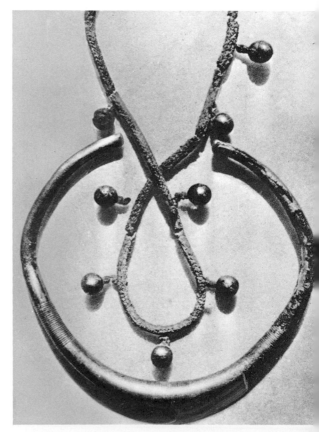

Bead necklaces of obsidian, carnelian,
quartz, amethyst, jasper colored glass,
and blue, green, and yellow faïence

A large silver dish engraved with
a figure of the Greek god Hermes

Wooden toilet flasks carved in the image of
a seated sphinx and the Egyptian god Ra

Silver ewers, 25 cm high

Silver earrings, set with amethyst
and coral, 9.5 cm long

Silver bracelets, one with lion head decoration and
the other set with amethysts, garnets, and beryls

A bronze human-headed hand lamp,
15 cm long; the eyes are
garnets set in silver

An iron knife, 25 cm
long, with an ivory
handle carved in the
form of the god Bes

A bronze bowl, 18.5 cm in diameter

A bronze censer, 17 cm high

Miniature bronze tables, 30 cm high

A bronze pedestal bowl, 11 cm high

Bronze standard lamps, each about 58 cm high

Bronze standard lamps, each about 64 cm high, and a hanging lamp in the form of a dove, 15 cm long

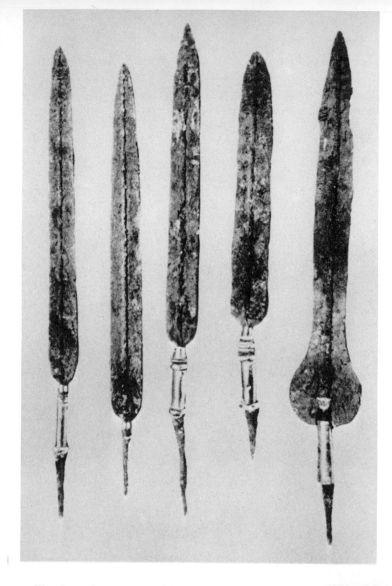

Five large iron spears with silver encased foreshafts

A circular leather shield, 70 cm in diameter

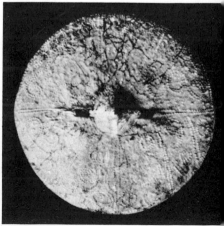

Two iron swords with silver hilts and
scabbards, and a leather arrow quiver

An archer's silver bracer

A wooden chest inlaid with painted ivory, 105 cm high

The west fortifications of the Middle Kingdom fortress;
workmen excavating the north ditch of the New Kingdom fortifications

The Middle Kingdom fortress, showing the north fortifications; and the north ditch

Loopholes in the lower ramparts of the fortress;
the remains of a round bastion

Dismantling the north wall of the sanctuary of the Temple of Hatshepsut; pillar drums loaded on wooden sleds ready for transport

One of the drums being pushed to the head of the ramp and (*below*) safely lowered down the ramp for the barge crossing of the Nile to the railroad

Excavating the Old Kingdom town site

A view of the great test trench we cut across the area

The great hill fortress as seen from the south

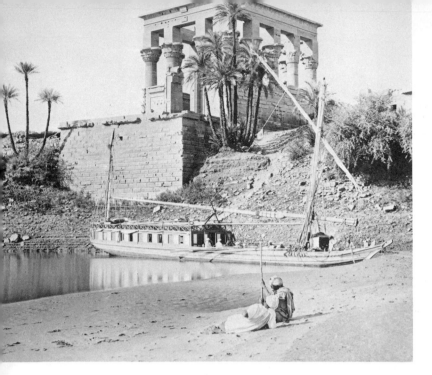

The palm-set "Kiosk"

The ruins of the outer court of
the Temple of Isis as they were
before the building of the first
Aswan Dam

The pylons of the Temple of Isis on Philae. A view taken from the "Kiosk" during the flood period

The Temple of Isis as it appeared at low water in 1964

The temple at Kalabsha before its removal in 1962

The colossi of the Great Temple and a close-up of the third colossus as seen from immediately below

The colossi of the Great Temple in profile and the façade of Queen Nefertari's
temple—both from photographs taken at the beginning of this century

The reconstruction of the Temple of Abu Simbel in 1966

Wooden models of an Egyptian
infantry company armed with
spears and shields, and of
a company of Nubian archers;
the latter, as seen in the close-up
of the first rank, carried bows
and arrows at the ready

3 OUTLINE OF NUBIAN HISTORY

I

The Archaic Period and the Old Kingdom

c. 3100–2160 B.C.

OF THE history of Nubia prior to a date contemporary with the rise of the First Dynasty in Egypt we know very little, perhaps because the country has hitherto never received any widespread attention from the prehistorian. Exploration has been almost exclusively devoted to the valley of the Nile and the desert edge, whereas the terraces of the high *gebel* have never been systematically explored. It is to be hoped that this omission in the search for Nubia's historical background will be rectified during the present archaeological effort to meet the modern threat to the country's existence.

A few palaeolithic flint implements are all that we have as relics of man's work in Nubia before the dawn of history. We have no knowledge of what Nubia was like at that remote period, but like Egypt it was probably very different from what it is today, or even from what it was like at the beginning of the historical period. Large areas of the country were probably watered and wooded and quite unlike the present barren and uninhabitable desert. Even in neolithic times, when the Early Predynastic culture was flourishing in Egypt, Nubia does not appear to have been anything but sparsely populated, and the only cemetery of this period, discovered during the exhaustive exploration of the Archaeological Survey, was No. 17 at Bahan, just south of the First Cataract. Farther south no earlier remains of civilized man have been found than a limited number of cemeteries between the cataract and *169*

Dakka which can be classed as contemporary with the Middle Predynastic period of Egypt.

But with the advent of the Dynastic Race in Egypt, and the unification of the country under the kings of the First Dynasty, the population of Nubia appears to have increased considerably and many cemeteries have been found in the north area of Lower Nubia which are undoubtedly contemporary with this period, although the culture they show is more or less identical with the Late Predynastic of Egypt. This culture, which lasted in Nubia until the close of the Second Dynasty (2700 B.C.), is known to the archaeologist as the A-Group and the people belonging to it were indistinguishable in physical characteristics from the Predynastic Egyptian; in fact, there is little doubt that they were the same people in a slightly different environment.

It is significant that prior to the invasion of Egypt by the Dynastic Race (*c.* 3100 B.C.), Nubia was very thinly populated and only showed connection with the northern Nile Valley by a few cemeteries located in the area immediately south of the First Cataract. Then suddenly we have a big increase in the population, and the advent of a new culture. The only possible explanation is the incursion of large numbers of Predynastic people in retreat from the pressure caused farther north by the invasion of the forerunners of the pharaonic Egyptians. Be that as it may, the archaeological remains of the A-Group people show that at that time Lower Nubia, at any rate, enjoyed a period of comparative prosperity; of conditions beyond the Second Cataract we have as yet little evidence.

In burying their dead, the A-Group people used two types of graves: one was a simple oval pit, nearly round, cut to an average depth of 0.80 meters and the other, less common, was a sort of lateral niche grave formed by an oval pit with a chamber sunk on one side, cut to an average depth of 1.30 meters (Figure 11). The bodies were laid in a contracted position on the right side with the head usually to the west. Surrounding the body were objects of daily use such as pottery vessels, alabaster grinding stones, palettes of alabaster and sandstone, wooden boomerangs, copper borers. Simple jewelry adorned the body, such as shell bracelets and bead

TYPES OF A-GROUP BURIALS

FIGURE II

necklaces of carnelian, blue-glazed steatite, and shell. The pottery in general was rather fine both in design and manufacture, and it shows a considerable variety of form and ware (Figure 12). The most common types were large pink-ware jars to contain liquid, large red-ware bulbous jars with a pointed base for storing food, and deep bowls and cups of thin polished red ware, black-polished inside with red-painted decoration outside, usually in imitation of basketwork; vessels of this type were probably used for eating purposes.

But the peace and prosperity of Nubia in the A-Group period was not undisturbed by war, and as early as the reign of Hor Aha, the first king of the First Dynasty, there are records of Egyptian conquests in the south. There is also evidence to show that Egyptian armies penetrated at least as far as the Second Cataract, for a rock-cut inscription on Gebel Sheikh Suliman, south of Buhen, records the invasion of this area by the pharaoh Zer, who succeeded   *171*

Hor Aha. The inscription shows a seated captive tied to the prow of a typical ship of the Dynastic people of Egypt—quite distinct in design from the boats of the Predynastic people (Figure 13). Below the boat are represented the drowned corpses of the defeated enemy and two crossed circles surmounted by a hawk and a crescent perhaps represent captured towns. Then comes the figure of a standing captive with his hands bound behind him, and finally the name of the king, Zer. To what extent this was a record of a

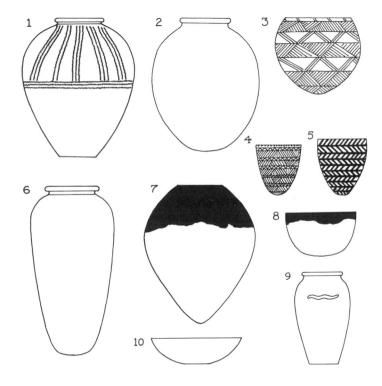

TYPES OF A~GROUP POTTERY

FIGURE 12 *1.* Pink ware with red-painted decoration; *2.* Red ware; *3* and *4.* Red ware with incised decoration; *5.* Thin polished red ware with red-painted decoration; *6.* Red ware; *7* and *8.* Red ware with black top; *9.* Red ware with wavy handle; *10.* Red ware

FIGURE 13   The inscription of King Zer at Sheikh Suliman

complete conquest of the region, or just the bombastic monument of a successful raiding party, is difficult to say, but at least it is evidence of Egyptian aggression in Nubia at a very early date. Further evidence of Egyptian penetration of Nubia in the First Dynasty is shown by fragments of archaic stone vases belonging to this period, which we have found during recent excavation in the fortress of Buhen, only a few miles north of the inscriptions of Zer.

It has been suggested that the A-Group culture of Nubia developed and prospered under Egyptian domination, but this would appear to be unlikely, for its disappearance is more or less contemporary with the first Egyptian conquest and colonization. It is significant that the apparently abrupt end of the A-Group culture came at a time when Nubia was invaded by the Egyptian king Khasekhemui at the end of the Second Dynasty. Whatever the cause, at this time the Nubian population lapsed into poverty, and although the so-called B-Group culture was partly descended from the A-Group, it also showed many different features, partly due to general decadence and perhaps because of the advent of new racial elements from the south. The period of existence of this poverty-stricken culture is roughly contemporary with the Old Kingdom in Egypt (2700–2160 B.C.), in whose great prosperity the Nubians had no share, being probably reduced to semislavery by the northern conqueror.

We are as yet uncertain if Khasekhemui's conquest was followed by colonization, but I think it very possible that tentative efforts were made in that direction. Be that as it may, the real subjugation of Nubia came when Sneferu, first king of the Fourth Dynasty, sent his armies on a campaign which cost the country 7,000 prisoners and 200,000 head of cattle. This blow must have had a devastating effect, and there was apparently no necessity for further military action for many years to come.

Lower Nubia was colonized, and the Egyptians found little difficulty in exploiting the country for its great mineral wealth, not the least important of which was copper. Recent discoveries at Buhen have revealed the existence of a large purely Egyptian settlement which certainly existed for more than 250 years during the Fourth and Fifth Dynasties without any interruption of its occupation. (See page 117.) Examination of the material from these excavations is only in its preliminary stages; but already there is sufficient evidence to show that the colonists, for a period of not less than 200 years, were working copper in well-organized foundries, the remains of which are still preserved. The names of some of the pyramid pharaohs—Khafra, Menkaura, Userkaf, Sahura, Kakai, and so on—have been discovered on papyrus sealings, probably from dispatches from Egypt. These, together with great quantities of pottery vessels which we know are of Egyptian manufacture, show that the town was a trading center of considerable importance.

Contemporary B-Group pottery has also been found in this Egyptian colony, but only in limited quantity, and it would not appear that Nubians formed part of the population of the town. With the Egyptian occupation of their homeland, the B-Group Nubians were probably reduced to extreme poverty, and even trade with their masters appears to have been nonexistent, for no longer do we find Egyptian products in the Nubian graves, and even the products of their own skill, such as pottery, showed a sharp decline in craftsmanship.

The graves of the B-Group people are usually shallow oval or round pits, with the sides sometimes lined with rough slabs of uncut stone or faced with mud plaster (Figure 14). In rare cases the graves of prosperous persons have been found with rough stone flooring, resting on a filling of sand. The burial was contracted, lying on either the right or the left side, and no particular attention appears to have been paid to orientation, although head to the west seems to have been the usual custom. Sometimes the body was laid on a mat and was covered by a goatskin or linen shroud. Only in the richer graves do we find any pottery, and this consists mostly of rather heavy bowls of red ware with a black top (Figure 15). Rough stone palettes and rubbing stones are fairly common, as are stone maceheads and axes; but copper implements, such as needles and awls, are rare. Bone tools are more common, as are poor quality beads of carnelian, shell, and blue faïence.

TYPES OF B-GROUP BURIALS

FIGURE 14

During the Fourth Dynasty (2620–2480 B.C.) Egyptian miners discovered the source of the fine diorite which was used for the royal statuary in the Old and Middle Kingdoms. The outcrop of this beautiful stone was located about 80 kilometers west of Toshka and from inscriptions found there we know that the quarries were worked by the pharaohs Khufu and Djadefra of the Fourth Dynasty and Sahura and Djadkasa-Isisi of the Fifth Dynasty.

On the rocks at Tumas on the west bank of the river inscriptions of the Sixth Dynasty kings Teti and Pepi I record the presence of Egyptian missions in this area, but there is no evidence of any organized settlement in Nubia, although it is possible that small military garrisons were stationed at strategic points to protect the Egyptian trade routes. The Pharaoh Mernera of the Sixth

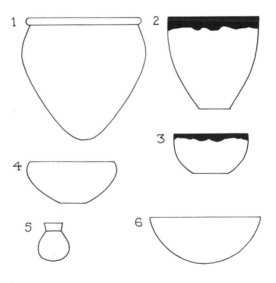

TYPES OF B-GROUP POTTERY

FIGURE 15   *1.* Brown ware; *2* and *3.* Red ware with black top; *4* and *5.* Red ware; *6.* Rough brown ware

Dynasty (2340–2160 B.C.) records in inscriptions at the First Cataract how he came to this district to receive the homage of the chiefs of Medju, Irtet and Wawat, which were probably at that time tribal areas in the northern part of Lower Nubia.

Throughout the reign of Mernera there was considerable Egyptian activity in Nubia ably directed by two of his officials, Uni and Herkhuf. Uni, a great noble, already had experience of Nubian affairs under Mernera's predecessor Pepi I, when he was commissioned to recruit Nubian soldiers for service in Pharaoh's armies, then engaged in warfare against the tribes of the eastern desert. The fact that such recruitment was possible shows that the Egyptian grip on northern Nubia was tightening and it is not surprising that in the succeeding reign it was considered necessary to improve the methods of communication with the lands to the south of the First Cataract. Uni, who was now governor of the south, organized the digging of five canals through the parts of the cataract that had proved to be the most difficult to navigation. The immediate purpose of the construction of these waterways was for the transport of granite for the royal pyramid at Memphis, and for this work Uni needed timber for the building of boats, which he had no hesitation in inviting the Nubian chiefs to supply. The fact that his request was promptly answered is a further indication of the advance of Egyptian power and influence in the northern areas of Nubia.

With the increase of Egyptian prestige in Nubia, the way was open for exploration into the far south and foremost in this was the nobleman Herkhuf, who may be considered the first explorer of whom history has any real record. Probably a younger man than Uni, Herkhuf was sent by Mernera to lead an expedition to open up communications with Yam, a country of whose location we are as yet uncertain, but which was certainly south of the Second Cataract; in fact, some authorities believe it was as far south as Darfur. This expedition, which was absent for seven months, was such a success that Herkhuf was soon sent on another journey through Nubia, taking what he describes as the "Elephantine Road," which has been identified as the desert road starting on

177

the west bank at Aswan which runs some distance out, but more or less parallel with the river. This road is still used extensively at the present time in the driving up of great herds of camels from the Sudan destined for the meat markets of Egypt. Herkhuf was understandably proud of his success as an explorer, for with reference to his second expedition he records that "Never before had any noble or caravan-leader who went forth to Yam done this."

After an interval, apparently of some years, Herkhuf undertook his third journey into the unknown south. This time he took a different route which he describes as the "What" road; it appears to have been farther out in the western desert, probably the Daraw-Kurkur track which is still used by express caravans today. It passes through the oasis of Kurkur, and here Herkhuf learned that the Chief of Yam had passed that way shortly before him, with the intention of waging war against the Temehu or Libyan inhabitants of the Kharga Oasis. For some reason not explained, Herkhuf felt it his duty to follow and act as a peacemaker, in which undertaking he succeeded, for he apparently enjoyed considerable influence and prestige with the people of Yam, who gave him a military escort on his return journey to Egypt. This escort was probably very necessary, for Herkhuf came back with 300 donkeys laden with valuable products of the south, such as incense, ebony, and ivory, which would have been welcome plunder for the inhabitants of Lower Nubia, through whose land he had to pass.

Herkhuf's fourth and last journey was made after the death of his royal master Mernera who had been succeeded by the boy king Pepi II. During his return journey he wrote to the king informing him that he was bringing a dancing dwarf from the land of Yam. This news delighted the young pharaoh and he sent a letter to the explorer saying: "Come northward to the court immediately, and bring with you the pygmy which you have brought living, in good condition and healthy, from the land of ghosts, for the amusement of the king, to rejoice and gladden his heart. When the pygmy is in the vessel, appoint trustworthy people to be on either side of him. Take care that he does not fall in the water. When he is sleeping at night, appoint trustworthy people to sleep beside him in his cabin, and make an inspection ten times a night. My Majesty desires to see this pygmy more than the gifts of Sinai and of Punt." There is some question as to whether Herkhuf's gift to the king was a real pygmy or just a dwarf, for the translation of the ancient Egyptian word is uncertain. If indeed it was a real pygmy, it would suggest that the expedition must have penetrated far into the southern Sudan, or alternatively that the little captive had been obtained through barter in the land of Yam.

The Egyptian penetration of Nubia was not always of the peaceful character of the expeditions of Uni and Herkhuf; for there were periods of revolt when Egyptian rule had been consolidated by force of arms. One such punitive expedition was led by the general Pepi-nakht, who records that he killed large numbers of the enemy, including the children of a Nubian chief as well as many of his nobles. After the pacification of the country, Pepi-nakht reorganized its government and brought the two chiefs of Wawat and Irtet to court to do homage to his royal master, the pharaoh Pepi II.

II

The First Intermediate Period
and the Eleventh Dynasty

c. 2160–1991 B.C.

EGYPTIAN rule in Lower Nubia was not to survive the death of Pepi II, for with him passed the power of the central government and a period of anarchy in the homeland followed, with the inevitable result that Egypt lost her possessions in the south. This period of Egyptian history, between the end of the Sixth Dynasty and rise of the Eleventh Dynasty, is known to Egyptologists as the First Intermediate Period.

Beyond the evidence of internal dissension, little is known of events in Egypt and still less in her lost possessions in Lower Nubia. The vacuum created by the withdrawal of Egyptian power was taken advantage of by the Nubians, who with a population increased by the addition of immigrants coming probably from the southwest, developed an independent culture known as the C-Group. The name and origin of these immigrants is still unknown, but it would appear probable that they were related, physically and culturally, to the older inhabitants of Lower Nubia; for both belonged basically to the brown or Mediterranean race, although certain Negroid characteristics have been noted in the anatomical material recovered from their graves.

Thus, although through this slight Negroid element, the newcomers differed anatomically from the A-Group and B-Group people, they inherited and developed the culture of their predecessors. Indeed C-Group pottery is related closely to the pottery of Predy-

nastic Egypt itself and we can perhaps see in their pastoral civilization what might have developed from the late neolithic culture
of the whole of the northern Nile Valley, had it not been inter-
rupted and destroyed by the invasion of the pharaonic Egyptians
at the end of the fourth millennium B.C. Although hundreds of
C-Group graves have been exhaustively examined by the archaeologists of the Archaeological Survey and other expeditions, our
knowledge of this people is still far from complete, and although
we can trace the evolution of their culture from its early beginning
in the First Intermediate period (2160 B.C.) to its final extinction
in the early New Kingdom (1575 B.C.), one vital question concerning them has as yet not been answered. This question concerns
the southern limit of their culture: did it end at the Second
Cataract, or did it continue into Upper Nubia, and if so, how
far south? The importance of this question lies in the fact that
until it is answered an important part of our knowledge of Nubian
history for more than 600 years must remain largely a matter of
theory.

The excavations of the Harvard-Boston Expedition at Kerma in
Upper Nubia revealed another Nubian culture which, although
resembling the C-Group, was yet definitely distinct and obviously
belonged to a different people. For want of a better term, archaeologists have called this the "Kerma" culture, and like the C-Group
its chronological and geographical limits are as yet not defined.
Even before any serious exploration had been made in Nubia,
archaeologists had been puzzled by the discovery, in various parts
of Egypt, of graves containing contracted burials of Nubian type
(Figure 16). Because the graves were usually shallow they were
called Pan Graves, and because they were frequently found in
districts that would have had military garrisons, their occupants
were identified as Nubian mercenary soldiers, of whose presence
in the pharaonic armies there is ample written evidence.

Now the Pan Grave culture can be definitely identified with
the Kerma people and not with the C-Group culture, and it would
thus appear that the black troops of the Egyptian army came from   *181*

Upper Nubia. In 1934 at the conclusion of the Second Archaeological Survey I said: "The C-Group people were not found in
Kerma, although as Reisner has pointed out, the cemeteries are
more or less contemporary with the C-Group. It is probable that
the C-Group peoples did not extend far south of the Second Cataract and that they confined themselves to Lower Nubia (Wawat)
leaving Upper Nubia (Kush) to their more warlike neighbors.
The similarity of the so-called 'Pan Grave' culture of Upper Egypt

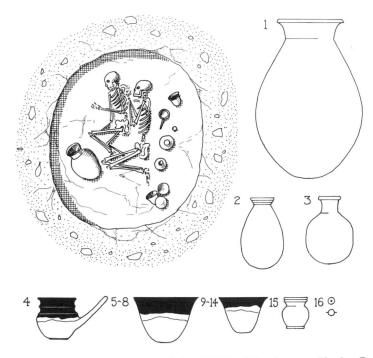

FIGURE 16   A Nubian pan grave of the Middle Kingdom at Abydos Burial:
male and female adults lying in a semicontracted position. Objects (scale ⅛):
1. Large pink-ware jar; *2.* Alabaster jar; *3.* Hard drab clay jar; *4.* Polished red-
ware black-topped spouted jar; *5–14.* Polished red ware, black-topped bowl;
15. Alabaster kohl pot; *16.* Nineteen spherical blue faïence beads

to the material found at Kerma, and its distinct difference from
the C-Group, forces one to the conclusion that it was not from
Lower Nubia that the pharaohs recruited their mercenaries, and
that Wawat and Kush were distinct both racially and culturally.
Furthermore, the anatomical material from the Egyptian 'pan'
graves undoubtedly has a more Negroid character than the Nubian
C-Group."

Since then, I have found no reason to modify this hypothesis,
but a hypothesis it must remain until Upper Nubia has been as
exhaustively explored as Lower Nubia, a task that is now being
undertaken because of the threat of the new High Dam reservoir.

The earliest C-Group contemporary with the First Intermediate
period are similar in many respects to those of the B-Group from
which they appear to have developed (Figure 17). The semicontracted body is found placed on its right side with the head to the
east, in an oval-shaped pit, and frequently wrapped in the remains
of a leather garment. In many cases the loins were covered with
the remains of a leather kilt, sometimes embroidered with beadwork, and it is evident that at this time, when trade with Egypt
was practically nonexistent, the inhabitants of Nubia were dependent on the skins of animals for their clothing. For personal adorn-
ment they wore bracelets of ivory, shell, and beadwork, earrings
of shell, and beadwork belts and necklaces. Cosmetics, such as
galena, were used, and shells and palettes of pottery were employed to contain and mix the pigments. In these early C-Group
graves it was usual to place the pottery offerings in the grave itself, a custom which was later abandoned in favor of placing
them outside the interment. After burial the grave was surmounted by a plain rough-stone circular superstructure. The pottery of the early C-Group people also showed a development
from that of the previous A- and B-Group cultures, but many new
forms and techniques are apparent, notably the bowls of red ware
with incised decoration and the small black-ware cups with incised decoration frequently filled with white, red and blue paint
(Figure 18). Unfortunately, few remains have survived of the
habitations of the C-Group people, and of those that have sur-   *183*

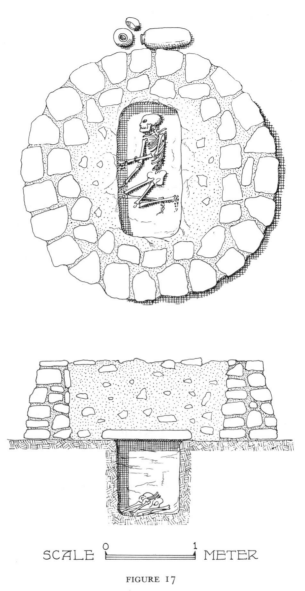

SCALE <u>0   1</u> METER

FIGURE 17

vived none can be considered as belonging to other than the poorer members of the community.

The homes of the richer citizens would probably be situated in 184 the fertile land areas near the banks of the Nile and in consequence would be obliterated without trace because of the intensive cultivation of such valuable land. And so only the humble settlements of the poorer class situated on the desert edge have survived and these only give an impression of a people living under very primitive conditions, whereas the character of many of the graves indicates that such was by no means the case. However, scanty as these domestic remains are, they do supply valuable evidence of the general character of the C-Group people.

The habitations of these more humble members of the community discovered on the desert edge consist of a series of irregularly shaped rooms, leading off from one another, built of rough flat stones set upright in the ground and bonded by means of dried mud "cement." No evidence remains of the method of roofing, but the presence of post holes in the flooring of rooms suggests a covering of reed matting or perhaps leather tenting. Certainly the rough stone walls would not support anything in the nature of stone roofing slabs. The flooring of these huts was of stamped mud, and corn bins also built of rough stone slabs were constructed against the walls.

To what extent the C-Group devoted themselves to agriculture is not known with any degree of certainty, for no implements for tilling the soil have been found in these graves. But they were certainly cattle owners on a large scale; rough clay models of cattle, sheep, and goats are frequently found in their settlements and with their burials; these animals are often drawn as decorations on their pottery and are shown in rock drawings which almost certainly belong to them. Nubia today has not the pasturage for cattle raising and we can only conclude that climatic conditions were very different when the C-Group people reared their herds of livestock on the banks of the Nile 4,000 years ago. Indeed, there are other indications that heavy rainfall was not uncommon at that time: witness the drainage systems which the Egyptians found it necessary to construct when they built their fortress towns in Nubia (see page 197).

Archaeologists differ in their views regarding the military qualities of the C-Group people, some authorities believing them to have   *185*

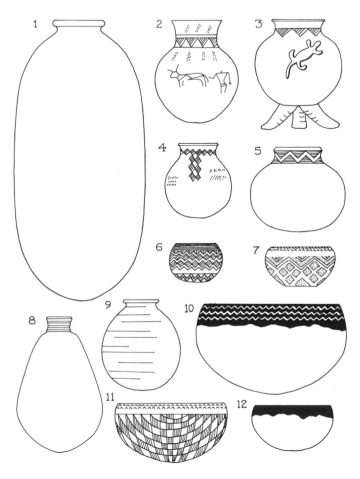

TYPES OF C~GROUP POTTERY

FIGURE 18   *1.* Buff ware; *2.* Rough brown ware with incised decoration; *3.* Rough brown ware with incised and relief decoration; *4.* Rough brown ware with incised decoration; *5.* Red ware with black top and incised decoration; *6* and *7* Black ware with incised and painted decoration; *8.* Red ware; *9.* Buff ware; *10.* Red ware with black top and incised decorations; *11.* Black ware with incised decoration; *12.* Red ware with black top

been a warlike race whom the Egyptians found to be a constant menace, while others consider them to have been nonaggressive, easily conquered and held in subjection; I must confess to subscribing to the latter viewpoint. It is a significant fact that among the variety of objects found in their graves for the use of the owner in the afterlife, weapons are almost entirely absent, a very strange thing if they were a warlike people. Moreover, as I have already pointed out, the Negroid troops in the Egyptian army were probably to be identified with the Kerma people who came from the lands south of the Second Cataract. Within such Egyptian forts as Kubban and Ikkur, situated in the heart of the C-Group homeland, we find relics of the Kerma people who served there as soldiers, but little or no trace of their C-Group relatives. On the other hand, we found ample evidence of C-Group habitations in the vicinity, but not in the forts themselves. In my view the obvious conclusion is that the C-Group were a peaceful people not considered suitable as military material by the Egyptians, who depended on the warlike people of the far south for their garrison auxiliaries.

A nonaggressive race of sedentary cattle owners: such I think were the inhabitants of Lower Nubia when with the re-establishment of a central government in Egypt, the Theban pharaohs of the Eleventh Dynasty (2134–1991 B.C.) commenced the reconquest of the south lands. It is true that there is evidence that even in the period immediately before the reunification of Egypt by the Theban kings, their forebears, princes whose rule did not at that time extend north of Asyut, claimed to "control the Gateway of the South."

Another inscription at Thebes records how a soldier named Jemy made Wawat pay tribute to the Prince of Thebes and although this so-called tribute probably represented only the spoil from a single expedition, it confirms that even when Egypt was weakened by internal dissension, her southern nobility still took an interest in Nubia and exerted some influence there. Nevertheless, it was not until the Theban princes had ascended the throne of a united   *187*

Egypt that large-scale and well-organized penetration of the south was possible.

Under Mentuhotep II (2060–2010 B.C.) of the Eleventh Dynasty, this unity was finally achieved, and with the end of her civil wars Egypt could at last turn her attention to her southern neighbor. Evidence of Egyptian military activity in Lower Nubia during the latter half of the Eleventh Dynasty is attested by numerous rock inscriptions, notably at Buhen, which show the extent of this penetration. But in general, these appear to have been punitive expeditions dispatched in reply to Nubian interference in Egyptian trading caravans and quarry work. For example, a rock inscription at Abisko records how a certain Thehmanu, who may have been a Nubian, became a soldier of Nebhepetra (Mentuhotep II) when the Egyptian king went upstream to Buhen, who "sailed through the whole land, intending to slaughter the nomads of Zati, who were preventing the cutting of stone."

But with Egypt herself still a prey to civil war, her hold on Lower Nubia was obviously precarious, and at the close of the Eleventh Dynasty it appears to have been almost nonexistent. However, as far as the Nubians were concerned, conditions seemed more or less peaceful, and on the archaeological evidence we may judge that the C-Group culture continued its slow development undisturbed. But beyond the Second Cataract in Upper Nubia things may have been very different and although we know little of conditions there during this period, later events suggest that during this time of Egypt's weakness a formidable military power was developing in the south, which the Egyptians called Kush. Thence-forward, Kush was a power that was a constant threat to the southern frontier and indeed to Egypt itself. So much so that when Egypt was once more unified under the great pharaohs of the Twelfth Dynasty, her rulers found it necessary to expend a large part of the national wealth in the construction of vast defense works, which I describe in the next chapter.

III

The Twelfth Dynasty

c. 1991–1786 B.C.

THE FOUNDER and first king of the Twelfth Dynasty was apparently not of royal blood, and there is reason to believe that he was partly of Nubian descent. A prophecy attributed to a priest of Bubastis during the reign of Sneferu (2620–2596 B.C.) foretold a period of disaster in Egypt which was only brought to an end when "a king shall come from the south called Ameny, the son of a woman of Ta-Sti [Nubia] a child of Khen-nekhen [Upper Egypt?]." The name Ameny is a recognized abbreviation of the name Amenemhat, and as the "prophecy" is written on a papyrus of Twelfth Dynasty date, we may conclude that it originated at that time as a form of royal propaganda. But although the age of this composition may be false, the birth and parentage of the hero Ameny is almost certainly correct. Having expelled an Asiatic infiltration in the delta, and restored prosperity, law, and order to Egypt, late in his life, Amenemhat faced up to the problem on his southern frontier. By this time, in the twenty-ninth year of his reign, his son Senusret had been associated with him as co-regent for nine years, and undoubtedly this Nubian campaign was conducted by him and not by Amenemhat, who was probably nearly eighty years of age. Of this war, the first of the long series of Twelfth Dynasty campaigns, no record has yet been found beyond a brief inscription on a rock near Korosko which reads: "Year 29 of King Sehetep-ib-ra [Amenemhat I] living forever. We came to overthrow Wawat." Only Lower Nubia (Wawat) is mentioned, and the war probably was mainly conducted to restore Egyptian control in the more or less peaceful area between the First and Second Cataracts, *189* preparatory to the more serious struggle with Kush farther south. I think the motives behind this Egyptian aggression were twofold: first, colonial expansion to exploit the mineral wealth and other products of the south; second, the vital necessity of preserving Lower Nubia as a buffer between Egypt and Kush.

Nine years after the pacification of Wawat, the main military operations commenced, and after a successful conclusion Senusret I (1971–1928 B.C.), apparently in possession of the Second Cataract, was in a position to commence the great task of starting the construction of a series of fortresses which were ultimately to become one of, if not the, greatest man-made military barrier of the ancient world. A sandstone stela found at Buhen, at the head of the Second Cataract, shows the king standing before the war god Mentu and addressing him: "I have brought for thee all countries which are in Nubia beneath thy feet, Good God." Then comes the conventional representation of the head and shoulders of a captive surmounting an oval enclosure in which is written the name of a conquered town or locality. There are ten of these names which represent the areas brought into subjection as a result of the campaign, and while no identification of them is possible, it is certain that they were situated in the cataract area, and were not part of Wawat. The inscription that follows is so mutilated that it becomes a jumble of such sentences as "Their life is finished," "Fire in their tents," "Her grain has been cast into the Nile." This monument of victory was set up by Senusret's general, who ends the inscription: "I myself swear, this happened in very truth; I, the general of the army, Mentuhotep." If we are to believe the general, the defeat of the Kushites was a major triumph, but it is significant that his figure standing behind the king was subsequently obliterated, which suggests that he was later disgraced. However, there is other and more detailed evidence of Senusret's Nubian victory of the year 18. This is supplied by an inscription in the tomb of a certain Ameny who was one of the most powerful men in Middle Egypt during the reign of Senusret I, since he was nomarch or feudal prince of the Oryx province (Beni Hassan). He says:

190

I followed my lord when he sailed southward to overthrow his
enemies among the four barbarians. I sailed south as the son of
a nomarch, a king's noble, a commander of troops, the great one
of the Oryx-nome, as a son representing his aged father in ac-
cordance with his favor in the king's house and the love for him
in the Court; I passed through Kush in sailing south and reached
the borders of the earth. I brought back tribute; my praise, it
reached heaven. Then His Majesty returned in safety, having
overthrown his enemies in Kush the vile. I returned, following
him as an efficient man. There was no loss among my soldiers.

Although the inscription is dated in the year 43 of the reign, it
undoubtedly records events during Ameny's youth, when his father
was still alive, and from his final statement that he had no casu-
alties among his troops it would appear that he accompanied
the king when victory had already been achieved by General
Mentuhotep.

After this victory the Egyptians were left in control of the region
of the Third Cataract, and Senusret started the construction of
the great series of fortresses which for many years were the barrier
holding the power of Kush in check. Choosing the natural barrier
of the Second Cataract region now known as the Batn el Hagar
(Belly of Stones) Senusret's military engineers designed a series of
strongholds on both banks of the river and on the islands, over a
distance of more than 100 miles, all within signaling distance of
each other. The sites of most of these forts have been located and
although some of them have been partly examined, only one, the
fortress of Buhen, has as yet been completely excavated. However,
they have been sufficiently investigated to show that they were all
built at more or less the same period and that they were all designed and built as part of a single tactical conception. Such a
gigantic task cannot have been completed during one reign, but
I think there is little doubt that the work on most of the forts was
started by Senusret I.

In 1896 James Quibell discovered a number of late Middle   *191*

Kingdom papyri in a tomb below the Ramesseum at Thebes. Among these papyri was one which had among its other contents a list of geographical names beginning with the names of the Nubian fortresses. Seventeen strongholds are named, of which eight undoubtedly belong to the Second Cataract group. The full list of these military centers, starting with the southernmost, is as follows:

1. Called "Repressing . . . " (the rest of the name is lost). This is probably to be identified with the remains of a large rectangular structure situated about 1 kilometer south of Semna, on the west bank of the Nile. It has not yet been excavated, but to judge from the size of the bricks and the thickness of its walls it would appear to be of Middle Kingdom date and contemporary with the other fortresses in this region.

2. Called "Khakaura-justified-is-powerful." This is to be identified with the fort of Semna on the west bank, which, with its twin stronghold on the east bank, holds command of the Nile, at this point cutting its way through a reef of hard rock at the narrowest part of the Second Cataract. From its name we may conclude that its final construction was completed by Khakaura (Senusret III), but excavation has shown that the eastern half of the structure was built at an earlier date, probably the time of Senusret I. It was built on an L-shaped rocky eminence immediately on the edge of the river and is thus rather irregular in plan. Surrounded by the usual wide dry ditch on its north, west, and south sides, its great enclosure walls of brick rest on a foundation of masonry. Divided at intervals by massive projecting towers, the walls are 6–8 meters thick. Two strongly fortified gates on the north and south sides give access to a congested town within the walls, which is bisected by an arterial road connecting the two gates. Although irregular in plan, the town yet shows the same careful layout which is apparent at Buhen (Figure 19).

3. Called "Warding off-the-Bows." This is the fortress situated opposite Semna on the east bank of the river and known as Kumma. Roughly rectangular in plan, it is considerably smaller than its counterpart across the cataract, and although also far simpler in design, there is little doubt that it is contemporary in date and

formed part of a single defensive unit with Semna. Here again, because of the uneven surface of the elevated rock on which it was
built, the brick walls, more than 6 meters thick, rest for the most
part on a bed of masonry. Unfortunately, the outer face of the
walls has for the most part been destroyed, and although we cannot be quite certain that they had not originally the usual projecting towers, it would appear probable that this feature was absent. There was apparently only one land entrance to the fort,
situated on the northeast side; but its character is not known, because most of the east side of the stronghold is denuded. In the
northwest corner a river gate leading down a covered way to the
river is still preserved (Figure 20).

4. Called "Repelling-the-Inu." This is to be identified with Uronarti, a small fort situated on an island in the cataract not far

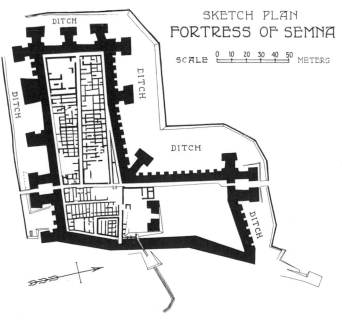

FIGURE 19

193

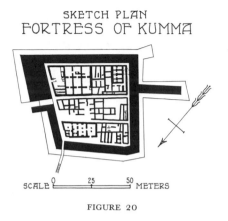

SKETCH PLAN
FORTRESS OF KUMMA

SCALE 0 25 50 METERS

FIGURE 20

north, and within signaling distance of the twin strongholds of
Semna and Kumma. A granite stela found on the site in 1899
records that the fortress was built by Senusret III, but here again
certain features of its construction, compared with Buhen, strongly
suggest that the structure was begun and designed by Senusret I.
The plan of the fort is roughly in the form of an elongated triangle
with a long tail, consisting of a great spur wall which extends to
the northernmost point of the island. To judge from the position of
big bastions on the west side of the spur wall and the town enclosure, it would appear that danger of assault was feared, as with
most of the other forts, from this direction. The exterior of the
walls which surround the small triangular enclosure have the usual
square towers, and at the south corner is a spur wall with the
square towers projecting from each side of it. The main entrance
through a large gatehouse is in the middle of the south wall, and
the small town is divided into two parts by the usual arterial road
which leads indirectly by a long descending stairway to the water
gate situated outside the fort on the east bank of the island
(Figure 21).

5. Called "Curbing-the-countries." This is almost certainly the
fortress situated on the west bank opposite Sarras, and now known as
Shalfak. Although smaller than Uronarti, it is strikingly similar
in design, consisting of towered walls surrounding the town, with
194   a long spur wall extending a considerable distance toward the

northeast. As with Uronarti, the strongly defended side of this long spur wall faces toward the desert. Two shorter spur walls extend from the north and south walls, and the main gate, similar in design to Uronarti, faces west (Figure 22).

6. Called "Subduing-the-Oasis-dwellers." This was perhaps the name given to the two strongholds of Mirgissa and Dabnarti, which from their relative positions show that they were probably considered as one unit. The larger fortress of Mirgissa is situated on the west bank, and Dabnarti, a far smaller structure, is built on an island, almost opposite and only a short distance away. Mirgissa strongly resembles Buhen both in size and design, and I think they were certainly the work of the same military architect. Rectangular in plan, on the river side the fortress has only one main wall, but on the northwest and south it is protected by double walls beyond which is a dry ditch. The site has as yet been only partly excavated and no detailed examination of the walls has been made. Comparing it with Buhen, I am inclined to think that the outer enclosure wall on the northwest and south sides is a later addition, perhaps the work of the New Kingdom pharaohs. It will be in-

SKETCH PLAN
FORTRESS OF URONARTI

SCALE 0 10 20 30 40 50 METERS

160 METERS →

STAIRWAY TO RIVER →

FIGURE 21

teresting to see, when the site is properly cleared, if a dry ditch exists in the areas between the two series of walls. Unlike Buhen, the two gates of the fortress are situated on the north and south sides and are connected with an arterial road running directly through the town. A water gate with a covered way leads from under the east wall down to the river, and this all-important feature was protected by spur walls at each end of the fortress (Figure 23).

The smaller stronghold on Dabnarti has not yet been excavated, but its general plan is ascertainable. It is rectangular in form with projecting towers or short spur walls situated at regular intervals on its exterior. The position of the entrance is uncertain, but an inclined way on the rising ground from the north and the south appears to meet at an opening in the west wall which may be the remains of the main gateway.

7. Called "Iken." This may perhaps be identified with a large fortified enclosure, about 900 meters long, which apparently surrounds a town, on the west bank of the Nile, opposite the island known as Mayanarti, at the head of the Second Cataract. This site has only been partly excavated, but sufficient has been uncovered to show a long line of rather roughly built fortifications, consisting of thick walls with semicircular bastions, projecting at

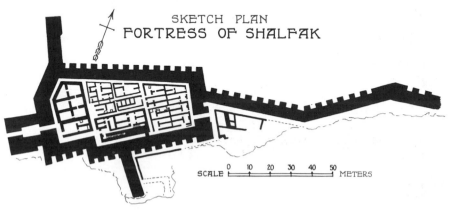

SKETCH PLAN
FORTRESS OF SHALFAK

SCALE 0 10 20 30 40 50 METERS

FIGURE 22

intervals from its western or outer face. Further excavations were carried out by the Egypt Exploration Society on this site in 1965 under the direction of H. S. Smith.

8. Buhen, on the west bank opposite Wadi Halfa, was the largest of the chain of Upper Nubian fortresses (Figure 24). It was the general headquarters for the administration of the garrisons of the other strongholds, and it was also probably the seat of the viceroy who ruled Nubia in the Middle Kingdom. It consists of an elaborate series of fortifications built on a rectangular plan, 172 by 160 meters, which enclosed a town containing domestic habitations, barrack buildings, workshops, a temple, and the governor's palace. Excavation of this great structure has been completed and has revealed a carefully laid out example of rectangular town planning with paved arterial roads, each with its own independent drainage system. On the river side of the fortress, two great gates in the

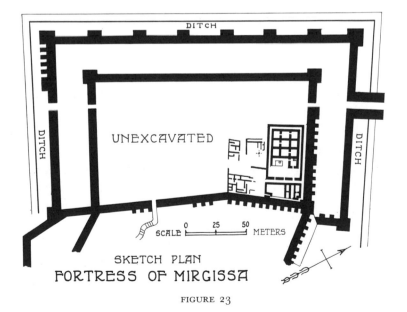

SKETCH PLAN
FORTRESS OF MIRGISSA

FIGURE 23

197

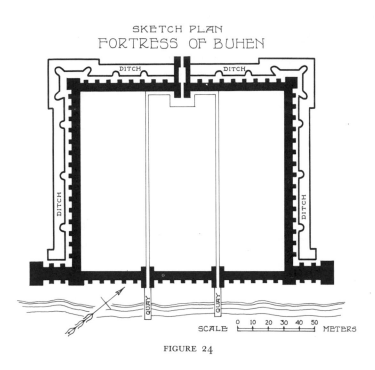

SKETCH PLAN
FORTRESS OF BUHEN

DITCH   DITCH

DITCH

DITCH

QUAY   QUAY

SCALE 0 10 20 30 40 50 METERS

FIGURE 24

walls lead directly to the stone quays from which ships were loaded with tribute and products of trade from conquered Nubia. The contents of tombs discovered outside the town and the condition of houses within it give ample evidence of a rich and even luxurious standard of living in this outpost of colonial Egypt.

The elaborate defense system which enclosed this small town consisted of a massive brick wall, 4.8 meters thick and 11 meters high, relieved at intervals on its outer face with the usual projecting rectangular towers. At the foot of the wall was a paved rampart with a firestep, protected by a loopholed parapet overhanging the scarp of a dry ditch about 9 meters wide and 7 meters deep. The counterscarp on the other side of the ditch was surmounted by a narrow covered way of brickwork, beyond which was a glacis rising from the natural ground level. Projecting into the ditch from the scarp were round bastions with a system of triple loopholes with single embrasures, through which archers could direct a cross-

198

fire which would completely cover the ditch. The most strongly fortified part of the structure was the great gate built in the center of the west wall facing the desert from which came the long trade roads leading to the mines and quarries. The gate was closed by double doors, beyond which was a wooden drawbridge which could be pulled back on rollers. The gate and bridge were flanked by two spur walls which extended over the dry ditch, forming a narrow corridor through which an attacking force would have to battle its way exposed to a rain of missiles from the battlements on three sides. Even when the storming party had broken through the gate, their difficulties would not be at an end, for they would find themselves in an enclosed square with exits giving access to the town only through narrow roads immediately under the inner sides of the walls of the fortification, thus coming under fire once again from the defenders.

The discovery of these complex and elaborate fortifications at Buhen shows that the Egyptian conquerors of the Twelfth Dynasty were holding their newly won territory against a well-organized enemy whose military prowess was by no means negligible.

9. and 10. These fortresses on the Ramesseum list have as yet not been identified. They were called "Embracing-the-two-lands" and "Repelling-the-Mezaiu" and are certainly located in the area of Nubia between Buhen (Wadi Halfa) and Ma'am (Aneiba). There are certainly large Middle Kingdom structures at Faras, just on the frontier line between Egypt and the Sudan, which were noted by F. Ll. Griffith in 1921, and I think that one at least of these units of the fortress chain was built here. This site was being explored by a Polish expedition in 1963–1965 and we may expect an early solution of this question.

11. Called "Ma'am." This is to be identified with the modern Aneiba, which since 1934 was again the capital of Egyptian Nubia. Here there are the denuded remains, little more than the foundations of vast fortifications, the nucleus of which was a stronghold certainly built by Senusret I. It is similar in design and size to that at Buhen. Rectangular in shape, it had the same towered walls, *199*

lower ramparts with semicircular bastions and dry ditch, as Buhen, and we may conclude with comparative certainty that it was the work of the same architect (Figure 25).

12. Called "Baki." This is certainly to be identified with the fortress of Kubban on the east bank of the Nile, which I excavated in 1930, at the time of the Second Archaeological Survey. This structure, again very similar in design to Buhen, has now completely disappeared beneath the waters of the present reservoir; but at the time of our excavations, it was wonderfully preserved, with a large part of the fortifications still standing to a height of more than eight meters. Inside, the buildings of the town were also well preserved, some with their barrel-vaulted roofing intact. On the opposite side of the river at Ikkur, a few miles north of Kubban, was another fortress of almost identical design, and as it is not

SKETCH PLAN
FORTRESS OF ANEIBA

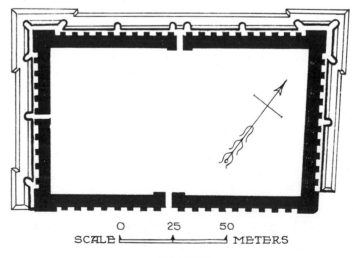

SCALE
O   25   50
METERS

200

FIGURE 25

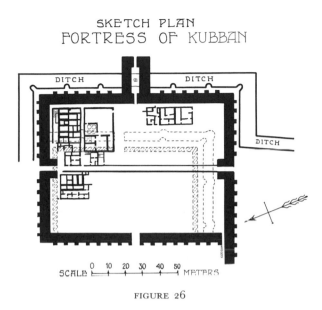

SKETCH PLAN
FORTRESS OF KUBBAN

DITCH   DITCH

DITCH

SCALE 0 10 20 30 40 50 METERS

FIGURE 26

mentioned in the Ramesseum list it would appear probable that it was considered as a single unit with that at Kubban and bore the same name, Baki. Both strongholds were built not only as a garrison station, but as trading stations, and as a dispatch post for the gold of the Wadi el Alaki mines. Moreover, it was necessary to guard the road to the north from any possible incursion of an invading force which might avoid the frontier forts on the river to the south, by taking the Wadi el Alaki road across the desert from Abu Hammad (Figure 26).

Of the remaining strongholds on the Ramesseum list, No. 13 was probably situated on the island of Biga and No. 14 on the island of Elephantine in the First Cataract, but their exact location has not yet been discovered. This also applies to numbers 15, 16, and 17, which were almost certainly situated north of the cataract in southern Egypt itself.

So much for the great system of Nubian fortresses which I think was founded by Senusret I; many of these strongholds were perhaps not finished in his reign and were finally completed by his successors, but the inception of the scheme was probably his. Why   *201* was the vast system of military fortifications made? Although many of the strongholds, such as Buhen and Kubban, served as dispatch posts and trading stations, this was certainly not the primary object of their construction. When we appreciate the elaborate nature and great strength of their fortifications, it becomes obvious that Senusret did not build them only as garrisons to hold down the sparse subject population of Nubia; particularly since, as I have pointed out, there is no evidence that the C-Group people of Wawat were warlike or would constitute anything of a military menace to the security of Egypt. Yet the forts were certainly designed and built to withstand attack from a first-class military power, and although this power has not yet been identified or its base located, I think we may assume it lay well to the south and was in fact the nation to which the Egyptians gave the name of Kush. We must appreciate that just as the Egyptians had good reason to penetrate the south in their search for gold, ivory, slaves, etc., so had the people of Kush equal incentives to force their way north to the more fertile parts of the Nile Valley. The building of the Nubian forts must have entailed a great national effort and considerable sacrifice on the part of the Egyptian nation, and we may realize from this that the menace of invasion from the peoples of the south must have been very real; indeed the records of Egypt's later history show how real it was.

And now let us examine what has been discovered regarding the soldiers who garrisoned the Nubian forts at the time of Senusret I and his immediate predecessors. The army, largely composed of free-born citizens, appears to have been formed in four distinct services, and in general resembled the military systems of Europe in the Middle Ages. The nomarchs, or chief magistrates of various provinces, like the barons of medieval Europe, were under an obligation to supply the king with militia or feudal levies when the necessity arose; but there was also a military force under the direct control of the monarchy. This standing army consisted of the "shock troops," the "recruits" and the colonial levies from Libya and Nubia. As with any modern army, the shock troops were, of course, the elite; they were professional soldiers, while the recruits formed the mass, probably conscripted. At this time, so early in the history of Egypt's empire, the colonial troops were probably limited in number and were only used in police duties in the newly conquered areas. In addition to this, the army of Senusret had a royal bodyguard known as the "Retainers who follow His Majesty," who were organized in companies of a hundred men.

Except in time of national emergency, the garrisons of the Nubian forts probably consisted in the main of recruits stiffened with shock troops. At a later date there is little doubt that a large part of the troops in Nubia were native levies, but in the Twelfth Dynasty there is no evidence that such troops were used to garrison the forts; in fact the remains of the period, such as pottery, strongly suggest that these strongholds were occupied almost exclusively by Egyptian personnel.

While the private soldier was simply called "a member of the army," there was a variety of titles of rank for the officer corps, such as "General," "Commander of the Shock Troops," "Commander of Recruits" or "Instructor of Retainers." There was also the "Army Scribe" who functioned in the quartermaster's department and the "Master of the Secrets of the King in the Army"— which surely indicates the existence of an intelligence corps attached to the command of major units.

The army of the Middle Kingdom consisted entirely of infantry variously composed of archers, slingers, spearmen, and axmen, who wore little in the nature of defensive body armor as we know it. The soldier wore a loincloth and sometimes webbing bands over the shoulders and across the chest, which would give some protection from sword cuts, but he depended most for bodily defense on bull-hide shields which appear to have varied in size according to whether the owner belonged to heavy or light infantry. Helmets were not worn, and the warrior was distinguished from the civilian by a shock of hair, on which he apparently depended for head protection. Troops wore distinguishing badges and are usually depicted with a feather in their hair. We have no reliable information regarding the size of the garrison of each of the Nubian forts, or of the proportion of combat troops to administrative of-

203

ficials, craftsmen, merchants, etc., but to judge from the size of such fortresses as Buhen, Aneiba, and Kubban, I would estimate that in time of war a minimum of 3,000 soldiers would be required.

With construction of the forts and the establishment of their garrisons the Egyptian hold on Nubia was firmly established as far south as Semna, which became the recognized frontier of Pharaoh's dominion in the south. However, the power and influence of Egypt undoubtedly extended beyond this frontier, and fortified trading stations were established even farther into the interior of Kush, in the same manner as the posts of the Hudson's Bay Company were maintained in the semi-hostile areas of Canada in the early days of the white penetration of the West.

The subject of the trading stations situated beyond the recognized frontier at Semna brings us to one, if not the most important, of the problems of Nubian history during the Middle Kingdom: that concerning the character of remains of this period discovered at Kerma, a short distance to the south of the Third Cataract and more than 100 miles beyond the southernmost limit of Egyptian domination. Discoveries made at Kerma in 1917 by the late Dr. George Reisner convinced him that here was an Egyptian colony called Inebu-Amenemhat, where a certain Prince Hepzefa of Asyut was established as governor by Senusret I. Excavation revealed a badly disturbed tumulus tomb of a type entirely foreign to Egyptian custom. In the complex of brick-built chambers below the tumulus were found remains of the burial of the owner, laid out on a bed, a recognized Nubian custom of the period. Surrounding the burial lay the bodies of the harem, servants, and other members of the household who had been buried alive so that they might continue their service to their lord in the afterlife. Among other objects found in the tomb was a magnificent statue of Prince Hepzefa and another of his wife Sennuwy, and Reisner came to the very reasonable conclusion that although this great noble had a magnificent tomb at Asyut in Egypt, he had died on duty in this Egyptian outpost and had there been buried according to local custom. This theory has been accepted by many Egyptologists, but others have questioned it on the grounds that the body of so important a person as Prince Hepzefa would certainly have been brought back to Egypt for burial. Undoubtedly the Egyptians had a fanatical distaste for foreign burial, particularly if it was not done according to their beliefs and the proper rites of purification. Indeed, although many Egyptian notables must have died on duty in Nubia during the hundreds of years of Egyptian rule, there is ample evidence to show that they were almost invariably brought home for burial in the homeland. In the case of Prince Hepzefa he had a very fine tomb at Asyut, but there is no evidence to show if it was used as his burial place, for it has been ransacked and damaged by generations of intruders.

In my view, the whole theory of the existence of the Egyptian colony of Inebu-Amenemhat is unsatisfactory on the following grounds. How could such a colony have maintained itself with more than 100 miles between it and the frontier of the Egyptian dominion, and would so important a person as a prince of Asyut be its governor?

The necessity for further excavation on the site at Kerma is vital, for I think there is a possibility that it was not an Egyptian colony but perhaps the capital of the Kushite power. It is true that vast quantities of Egyptian objects, such as statuary, furniture, beadwork, scarabs, and stone vessels were discovered in its ruins and tombs; but may these not have been plunder taken by the Kushites from their northern enemies?

Following the conquest of Nubia, Senusret I appointed the nomarch of Elephantine, Sarenpuwt, as governor of his new dominions in the south. In his tomb at Aswan, Sarenpuwt describes himself as "the hereditary prince, the nomarch, the king's noble, sole friend, overseer of the priests of Satet, mistress of Elephantine, great controller of Nubia, overseer of all foreign lands, the nomarch Sarenpuwt." We may see in him the first of the long line of viceroys who ruled Nubia for the pharaohs, with intervals, for nearly 1,000 years, and it was probably he who supervised the early stages of the   *205* gigantic task of building the elaborate complex of Nubian forts. Unfortunately, the tomb is very badly preserved and the inscriptions defaced, but there are vague references to what may be a second campaign undertaken by Senusret in Nubia. However, if indeed this did occur, it was probably of a minor character and probably little more than a punitive expedition, for there is evidence that during the latter part of the reign conditions remained peaceful in the south and continued so during the reigns of his successors Amenemhat II (1929–1895 B.C.) and Senusret II (1897–1877 B.C.).

An official named Sihathor of Abydos, who held a position of "assistant treasurer" during the reign of Amenemhat II, records on his funerary stela that "I visited the Mine-land as a youth, and I forced the [Nubian] chiefs to wash gold. I brought malachite, I reached Nubia of the Negroes. I went overthrowing [?] by fear of the Lord of the Two Lands; I came to Heh, I went around its islands, I brought away its produce."

That some of the forts were complete and occupied is indicated by the rock inscriptions at Aswan of a certain Hapu, who records that in the third year of Senusret II he visited Nubia "in order to make an inspection of the fortresses of Wawat." All this suggests that the collection of the products of Nubia and the general routine of administration of the area was established in the newly conquered land.

But the real pacification of Nubia was finally accomplished by Senusret III (1878–1843 B.C.), who by a series of successful campaigns stamped out any lingering resistance and firmly established the frontiers of Egypt's new dominion, dissipating for many years the haunting menace of Kushite invasion. Senusret III, by virtue of his accomplishments as a soldier and administrator, became in later times the patron deity of Nubia, and as such was worshiped in the temples of Nubia by the Egyptians of the New Kingdom hundreds of years after his death.

With a view to future military action in the south, Senusret III early in his reign had a canal cut through the rocks of the First Cataract which, apart from its commercial value, would give pas-

sage for his war fleets. This canal, which was called "Beautiful-
are-the-Ways of Khakaura" (Senusret III), was used by the navies
of the pharaohs for hundreds of years during their intermittent
struggles with Kush and can be reckoned as one of the great king's
major achievements. An inscription on the rocks of the island of
Sehel in the First Cataract, dated to the eighth year of his reign,
gives the dimensions of the waterway as being 150 cubits long
(250 ft.), 20 cubits wide (34 ft.), and 15 cubits deep (25 ft.).

That the threat from the south even to Egypt's natural frontier
was still a matter of concern is shown by the fact that the fortifications at the First Cataract were strengthened; it is also possible
that a great brick wall, remains of which still exist on the east side
of the cataract at Shellal, was also part of the military precautions
taken at this time. The cutting of the canal must have taken some
time, and was perhaps at first not entirely satisfactory, for in the
year 8 of Senusret III we have a record that "His Majesty commanded to make the canal anew." It is uncertain whether this refers to repairs or to the renewal of an abandoned project, but it is
significant that it was in the year of his reign that he undertook his
first campaign in Nubia. The necessity for these military operations,
and even for those which followed, is not apparent, for as far as
can be ascertained from the archaeological evidence, the peace of
Lower Nubia (Wawat) had not been disturbed for many years. But
beyond the Second Cataract may have been a different matter, and
the pressure from Kush may have become menacing. Whatever the
cause, the campaign was successful, and the frontier was established
some thirty-seven miles south of Buhen; but even so, it is obvious
that the struggle continued at intervals. Senusret III had to take
the field again in the years 12 and 16, campaigns in which he
finally established Egyptian rule as far south as Semna. Some
conception of the Egyptians' fear of the continuous pressure from
the south is shown first by Senusret's boundary stela set up at
Semna at the end of his first campaign. It runs as follows:

Southern boundary, made in the year 8, under the majesty of
the King of Upper and Lower Egypt, Khakaura Senusret III   *207*

who is given life forever and ever; in order to prevent that any Negro should cross it, by water or by land, with a ship, or any herds of the Negroes; except a Negro who shall come to do trading in Iken, or with a commission. Every good thing shall be done with them, but without allowing a ship of the Negroes to pass by Heh, going downstream, forever.

So it is evident that although the Kushite was permitted to pass through the cataract area by land in order to trade, he was not allowed to penetrate this fortified area by river. The fear of this people can, I think, also be read between the lines of the King's final victory stela which was set up at Semna with a duplicate on the island of Uronarti:

Live the King of Upper and Lower Egypt, Senusret III, who is given life, stability, satisfaction forever. Year 16, third month of the second season, occurred his majesty's making the southern boundary as far as Heh. I have made my boundary beyond that of my fathers; I have increased that which was bequeathed to me. I am a king who speaks and executes; that which my heart conceives is that which comes to pass by my hand; one who is eager to possess, and powerful to [?]; not allowing a matter to sleep in his heart . . . attacking him who attacks, silent in a matter, or answering a matter according to that which is in it; since, if one is silent after attack, it strengthens the heart of the enemy. Valiance is eagerness, cowardice is to slink back; he is truly a craven who is repelled upon his border; since the Negro hearkens to the [?] of the mouth; it is answering him which drives him back; when one is eager against him, he turns his back; when one slinks back, he begins to be eager. But they are not a people of might, they are poor and broken in heart. My Majesty has seen them; it is not an untruth. I captured their women, I carried off their subjects, went forth to their wells, smote their bulls; I reaped their grain, and set fire thereto. [I swear] as my father lives for me, I speak in truth without a lie therein coming out of my mouth. Now, as for every son of mine who shall maintain this boundary, which my Majesty has made, he is my son, he is born

to my Majesty, the likeness of a son who is the champion of his
father, who maintains the boundary of him that begat him. Now,
as for him who shall relax it and shall not fight for it; he is not
my son, he is not born to me. Now behold, my Majesty caused
a statue of my Majesty to be made upon this boundary, which
my Majesty made in order that ye might prosper because of it,
and in order that ye might fight for it.

The reference to Egypt's enemies as "Negroes" is misleading, for
the people of Kush were not Negroes as we understand the term
as applied to this racial group today. The Egyptians used the term
"Negro" (*nḥsi*) to designate all the dark-skinned peoples of the
south, whatever their race.

Following the great king's conquest of Nubia, Egyptian rule
appears to have been maintained without interference, at least as
far as the frontier at Semna and throughout the reign of his successors Amenemhat III (1842–1797 B.C.), Amenemhat IV (1798–
1790 B.C.) and Queen Sebek-neferura (1789–1786 B.C.); there is no
reference to any military activity in the area. Lower Nubia (Wawat)
remained undisturbed, and the native population, still largely free
of Egyptian cultural influence, was able to develop its own way
of life, with the result that what we call the C-Group civilization
now reached its zenith. The passage of Egyptian armies and the
garrisons of the forts and trading posts appears to have had little
influence on the natives, who as a nonaggressive people were not
recruited for service as soldiers. It is significant that in the fortified
areas such as Kubban, what remains of Nubian material discovered
there does not belong to the C-Group people but to the people of
the lands south of the Second Cataract. The only explanation of this
is that the Egyptians employed the warlike people of Kush as
colonial troops and exempted the unwarlike people of Wawat from
military service. Of course, many of the inhabitants of Lower Nubia
must have been forced to work in the mines and quarries, but in
general the Egyptian occupation, and the stable administration
that came with it, gave the land a long period of peace in which *209*

the native culture could develop to its maturity. So it is that the remains of the C-Group culture of this period show the greatest wealth and individuality, with little or no evidence of foreign influence. As I have previously pointed out, we are largely dependent on the cemeteries for our knowledge of the C-Group people, for their towns and settlements would be situated in close proximity to the river and consequently, lying in the area of cultivation, were destroyed leaving no trace. Small settlements on the desert edge have been preserved, but these were probably the temporary habitations of poor herdsmen, and the evidence of poor living conditions gives no indications of the domestic life of a people whose culture was obviously by no means negligible.

The size and number of the cemeteries show that the native population of Lower Nubia was at this time larger than at any subsequent period until Meroitic rule more than 1,000 years later. It is obvious from rock pictures and from pictorial decoration on their pottery that the C-Group people were cattle breeders on a large scale and that large herds must have had adequate grazing ground on the banks of the Nubian Nile, a condition which would not be possible today. This fact, in conjunction with other evidence, such as the existence of drainage systems in the streets of the Egyptian fortress towns and the discovery of water runnels for cultivation buried beneath desert sand, shows that climatic conditions in Nubia during the Middle Kingdom must have been far less harsh than at the present time. Under these conditions, protected by the military strength of the pharaohs from incursions from the south, Lower Nubia prospered, and this prosperity is reflected in the graves of its people. All C-Group graves of this period were surmounted by circular superstructures of roughly hewn stone, and although in most cases only the lower part of these structures remains, we may judge from the slight batter of their outer walls that they originally had a rounded top. The larger, and we may presume the richer, tombs sometimes had a mud-brick chapel built against the east side of the superstructure, in which pottery vessels containing food and drink were placed as offerings to the dead

210

(Figure 27). In burials of lesser importance, where no offering
chapel had been built, the food vessels were just placed outside
the superstructure, soon becoming covered by sand. It is not uncommon to find tall stone stelae or boundary stones placed at intervals in the cemeteries; but at the present stage of our knowledge, the significance of these is still uncertain. They take the form
of a flat slab with a rounded top tapering inward toward the base,

TYPE OF C~GROUP BURIAL

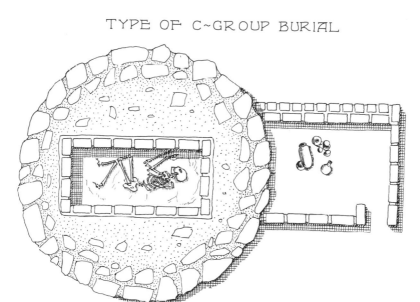

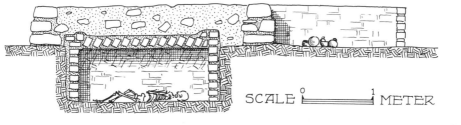

SCALE ⊢———⊣ METER

FIGURE 27

211

and they vary from about 2 ft. to as much as 6 ft. in height. They are frequently inscribed or painted with figures of cattle, and although traces of burnt offerings have been noted on the ground surfaces of the cemeteries, these appear to have no direct relation to the stelae.

TYPE OF C~GROUP BURIAL

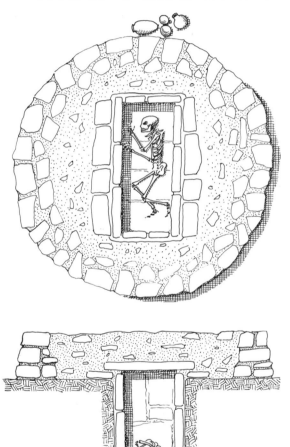

SCALE 0 ⟼ 1 METER

FIGURE 28

TYPE OF C~GROUP BURIAL

SCALE |———| METER

FIGURE 29

The grave, cut in the ground below the superstructure, varied according to the importance and wealth of the owner. The average grave consisted of an oval pit sometimes roofed with matting or rough stone slabs, but interments of the richer citizens sometimes had the walls of the grave lined with flat stone slabs, with roofing of the same material, or a lining of brick with a barrel-vaulted roof (Figures 28 and 29).

The burial was placed in a semicontracted position on the right side, usually with the head to the east. The body was wrapped in leather, and numerous examples have been found where a leather kilt embroidered with beadwork was worn. Sandals and leather caps have also been found, but these are not common. Usually a leather pillow stuffed with straw was placed beneath the head, and in some of the more important burials the body had been placed on a wooden bed, the legs of which were sunk in specially cut holes, so that the frame rested on the floor of the grave (Figure 30).

Of jewelry adorning the bodies of the dead, we find bracelets of gold, silver, ivory, shell, alabaster, and beadwork; necklaces and belts of beadwork with amulets of gold, silver and shell. Shell earrings and finger rings are not uncommon and sometimes, but rarely, we find Egyptian scarabs of steatite and faïence. Objects for the toilet were also placed with the dead, such as bronze mirrors with handles of wood and ivory, shells to contain face paint, and bronze tweezers and pins.

But of all the material found in the cemeteries of the C-Group people, by far the most spectacular and informative was the pottery, the offering vessels found outside the superstructures of their graves. Roughly it may be divided into four categories: first, there are the large buff-ware water jars; second, red-polished black-topped bowls; third, small black-ware cups with incised decoration filled with white or colored pigment; and fourth, jars of pebble, smoothed rough brown ware, many of which have incised patterns of geometric design, while others, more rare, have human and animal figures which in conjunction with the rock drawings give us a valuable glimpse of the appearance and habits of the C-Group people

214

TYPE OF C-GROUP BURIAL

SCALE 0 ⊢━━━━━┥ 1 METER

FIGURE 30

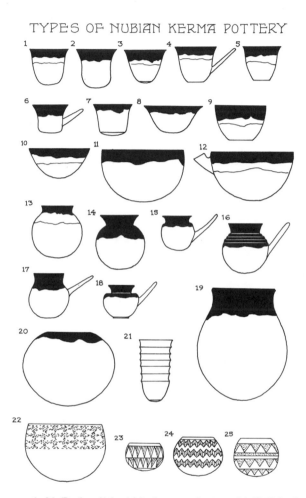

TYPES OF NUBIAN KERMA POTTERY

FIGURE 31   *1–20.* Red polished black-topped ware; *21.* Polished red ware;
22–25. White filled, incised, black polished ware

at the time of the Egyptian conquest. Such a picture is that taken
from one of these jars shown on Figure 18 on page 186.

Until we have the results of excavations now in progress in Up-
216   per Nubia, we know very little of living conditions at this time

in the area south of the Second Cataract. It will be of great interest to know if remains of the C-Group culture extended into
the south lands, and if so, where its frontier was. As I have pointed
out, although akin to the material found at Kerma, it is nevertheless distinct and certainly belongs to a different people.

This Kerma culture, so distinctly marked by its pottery, I tenta-
tively identify with that of Kush, while I think the C-Group material belongs to the people of Wawat. One fact is already firmly
established, and that is that the Kerma material is identical with
that found in the so-called pan graves found sporadically in
Egypt itself, usually in areas that we have reason to suppose had
military garrisons (Figure 31). The pan graves almost certainly
contain the bodies of Nubian soldiers who had found service in
the Egyptian army and who at a later date became the backbone
of Pharaoh's military strength. They date from the Twelfth Dynasty, through the Second Intermediate Period down to the days of
the Empire in the Eighteenth Dynasty. It must be noted that the
material from these graves definitely belongs to the Kerma people
and shows no connection with the C-Group culture of Lower Nubia.
We may therefore conclude that even as early as the Twelfth Dynasty, the pharaohs were recruiting colonial troops from among the
warlike people of Kush. This perhaps explains the quantity of
Egyptian objects found at Kerma, in comparison with the lack of
them in contemporary C-Group graves farther north.

217

IV

The Second Intermediate Period

c. 1786–1575 B.C.

THE END of the Twelfth Dynasty, following the death or deposition of Queen Sebek-neferura in 1786 B.C., does not appear to have caused any immediate weakening of Egyptian rule in Nubia. The names of the first two kings of the Thirteenth Dynasty, Sekhem-rekhutowi and Sekhemkara, are recorded on the Nilometer at Semna where the river levels were recorded; so it is obvious that the forts were still occupied. Even later in the dynasty, we find the name of the twenty-first king called Neferhotep inscribed on the rocks at the First Cataract and on a steatite plaque which was discovered in the fortress of Buhen. A colossal statue of his successor Khaneferra Sebekhotep has been discovered on the island of Argo just south of Kerma; but its location so far south of Senusret's frontier is, I think, suspect, for we have ample evidence of Egyptian monuments being removed to other sites by the Kushites during the periods of their supremacy which came in later ages. Nevertheless, the statue must have been sited in Nubia; so we may conclude that, at least in Khaneferra Sebekhotep's time, the Egyptian hold on the south was still maintained.

But the shadow of future events which would have a vital effect on Nubia's history was already in the north of Egypt. Even toward the end of the Twelfth Dynasty, infiltration into the Delta of Semitic tribes from Palestine was causing uneasiness, and with the weakened central government of the Thirteenth Dynasty, this infiltration gradually assumed the form of an invasion. The leaders of these invaders were known to the Egyptians as Hik-khase, *218* "Rulers of Foreign Countries," from which was derived the name

Hyksos which in later times was used to describe the whole race.
Gradually, as their power increased, the Hyksos made themselves
masters of all Egypt as far south as Cusae. Some conception of the
magnitude of the disaster which had come to Egypt can be appreciated in Manetho's account, recorded by Josephus:

> Tutimaios. In his reign, for what cause I know not, a blast of
> God smote us; and unexpectedly from the regions of the East
> invaders of obscure race marched in confidence of victory against
> our land. By main force they easily seized it without striking a
> blow; and having overpowered the rulers of the land, they then
> burned our cities ruthlessly, razed to the ground the temples of
> the gods, and treated all the natives with a cruel hostility, mas-
> sacring some and leading into slavery the wives and children of
> others. Finally, they appointed as king one of their number
> whose name was Salitis. He had his seat at Memphis, levying
> tribute from Upper and Lower Egypt, and always leaving gar-
> risons behind in the most advantageous places. . . .

The identity of Tutimaios is uncertain, but he is probably the
pharaoh Dudy-mose, one of the later kings of the Thirteenth Dynasty, who reigned about 1675 B.C. Thus most of Egypt came under
the rule of these Hyksos pharaohs, the native rulers preserving a
rather shadowy rule in the southern part of Upper Egypt with
their capital at Thebes. Even so, in the early years of Hyksos'
rule, these native rulers were apparently tributary to the foreign
conqueror in the north.

Under such conditions Egypt's power in Upper Nubia was overthrown, the forts being captured and in some cases destroyed.
Buhen, headquarters of the cataract fortifications, was left a smok-
ing ruin, to remain derelict for more than a hundred years, although parts of it may have been occupied and used by its Kushite
conquerors. Evidence of this is shown by the stela of Sepedher
whereon he states that "I was a valiant commandant of Buhen
and never did any commandant do what I did; I built the temple
of Horus, Lord of Buhen, to the satisfaction of the ruler of Kush."
Sepedher would appear to have been, with others, an Egyptian   *219*

who had taken service with the chieftains of Kush, whose rule had by then extended over a large part of Nubia. We have not found the temple he claims to have built at Buhen, but with studies now in progress it may yet be identified. It is important to learn from this inscription that the Kushite ruler was interested in the construction of a temple to Horus, an Egyptian god, for it indicates that by this time Egyptian customs and culture were well established and accepted by the ruler of an independent Kush.

How far north Kushite rule extended is uncertain, but I am inclined to think that a large part of Lower Nubia (Wawat) was still controlled by the Egyptians, or at least was very much under their influence. My reason for this belief is the evidence of the rapid adoption of Egyptian burial customs by the C-Group inhabitants of this area which took place at this time. It is in fact so marked that it might well indicate fairly large scale immigration by Egyptian settlers coming as refugees from Hyksos pressure. During the first part of the Second Intermediate Period, the conventional circular superstructure tomb with its semicontracted burial survived; but by the close of the Thirteenth Dynasty the whole character of the C-Group burial grounds had changed. No longer do we find the curious stelae, but in their place are offering pits scattered sporadically throughout the cemetery, but showing no certain relation to any particular grave. These small pits usually contained the forepart of the skulls of gazelles, decorated with red and black paint, and offerings usually in the form of pottery vessels. In many cases, the pits were covered by small vaulted superstructures of mud brick. With regard to the burials, the body, lying on the right side in a flexed position with the head to the west, was placed in a rectangular pit with rounded ends. No covering stones were used, and after the interment the grave was filled with sand. Over it was built a rectangular vaulted superstructure of mud brick with a stone offering slab at the head end. In some cases a hole was cut in the wall of the superstructure to connect the grave with the offerings resting on the slab (Figure 32). There is evidence that these superstructures were frequently built

some considerable time after the interment; for in many cases
they are found out of alignment with the grave below them.

Apart from the pottery placed on the offering slab at the head of
the superstructure, vessels were frequently placed in the grave at

TYPE OF C~GROUP BURIAL

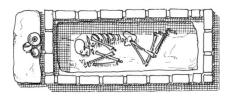

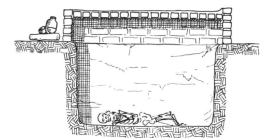

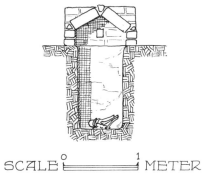

SCALE METER

FIGURE 32

221

the head and feet of the body. Egyptian influence is shown by the contents of the grave, such as scarabs of steatite, carnelian, and amethyst, amulets of faïence attached to the fingers and neck. Typical Egyptian kohl pots of alabaster were popular, as were bronze mirrors and razors, and although weapons were rare, daggers of Egyptian type are sometimes found. In fact, with the exception of the pottery, most of the grave contents, such as jewelry, toilet articles, tools, and weapons, show an unmistakable Egyptian origin.

It is evident that at some period, an alliance was established between the Hyksos kings and the chieftains of Kush; thus placing the native princes of Thebes and their dominions between two fires. Little wonder that for many years they were compelled to stand on the defensive. This state of affairs continued until, with the advent of the Seventeenth Dynasty (1650–1575 B.C.), a gradual rebirth of Egyptian strength took place, and a war of liberation commenced under the last king of the dynasty, Kamose. In the third year of his reign, he called a council of his courtiers at Thebes and addressed them as follows.

> I should like to know what serves this strength of mine, when a [Hyksos] chieftain is in Avaris [Tanis?] and another in Kush, and I sit between an Asiatic and a Nubian, each man in possession of his slice of this Egypt, and I cannot pass by him as far as Memphis. See, he holds Khmūn (Ashmunen) and no man has respite from his spoliation through to the Setyu [a name for the Hyksos]. I will grapple with him and slit open his belly. My desire is to deliver Egypt and to smite the Asiatics.

According to the record, the king's advisers appear to have been rather timid, or at least cautious, and among other reasons they advance against taking the offensive is that "Elephantine is strong." This indicates that they considered their southern frontier to be at the First Cataract; in which case Lower Nubia (Wawat) must have been independent, or subject to Kush. However, as I have

222

pointed out, the archaeological evidence shows that Egyptian influence was so strong at that time in Lower Nubia that even if
the area was not actually part of the dominion of the Theban
kings, probably it was friendly territory, with Egyptian colonists
as part of its population.

Kamose paid no heed to the cautions of his advisers, and carried out a successful campaign against his Hyksos enemy. In the
record of his victory, we again have evidence that at least some
part of Nubia was still under Egyptian influence, for mention is
made of Nubian troops in his army. Hyksos resistance to the liber-
ating armies of Thebes was so weakened that their king Apepi
sent to Kush for help. Kamose's record of events continues:

> I captured a messenger of his, high up over the Oasis, traveling
> southward to Kush for the sake of a written despatch, and I
> found upon it this message in writing from the chieftain of
> Avaris: "I Aaweserre, the son of Ra, Apepi greet my son the
> chieftain of Kush. Why have you arisen as chieftain without
> letting me know? Have you [not] beheld what Egypt has done
> against me, the chieftain who is in it, Kamose the Mighty,
> ousting me from my soil and I have not reached him—after the
> manner of all that he has done against you, he choosing the
> two lands to devastate them, my land and yours, and he has
> destroyed them. Come, fare north at once, do not be timid. See,
> he is here with me . . . I will not let him go until you have ar-
> rived. Then we will divide the towns of this Egypt between us."

From the wording of this appeal by the Hyksos king, particularly the reference to "after the manner of all that he has done
against you," there is, I think, reason to suppose that Kamose had
struck south into Nubia before turning his attention to his principal
enemy in the north. Although there is no concrete evidence of this,
some support is given to the theory by the fact that his name, together with that of his successor Ahmose, appears on an inscription found at Tushka. But if any military effort was made in Nubia

223

by Kamose, it can only have been of a minor character, as a preliminary precaution to safeguard his southern frontier before em-
barking on major warfare against the Hyksos power. It was his
successor Ahmose who inaugurated the southern wars which were
to end with the reconquest of Nubia and its ultimate colonization
by the Egyptians.

V

The Eighteenth Dynasty

c. 1575–1308 B.C.

THE FOUNDER of the Eighteenth Dynasty, Ahmose I, came to the throne in 1575 B.C., and throughout the major part of his reign he was engaged in the expulsion of the Hyksos from the delta of Egypt, finally driving them into the southwest of Palestine. This accomplished, in the twenty-second year of his rule he turned his attention to his southern frontier, and the second conquest of Nubia commenced.

The principal source of our information concerning this campaign and those of the succeeding reigns comes from the autobiography of the king's namesake, the admiral Ahmose, which he inscribed on the walls of his tomb at El Kab. Ahmose, son of Ebana, came of a noble family who for some generations had been the nomarchs of the district of El Kab. Throughout the period of the Hyksos struggle, they had shown complete loyalty to the Theban kings, and consequently were high in the royal favor. Ahmose even as a youth was given officer status, apparently in the royal bodyguard, for he tells us that "I followed the King on foot when he rode abroad in his chariot."

By the time of the Nubian campaign, Ahmose was a veteran with a long record of distinguished service behind him, and was probably already in command of the Egyptian warships which must have passed through the canal of Senusret III to aid in the reconquest of Nubia. Ahmose relates how "His Majesty made a great slaughter among them" (the Nubians) and how "His Majesty sailed downstream, his heart joyous with the might of victory [for] he had seized the Southerners and the Northerners." We do

225

not know how far south the Egyptians penetrated in this campaign, but there is no doubt that the whole of Nubia as far as the Second Cataract was firmly in their hands and that the ruins of the great fortress at Buhen were occupied. A certain Thuwre was appointed commandant of Buhen, and in the following reign this individual was to become the viceroy of Kush. It was probably under the direction of Thuwre that the reconstruction and enlargement of the fortifications of Buhen were commenced; for we have evidence that the pharaoh Ahmose built a temple north of the Middle Kingdom fortress outside its defenses, which suggests that he had in mind the enlargement of the fortifications which would enclose both his temple and the older stronghold. Amenhotep I succeeded his father Ahmose in 1550 b.c., and although there is only record of one campaign, he succeeded in establishing his frontier at least as far south as Semna. For the record of his expedition we are again indebted to the admiral Ahmose, who tells us: "I sailed with the King Zeserkara [Amenhotep I] triumphant, when he ascended the river to Kush, in order to extend the borders of Egypt. His Majesty captured that Nubian chieftain in the midst of his army." After a description of his fighting abilities, Ahmose continues: "I brought His Majesty in two days to Egypt from the upper well; one [the king] presented me with gold." If, as would appear likely, the "upper well" describes the Second Cataract or somewhere in the vicinity, we can only conclude that all territory north of the frontier at Semna was considered Egyptian, for it would be impossible to cover any great distance by ship in two days.

We do not know the date of this war against Kush, but it must have occurred in the earlier half of Amenhotep's reign, for there is an inscription of the year 8 of this king on the rocks at Ikonarti. Following this victory came the decision to colonize Nubia and the foundation of the office of Viceroy under the title of "King's Son of Kush." First of a long line of these viceroys, many of whose names are now known to us, was Thuwre, who as commandant of Buhen would at that time be already holding the most senior administrative post in Nubia. Amenhotep I was succeeded by Thotmose I (1528–1510 B.C.), whose first act was to send a dispatch announcing the fact to Thuwre, who was still viceroy of Nubia. Thuwre caused this coronation decree to be cut on stelae which were set up at Kubban and at Buhen. It runs as follows:

> Royal command to the king's-son, the governor of the south countries, Thuwre triumphant. Behold, there is brought to thee this command of the king in order to inform thee that My Majesty has appeared as King of Upper and Lower Egypt upon the Horus-throne of the living, without his like forever. Make my titulary as follows:
>
> Horus title: "Mighty Bull, Beloved of Maat."
>
> Two Ladies title: "Shining in the Serpent-diadem, Great in Strength."
>
> Golden Horus title: "Goodly in years, Making Hearts live."
>
> King of Upper and Lower Egypt title: "Akheperkara."
>
> Son of Ra title: "Thotmose, living forever and ever."
>
> Cause thou oblations to be offered to the gods of Elephantine of the South as follows: "Performance of the pleasing ceremonies on behalf of the King of Upper and Lower Egypt, Akheperkara, who is given life." Cause thou that the oath be established in the name of My Majesty, born of the king's-mother, Seniseneb, who is in health. This is a communication to inform thee of it; and of the fact that the royal house is well and prosperous. . . .
>
> Year 1, third month of the second season, twenty-first day; the day of the feast of the coronation.

Within two years of his coronation Thotmose I had indeed earned his Horus title of "Mighty Bull," for he achieved the conquest of Kush and as he claimed on an inscription at Tombos south of the Third Cataract he had "penetrated valleys which the royal ancestors knew not, which the wearers of the double diadem had not seen." Indeed, there is evidence that strongly suggests that the Egyptian armies penetrated the whole of the Dongola reach of the Nile, for Thotmose set up a boundary inscription at Kurgus at the southern end of the Abu Hamed road which was the ancient overland route to Kubban in Lower Nubia. It is, of course,

227

possible that this inscription was set up by a raiding expedition coming from Kubban across the desert and does not necessarily prove that all the river areas downstream were firmly in Egyptian hands. Nevertheless, there is little doubt that the power of Kush was destroyed, and once again we are indebted to the biography of the old veteran Ahmose of El Kab, who was in command of the war fleet of Pharaoh. He tells us:

> I sailed the king Akheperkara [Thotmose I] triumphant, when he ascended the river to Khenthennofer, in order to cast out violence in the highlands, in order to suppress the raiding of the hill region I showed bravery in his presence in the bad water, in the passage of the ship by the bend [Dongola Reach?]. One [the king] appointed me chief of the sailors. His Majesty was. . . . His Majesty was furious thereat, like a panther; His Majesty cast his first lance, which remained in the body of that fallen one. This was . . . [the chief of Kush?] powerless before his flaming uraeus, made so in an instant of destruction; their people were brought off as living prisoners. His Majesty sailed downriver, with all countries in his grasp, that wretched Nubian chieftain being hanged head downward at the prow of the ship of His Majesty, and landed at Karnak.

But before the king could sail his fleet in triumph to his capital at Thebes, Thuwre, the viceroy, records on an inscription at the First Cataract that he was compelled to clear Senusret's canal which had become filled with stones. This work was done in the year 3, at the end of the campaign, and it is peculiar, for one would suppose that the canal would have been clear enough for the passage of the fleet at the outset of the war. The only possible explanation is that at the start of hostilities the warships were built in Nubia south of the First Cataract, and with its conclusion were considered essential for service in Egypt itself.

There is evidence suggesting that Thotmose I built forts at Tombos, and on the island of Sai, and there is no doubt that by the end of his reign the whole of Nubia, including the Dongola reach, was firmly held. Many of the ruined fortresses of the Middle

228

Kingdom farther to the north were rebuilt and enlarged; this gigantic task was probably done under the direction of the viceroy Thuwre. Buhen, at the head of the Second Cataract, was at this time once again selected as the administrative center. The old fortress walls were rebuilt and strengthened, the lower ramparts and ditch being filled in and covered by a brick paved road which surrounded the whole structure, making it a citadel in the center of the new fortifications, which were built on a much larger and more elaborate scale. A ditch, 6 meters wide and 2 meters deep, was dug, forming a perimeter of about one mile, and behind this were built the walls which enclosed the new town. These were of great strength: 5 meters thick, at least 12 meters high, with rectangular towers set at intervals on the exterior face. The plan of these fortifications, unlike that of the Middle Kingdom structure, was irregular in shape with wide salients, the largest of which was situated approximately in the center, on the western side facing the desert. Within this salient was a great gatehouse with a rock-cut causeway which crossed the ditch and was the principal entrance to the fortress.

Other military strongholds in Lower Nubia, such as Kubban, Ikkur, and Aneiba, were strengthened; but the forts beyond the Second Cataract in the Batn el Hagar appear to have received little attention and indeed some of them appear to have been left unoccupied. We can only conclude that with the area of conquest pushed so far to the south, they were to a certain extent now considered redundant and the main effort of military building had to be concentrated in the newly acquired territories beyond the Second Cataract. Numerous sites have been noted in the Dongola reach which may cover the remains of such buildings, but until they receive the attention of the excavator we cannot be certain on this point. The necessity for the reconstruction of Buhen (Halfa), Ma'am (Aneiba), and Baki (Kubban) in Lower Nubia is obvious. Buhen, at the head of the Second Cataract, was the headquarters for all military units in this vital area, and it was the clearing house for the products of the south which were loaded on the ships moored to its large stone quays. Ma'am as the future center of administration and seat of the Viceroy, was of even greater importance, as the ruins of its vast walls testify, and Kubban, situated at the river end of the vital road to the Wadi el Alaki gold mines, was also essential to check any attempt at invasion from the south which might try to avoid the river fortifications by taking the Abu Hamed road across the desert.

And now let us look at the Egyptian army which had so rapidly re-established the power of the pharaohs in Nubia. The military organization of the time of Thotmose I was very different from that of Senusret I, for no longer was it based on a feudal system. Egypt now had a truly national army with an elaborate structure of command of which there is no evidence in the Middle Kingdom. The wars of liberation against the Hyksos usurpers had taught the Egyptians that a professional army was a necessity, and that Egypt could no longer depend on partly trained levies led by members of the local nobility. She had become a first-class military power with a large standing army officered by professional soldiers.

As always, in any major campaign the pharaoh was the commander-in-chief, aided by the vizier in his capacity of Minister of War and by an army council. The army was organized into divisions of 5,000 men and each division was a complete army corps in itself, for it was made up of both infantry and chariotry with a general in command. The infantry, consisting of three classes, "recruits" (conscripts and volunteers), "trained men" (regulars), and "braves" (elite shock troops), were divided up into regiments of 250 men under the command of an officer who carried their standard both on parade and in combat. Under him was a junior officer who was known as "the greatest of fifty"—which was obviously the smallest unit in the army. With regard to armament, the troops were equipped with weapons, according to their class as heavy or light infantry and archers, with bow and arrow, club, ax, spear, and sword. The two-wheeled two-horse chariotry was divided into squadrons of twenty-five vehicles, each holding a driver and soldier; each of these squadrons was commanded by a "Charioteer of the Residence" under the over-all direction of the "Lieutenant-commander of Chariotry." The soldier in the chariot was usually armed with bow and arrow, javelin, sword and shield.

Apart from the native troops, the army even in the early days of the empire incorporated units of foreign mercenary troops which were ultimately to form its backbone. At this time, these foreign units were largely recruited from the tribesmen of Nubia, serving exclusively as infantry. It is interesting to note in this connection that in the course of excavations on the fortress sites, only very limited amounts of Nubian pottery have been found within the actual strongholds and nearly all of this is Kerma ware from Kush; little or nothing is of the late C-Group ware from Wawat. All this suggests that, as in the Middle Kingdom, the military commander of the empire considered it hazardous to employ Nubians as garrison troops in the land of their origin.

The administration of an army invading so rugged a country

TYPE OF NEW KINGDOM BURIAL

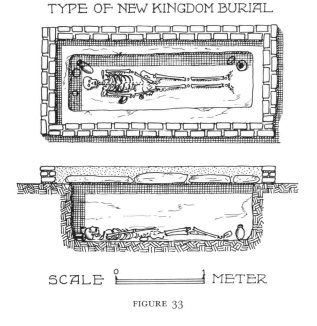

SCALE ⊢———⊣ METER

FIGURE 33

231

as Nubia must have been complicated; communication between the military posts was difficult and the "heralds" (dispatch carriers) must have been a vital part of the organization. Attached to the army were the military scribes, who were probably civilians, and we read of such titles as "Scribe of Assemblage" and "Scribe of Distribution," whose duties were obviously connected with the quartermaster's office.

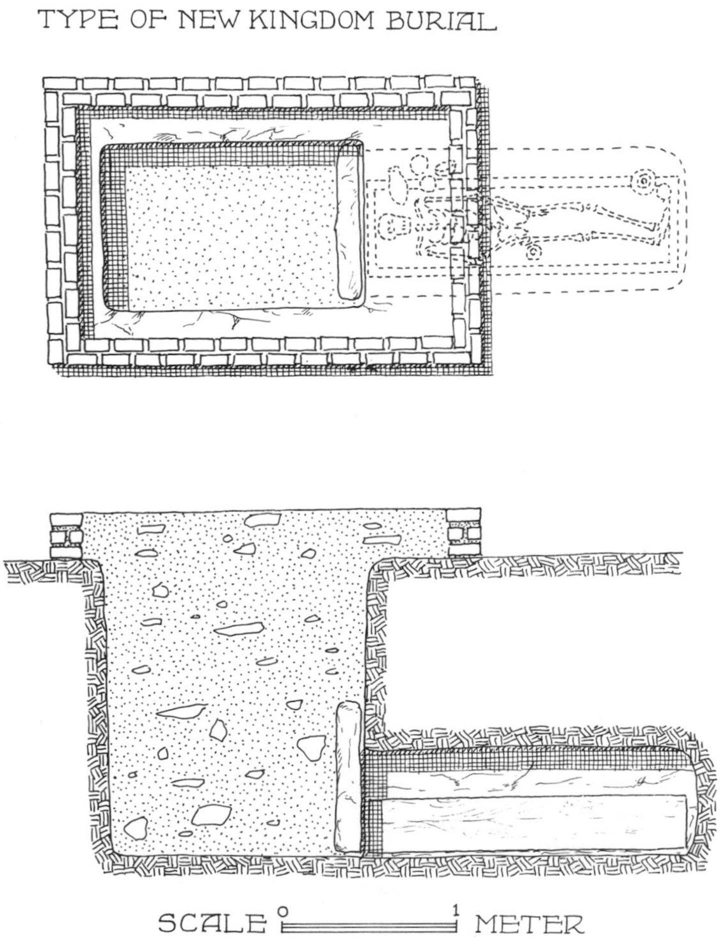

TYPE OF NEW KINGDOM BURIAL

SCALE ⌐————————┐ METER

FIGURE 34

The passage of the armies through Lower Nubia to the battle
areas in the south, in conjunction with an increasing number of
colonists connected with the military and trading stations, soon
had an effect on the manners and customs of the native popula-
tions, and all remnants of the C-Group culture disappeared. This
change is particularly noticeable in the burial of the dead. No
longer do we find the body laid out on its side in a semicontracted

TYPE OF NEW KINGDOM BURIAL

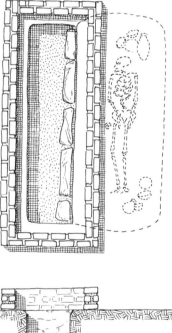

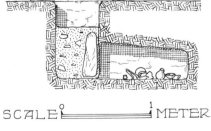

SCALE |0_____|1 METER

FIGURE 35

233

position; instead, following Egyptian custom, the deceased was laid fully extended on his back, and in richer interments was placed within plain wooden coffins. The graves were of three types: a plain rectangular pit (Figure 33), a rock-cut pit with a subterranean end chamber for the burial (Figure 34), and a rectangular pit with a lateral niche cut on one of the long sides (Figure 35). In most of the graves, the grouping of the burial equipment appears to follow a certain system, so that in the New Kingdom period we find pottery and other objects arranged as follows (see Figure 36):

Red-ware dish	AT THE HEAD
Large red-ware drop pot	
Small red-ware drop pot	
Toilet objects, such as	
bronze mirrors and wooden combs	
Painted buff-ware unguent pot	NEAR THE LEFT ARM
Red-ware dish	
Alabaster kohl pot and stick	
Red-ware dish	AT THE FEET
Large red-ware drop pot	
Small red-ware drop pot	
Poor-class *ushabtis* of pottery, clay,	BETWEEN THE KNEES
faïence	

Jewelry consisted of earrings of bronze, carnelian, and jasper, finger rings of gold and bronze, scarabs and amulets of carnelian, steatite, glass, jasper, and faïence, and bead necklaces of faïence, gold, carnelian, glass, and shell. Weapons, such as bronze spearheads, arrowheads, axheads, and daggers, are sometimes found with the dead, but these are a rarity, particularly in Lower Nubia (Wawat). Except in the limited rock-cut tombs of more prosperous citizens, such objects are usually of poor quality and the general impression given from the evidence of burial installations other

than those in the vicinity of the military stations is that Nubia
after the conquest was populated by a poor subject race largely
dependent on poor-class imports from Egypt, with little or no
cultural background of its own. Near colonial settlements such as

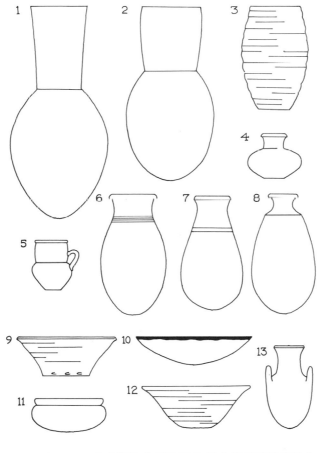

TYPES OF NEW KINGDOM POTTERY

FIGURE 36   *1* and *2*. Red ware; *3*. Rough red ware; *4*. Red ware; *5*. Cream ware;
6–8. Red ware; *9*. Rough red ware; *10*. Red ware with red painted rim; *11*. red
ware; *12*. Rough red ware; *13*. Cream ware

235

Ma'am and Buhen the case was obviously different and the evidence obtained from even the badly plundered burial installations shows that the population of such areas was accustomed to a fairly high standard of living.

Such were conditions in Nubia at the end of the reign of the great conqueror Thotmose I, and it is not surprising that as soon as news of his death in 1510 B.C. was received, rebellion broke out in the south, and his son Thotmose II was faced with a campaign against Kush in the first year of his reign. An inscription on the rocks between Aswan and Philae records:

> One came to inform His Majesty as follows: The wretched Kush has begun to rebel, those who were under the dominion of the Lord of the Two Lands purpose hostility, beginning to smite him. The inhabitants of Egypt [the colonists] are about to bring away the cattle behind the fortress which thy father built in his campaigns, the King of Upper and Lower Egypt Akheperkara [Thotmose I], living for ever, in order to repulse the rebellious barbarians, the Nubian Troglodytes of Khenthennofer, for those who are there on the north of the wretched Kush. . . .

The reference to the north of Kush suggests that the revolt started below the Second Cataract; so the unnamed fortress which served as a refuge for the threatened colonists was perhaps Buhen, which alone among the strongholds in that area was big enough to accommodate large numbers of people and their cattle.

On hearing the news, Thotmose II dispatched a large army to Nubia, but apparently did not accompany it in person, perhaps because of his youth. The Aswan inscription continues:

> Then this army of His Majesty arrived at wretched Kush. . . . This army of His Majesty overthrew those barbarians; they did not let live anyone among their males, according to all the command of His Majesty, except one of those children of the Chief of wretched Kush, who was taken away alive as a living prisoner with their people to His Majesty. They were placed under the

feet of the Good God; for His Majesty had appeared upon this throne when the living prisoners were brought in, which this army of His Majesty had captured. This land was made a subject of His Majesty as formerly. . . .

Thus ended this punitive campaign, and with the taking of royal hostages of Kush, peace was restored and firmly established in the south for some years to come. The name of Thotmose II has been observed at Barkal and at Dakka, where he perhaps built a temple, the foundations of which are suspected to exist below a temple later built by the Meroitic king Arkamen and Ptolemy II. His name also appears with that of his father at Semna, where they are recorded as giving gifts to the god Amon. Queen Hatshepsut, who succeeded Thotmose II in 1490 B.C., found no necessity for military action in Nubia, for the south lands remained at peace throughout her reign. In the fortress of Buhen the queen built a garrison temple, which, although now in a very ruined state, retains architectural features and painted reliefs which can be counted among the finest in Nubia. In plan it follows the conventional design of the small temple of the period, with a closed and roofed building of stone containing the sanctuary, side rooms and the pronaos (Figure 37). This building is flanked by an open colonnade on two sides of round pillars of the "proto-Doric" type which are a feature of Hatshepsut's temple at Deir el Bahri. Pillars of the same design flanked the open forecourt, and the whole area was encircled by a brick wall with an entrance gate facing east. Unfortunately, the symmetrical plan of the temple has been marred by additions and alterations made by the queen's husband and successor Thotmose III (1490–1436 B.C.) who, following his policy of obliterating all traces of her existence, has erased her cartouche wherever it could be found. The names of both Thotmose I and Thotmose II appear on the reliefs, and it would appear probable that work on the temple had begun prior to the accession of Hatshepsut; nevertheless, it is certain that the main structure was built by her.

237

The reliefs, dedicated to the local god Horus of Buhen, are entirely religious in character, showing the nomarchs making offerings to the patron god and to other deities such as Amon-re, Isis, Satis, Anubis, and Mentu. Queen Hatshepsut also built a temple dedi-

SKETCH PLAN
OF THE TEMPLE OF BUHEN

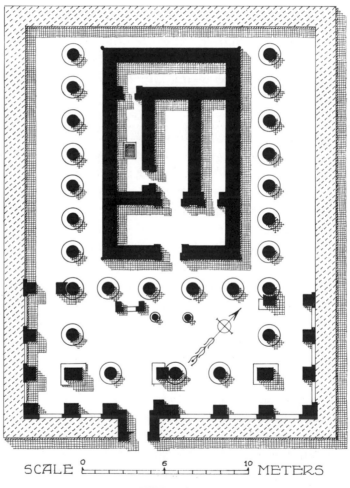

SCALE 0 ⸻ 5 ⸻ 10 METERS

238

FIGURE 37

cated to the goddess Hathor at Faras; but only the foundations and scattered inscribed blocks of stone remain.

Peaceful conditions continued throughout the reign of Thotmose III, and although the great conquering pharaoh undertook an expedition to the south in the final years of his reign, it was probably little more than a military demonstration; the fame of his victories in Syria would certainly check any thoughts of aggression in Kush, and Wawat was by now almost an integral part of Egypt. The viceroy Nehi ruled the land wisely and saw to the regular transmission to Egypt of the Nubian tribute. In the *Annals of Thotmose III* the tribute of Wawat and Kush is listed as follows:

Wawat

Year 31. 92 cattle, 1 harvest.

Year 33. 20 slaves, 104 cattle, 1 harvest.

Year 34. 254 deben of gold, 10 slaves, and an unknown number of cattle.

Year 35. 34 slaves, 94 cattle, 1 harvest.

Year 38. 2844 deben of gold, 16 slaves, 77 cattle.

Year 39. 89 cattle, ivory and ebony.

Year 41. 3144 deben, 3 kidet of gold, 114 cattle, and an unknown quantity of ivory.

Year 42. 2374 deben, 1 kidet of gold, and 1 harvest.

Kush

Year 34. 300 deben of gold, 60 Negro slaves, 275 cattle, ivory and ebony.

Year 35. 70 deben, 1 kidet of gold, an unknown quantity of slaves, cattle, ivory and ebony, and 1 harvest.

Year 38. 100 deben, 6 kidet of gold, 36 Negro slaves, 306 cattle and ivory and ebony, 1 harvest.

Year 39. 144 deben, 3 kidet of gold, 101 Negro slaves and an unknown quantity of cattle.

Year 41. 94 deben, 2 kidet of gold, 21 Negro slaves and an unknown quantity of cattle.

1 deben = 0.035 ounces; 1 kidet = 1/10 of a deben

Although the total amount of gold—more than 9345 deben—is impressive, the other articles of tribute are strangely small; which perhaps suggests a poverty-stricken land devastated by war. Whichever way we interpret it, the hand of Pharaoh does not appear to have been unduly heavy. Under the rule of Thotmose III, the administration of Nubia, in the able hands of the Viceroy Nehi reached its highest level, and it is evident that the working of the gold mines and the security of the trade routes were not disturbed by desert raiders. It was typical of the far-sighted policy of the king that once again he had the canal of Senusret III, at the First Cataract, cleared and repaired, ordering the fishermen of Elephantine to dredge it every year. The monuments of Thotmose III in Nubia are very numerous, perhaps because of his veneration of his great ancestor Senusret III, now deified as the hero who conquered Nubia. In the Middle Kingdom fortress of Semna he leveled the ruined brick temple of Senusret III and rebuilt it in stone. The original structure had been dedicated to Khnum and Dedun, the latter being the principal god of Kush; but in the restored sanctuary Thotmose added to them Senusret III, thereby making it a trinity. In the dedication scene which is inscribed on the west wall of the temple, a statue of Senusret III is depicted in a shrine on a sand barque, and behind it is Thotmose III being embraced by the god Dedun. The inscription recording the words of Dedun is as follows:

> My beloved son, Menkheperra [Thotmose III], how beautiful is this beautiful monument, which thou hast made for my beloved son, King of Upper and Lower Egypt, Khakaura [Senusret III]. Thou has perpetuated his name forever, that thou mayest live.

The words of Dedun continue on the opposite wall:

> Thou has renewed his birth a second time in a monument in memoriam. Thou hast presented to him many offering tables of

silver and gold, bronze, and Asiatic copper. The reward thereof for thee is satisfying life, like Ra, forever.

On the outside of the west wall of the temple is the dedication inscription which reads:

> The Good God, Menkheperra [Thotmose III]. He made [it] as his monument for his father Dedun, president over Nubia, and for the King of Upper and Lower Egypt, Khakaura [Senusret III], making for them a temple of fine white stone of Nubia, although my Majesty found it of ruinous brick; as a son does according to the desire which his father desired, who assigned to him the Two Regions, who brought him up to be Horus, lord of this land. I have set it in my divine heart that I should make his monument; that I should make him mighty according as he gave; that I should perpetuate his house forever, according as he has become greater than any god. He hath given to me all life, stability and satisfaction like Ra, forever.

Although the apotheosis of Senusret probably took place at an earlier date than in the reign of Thotmose III, the dedication of the restored temple at Semna appears to be the first official recognition of his deification. Other monuments of Thotmose III were built in Upper Nubia (Kush). Besides Semna, he built fortress temples at Kumma and Uronarti, and it is possible that part of the foundations of the great temple of Soleb were laid bare in his reign. It is also probable that he built a temple on the island of Sai which has long since disappeared, and a stela discovered at Barkal records that the southern frontier of his dominions reached the "Horns of the Earth," a locality still unidentified with certainty, but probably south of the Fourth Cataract.

In Lower Nubia (Wawat) at Kalabsha, a granite statue of Thotmose III was seen near the quay which led to the Temple of Augustus, thus suggesting that the Pharaoh may have had some part in the building of the earlier temple which once occupied this site. He probably built a temple at Qurta, for as late as the middle   *241* of the last century, a gateway inscribed with his name was still standing, and at Amada he started to build the temple to Re-Harmachis which was finished by his son Amenhotep II. At El Leisiya, Thotmose constructed a small rock-cut temple in which he is shown worshiping Horus, Dedun, and Senusret III, and a stela dated to the year 50 shows him before Horus of Ma'am and the goddess Satis. Two of the four shrines cut in the rock below Kasr Ibrim must be assigned to Thotmose, although both were probably not his original work, the first one belonging originally to the viceroy Nehi; the second may have been the work of Hatshepsut. Blocks from a sanctuary built by him have been found at Faras, and he was, as stated above, responsible for the alterations to the fortress temple of Queen Hatshepsut at Buhen. It was at Buhen that the viceroy Nehi erected Thotmose III's record of victory, on a great stela which still stands in the forecourt of the temple.

During the reign of Amenhotep II, who succeeded his father Thotmose in 1436 B.C., peaceful conditions continued in the south, and the king was able to give his entire attention to a career of conquest in Syria. He completed the building of the temple of Amada, begun by his father, and there in a stela he records his triumphal return from his Asiatic campaigns and his personal sacrifice of seven captive princes, six of whom were hanged before the walls of his capital at Thebes. Of the seventh prince, the inscription reads:

> Then the other fallen one was taken upriver to Nubia and hanged on the wall of Napata, in order to cause to be manifest the victories of His Majesty, forever and ever in all lands and countries of the land of the Negro.

The extensive building operations of his predecessor were continued by Amenhotep II in Nubia, and it is probable that he completed the construction of the early temple at Kalabsha. The fourth rock-cut shrine at Kasr Ibrim belonged to him, although it was probably built by the viceroy Wesersatet, who had followed the famous Nehi. Amenhotep II also added to, and completed, the small brick temple which, in the early days of reconquest, the pharaoh Ahmose I had built outside the north wall of the ruined Middle Kingdom fortress at Buhen. Two kneeling statues of Amenhotep were found at Wad-ba-Nagaa, about seventy miles north of Khartoum; but it is unlikely that this was their original location.

There is no evidence of warfare in the south until the year 8 of Thotmose IV, who succeeded Amenhotep II in 1413 B.C. According to a rock inscription on the island of Konosso in the First Cataract, the king received news of a revolt in Wawat possibly occasioned by a raid from Kush. The danger does not appear to have been very great, for the progress of the Egyptian army to the south appears to have been very leisurely, with Pharaoh stopping at all the great temples to intercede and receive the blessing of the gods. The revolt was suppressed, and the king returned to his capital with presumably numerous important captives, who were apparently placed in a concentration camp in his mortuary temple at Thebes. A tablet found in the temple enclosure bears the words: "Colony of Kush the wretched, which His Majesty brought back from his victories."

As far as is at present known, the only building activity of Thotmose IV in Nubia was the construction of the hypostyle hall in front of the main building of the temple of Amada. He died in 1405 B.C., and was succeeded by his son Amenhotep III, who undertook a campaign against the Negro tribes in the far south. This event took place in the fifth year of his reign, and his conquests mark the extreme limit of Egyptian power in the Sudan. For this campaign, which appears to have been more a punitive expedition than a full-scale war, the viceroy Mermose was entrusted with the recruitment of a Nubian contingent in the districts between Baki (Kubban) and Ma'am (Aneiba); but beyond the conscription of man power, Wawat was probably little affected by these events. A record of this expedition, on a stela found at Semna, gives a list of prisoners and killed and from the small numbers we may appreciate the minor character of the campaign. The list is as follows:

243

Living Negroes	150 heads
Archers [military personnel?]	110 heads
Negresses	250 heads
Servants of the Negroes	55 heads
Their children	175 heads
	Total 740 living heads
Hands thereof (i.e., the slain)	312
United with the living heads	1,052

Although Amenhotep III's military exploits in Nubia appear to have been mainly a matter of vainglorious posing over a land which was helpless and already subject to him, his building activities in this part of the Empire are worthy of the greatest praise, for at Soleb he erected one of the finest temples in the south. Built of sandstone on the most insecure foundations, even today in its ruined state the remains of this great temple are an impressive sight. At the time of its dedication, the temple of Soleb must have compared very favorably with other great temples at Luxor, and indeed it is possible, even probable, that both structures were the design of the same architect. The approach to the temple was bordered by an avenue of granite rams and two lions, the latter now being among the artistic treasures of the British Museum. These statues were not found at Soleb but at Barkal, where they had been removed during the time when the Kushite kings ruled both Egypt and Nubia as the Twenty-fifth Dynasty (751–656 B.C.).

Amenhotep III also built a temple for his queen, Tyi, at Sedenga, thirteen miles north of Soleb; but only one of the pillars of this edifice has survived.

The religious revolution of Amenhotep IV (1367–1350 B.C.) affected Nubia very little, and the tranquillity of the country was undisturbed by the political upheaval in Egypt. It is indeed indicative of the strength of Egypt's grip in the south that the Kushite chiefs apparently made no attempt to take advantage of the chaos which must have prevailed in the government administration of the empire at this time. In the early years of his reign,

Amenhotep IV, before he changed his name to Akhenaton, built a group of three temples on a common substructure at Sesebi, near Soleb. These formed the nucleus of a small walled town which included a shrine dedicated to the new god, Aton. It is probable that Akhenaton also founded the town of Gematon which was situated at Kawa opposite Dongola. This settlement may well have been a creation of the heretic pharaoh late in his reign, for no building of an earlier date than Tutankhamen, who built a small temple there, has been identified.

During the short reign of Akhenaton's successor, Semenkhkara, peaceful conditions continued in Nubia, under the administration of the viceroy Thotmose, and this was maintained under his successor Tutankhamen, who became pharaoh in 1347 B.C. Tutankhamen's viceroy in Nubia, Huy, built his tomb at Thebes, the wall paintings of which are of the greatest importance, for they portray his investiture as viceroy and give details of the tribute of the south. From these paintings and the inscriptions which accompany them we learn the limits of the area which came under the control of the viceroy, and we can appreciate the vast responsibility and power of the holder of this office; a power which was to be used with great effect in later times by Huy's successors. The investiture scenes show Huy accompanied by courtiers, brought before the enthroned Tutankhamen, in front of whom stands an official who is called Overseer of the White House. Addressing Huy, he says: "This is the seal from the Pharaoh, Life, Prosperity, Health, who assigns to thee [the territory] from Nekhen to Napata." The distance by river from Nekhen, the modern El Kab, north of the First Cataract, to Napata in Dongola Province in the Sudan, is more than 800 miles. The seal of office is then given to Huy, who is addressed as "King's son of Kush" and a further scene depicts Huy's reception by his family and officials—the text above him reads: "The coming forth, favoured, from the court, having been appointed in the presence of the Good God to be King's-son and governor of the southern countries, Huy."

In the tribute scenes which follow, there is one puzzling feature, for two viceroys are shown, one being Huy and the other being his

245

brother, Amenhotep, who is also called King's-son of Kush. It is of course possible that the viceroy had a deputy, but if so, it would appear unlikely that the deputy would also have the title of King's-son. We can only conclude that the southern territory was so vast that it was necessary to have two viceroys, one perhaps for Wawat and the other for Kush.

In the first of the tribute scenes, the king is shown enthroned, with the tribute of Nubia before him. This consists of gold and silver ingots, gold and silver vessels, a chariot, shields and furniture. The second scene shows the viceroy receiving three lines of Nubians and a line of Egyptians. The top line depicts three Nubian princes, two kneeling and one prostrate. Only one of these men is named: Hekanefer, Prince of Ma'am, whose tomb at Toshka has recently been recorded and excavated by the Pennsylvania-Yale Expedition (see page 104). The group includes two Nubian princesses; one riding in a chariot drawn by small oxen (Figure 38). It is interesting

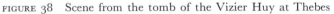

246   FIGURE 38   Scene from the tomb of the Vizier Huy at Thebes

to note that the Nubian chiefs wear Egyptian dress, whereas in a similar scene in the tomb of the Vizier Rekhmire of the time of Thotmose III, they are shown in native costume. It would thus appear that within a hundred years the Egyptianization of the south lands had made considerable progress. With other tribute which the Nubian chiefs have brought are elaborately decorated cattle, and behind all these figures are six ships, above which is the text: "Arrival from Kush bearing this good tribute of all the choicest of the best of the south countries. Landing at the city of the South [Thebes] by the King's-son of Kush, Huy." The final scene of the tribute series shows Huy leaning on his staff and accompanied by his family, waiting to embark on a ship which has its sails spread ready to leave for Nubia. A second ship, not yet ready to sail, has his chariot and horses, and it is evident that his official duties in the capital are at an end; the viceroy is preparing to return to the south.

Building operations continued in Nubia, under Huy's administration, and he built for his master a small walled town and temple at Faras which he called Sehetep-enter, "the Conciliation of the Gods," obviously commemorating Tutankhamen's reconciliation with the old religion and the end of the Aton heresy.

The troubled close of the Eighteenth Dynasty appears to have had no effect on the stability of Egyptian rule in Nubia, and the evidence of the cemeteries shows that the Egyptianization of the country had been largely successful.

At Adda, a few miles south of Abu Simbel, is the rock shrine of Paser, viceroy of Tutankhamen's successor, Ai, who was the last king of the dynasty. On its walls is shown the figure of a king who is probably Ai, worshiping Amon, Ra, Ptah, Mentu, and Satis.

247

VI

The Nineteenth Dynasty

c. 1308–1194 B.C.

WHATEVER weakening of Egyptian power there was in Nubia due to the disorganization of government during the four preceding reigns was speedily restored by Horemheb, who ascended the throne in 1335 B.C. Nevertheless, the decline had set in, and Egypt never again held the country as securely as she had done under Amenhotep III. Horemheb apparently visited Nubia on two occasions, once as a general of the army before he usurped the throne, and later as Pharaoh. Although, on the walls of a commemorative chapel at Silsileh, this expedition is recorded as a full-scale campaign, it was probably little more than a royal progress in which the usurper could assess the loyalty or otherwise of his southern subjects. No one would know better than he the political value of the Kushite warriors now being enlisted in increasing numbers in the Egyptian army, and to secure their allegiance and the support of their leaders would indeed be of vital importance to him. Paser, who served as Viceroy in the previous reign, continued in office under Horemheb; so we can presume that the new pharaoh received the loyalty of the Egyptian administration of Nubia.

During the short reign of Rameses I (1308–1309 B.C.), who succeeded Horemheb, we have no records of warfare in Nubia, and the only evidence of his activities there is contained on a stela which was found by Champollion in the temple of Hatshepsut at Buhen. The inscription records his pious gifts to the temple, consisting of an increase in the number of priests and temple slaves, male and female, together with the addition of new buildings to the edifice.

The next king, Seti I, who ascended the throne in 1309 B.C., paid considerable attention to the working of the Nubian gold mines; in an effort to increase the output of the workings in the Wadi-el-Alaki, which was reduced through the lack of water, he dug a well somewhere in the vicinity. He failed to reach water, but the fruits of his labors were reaped by his successor, Rameses II (1290–1224 B.C.) as described on the famous Kubban stela. Seti I built a town at Amara, which later grew to be a center of government in Kush, as the residence of the deputy viceroy. Of his military activities there is little concrete evidence, and although small punitive expeditions may have taken place, they cannot have been of any importance, for no mention is made of war in the south on the extensive series of war reliefs which occupy the exterior north wall of the hypostyle of the temple of Karnak at Thebes. There is some reason to suppose that the most magnificent monument of pharaonic Egypt, the temple of Abu Simbel, was started by Seti I. The evidence for this lies in the fact that on an internal doorway there is an inscription dated to the first year of his successor Rameses II, which shows that the vast excavation of the interior must have been largely accomplished at the time the inscription was made. There are many representations of military activity in Nubia during the long reign of Rameses II, but both dates and the localities of these supposedly important campaigns are lacking and the general impression is that much of this material is fictional, for it now appears to be necessary for Pharaoh to have his victories in Nubia to balance his victories in Asia. Undoubtedly, punitive action on the southern borders of the empire would be necessary from time to time, but in general, peace prevailed in the south lands; as witness his widespread building activity, which would have been impossible if Nubia had been continuously torn by warfare.

In the year 3 of his reign Rameses turned his attention to the development of the Nubian gold mines, and above all to those of Akita, now identified with the Wadi el Alaki. According to inscriptions on a stela found at Kubban, which is situated at the river end of the road to these mines, the King was in Memphis when *249*

. . . it came to pass that, lo, His Majesty was sitting upon a great throne of electrum, diademed with the double-feathered crown, recounting the countries from which gold is brought, and devising plans for digging wells on a road lacking in water, after hearing said that there was much gold in the country of Akita, whereas the road thereof was very lacking in water. If a few of the caravaneers of the gold washing went thither, it was only half of them that arrived there, for they died of thirst on the road, together with the asses which they drove before them. There was not found for them their necessary supply of drink, in ascending and descending, from the water of the skins. Hence no gold was brought from this country, for lack of water.

Summoning his court for consultation, the king was informed by the Viceroy of Kush that:

As for the country of Akita . . . it has been in this manner lacking in water since the time of the god. They die therein of thirst, and every earlier king desired to open a well therein, but did not succeed. King Menmare (Seti I) did the like, and caused to be dug a well of 120 cubits depth in this time. It is [however] forsaken on the road, [for] no water came out of it.

Thereupon Rameses gave orders for a renewed attempt on his father's borings, and later he was informed by a letter from the viceroy that the project was a success, for water had been reached only 12 cubits below the depth dug by Seti I. The location of this famous well has been lost, and it is interesting to speculate if its rediscovery might warrant the reopening of the Wadi el Alaki mines; for they are known to be still productive, but uneconomic because of the lack of water.

As in Egypt, the building activities of Rameses II were on an immense scale, and in addition to the masterpiece at Abu Simbel he built temples at Beit el Wali, Gerf Hussein, Wadi es Sebua, Aksha, and Derr in Lower Nubia (Wawat) and at Amara in Upper Nubia (Kush). It is possible, even probable, that more monu-

250   ments of this king exist beyond the Second Cataract, but they

have not yet been found, for there are still large areas which have not yet been explored by the archaeologist.

The temple of Abu Simbel, one of the largest rock-cut structures in the world, is indeed a masterpiece of ancient architectural design and engineering (Figure 39). Carved in a great head of rock on the west bank of the Nile opposite the modern village of Farek, its setting is magnificent; but this was not the only reason for the selection of this site, for there is evidence to show that these hills, even before the construction of the temples, were considered important and sacred. Farek, on the east bank of the river, is set in wide stretches of cultivation, and there is no reason to suppose that the character of the land was any different in ancient times, when it was the site of the town of Maha facing the great temple across the Nile. Near the temples there was another small town called Abshek, so we may conclude that in the days of Rameses II these great structures were situated in a well-populated district. Even so, it is difficult to understand why such magnificent monuments should be located in such a distant part of the country. Only two explanations seem plausible: either as I have just said, the hill at Abu Simbel was for some reason considered sacred, or, at a point near the head of the Second Cataract, which by that time was considered the frontier of Egypt proper, the pharaoh wished to impress his unruly neighbors farther south with his power and wealth. If this was his purpose I feel sure he must have succeeded. Opinions differ among artists, architects, and archaeologists on the merits of the temple as an artistic treasure—indeed one famous Egyptologist described it as "that gigantic abomination"—but others, particularly those who have seen it a number of times, are overwhelming in their admiration, and many regard its gigantic façade as one—if not the greatest—manifestation of the power and grandeur of ancient Egypt still preserved (Figure 39).

As stated above, there is evidence suggesting that the original conception of a temple at Abu Simbel was made by Seti I, and certainly a large part of the interior excavation must have been complete before Rameses ascended the throne in 1290 B.C. But to what extent Seti was responsible for the final design, particularly

251

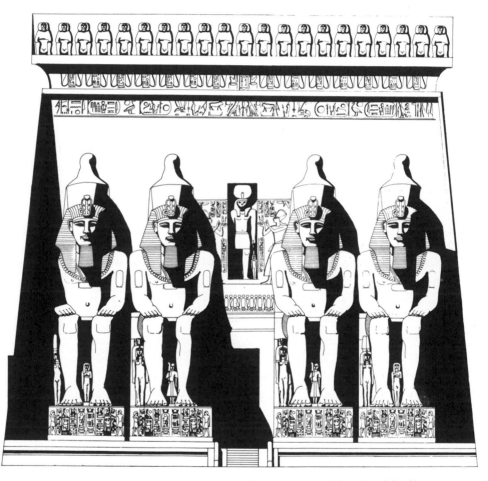

FIGURE 39   Attempted reconstruction of the ancient architect's original conception of the façade for the Great Temple at Abu Simbel

the façade, is not known, and as usual Rameses gives no credit
to his predecessor. However, when he took over, the work must
252   have been far advanced, and as it was usual in the construction

of such rock-cut monuments to complete the façade before excavating the interior, we must consider it possible that the four colossal statues which are the principal feature of its design are portraits of Rameses' predecessor. However, he takes the sole credit for the creation of this magnificent edifice, for in the building inscription he is shown instructing an official called Rameses-eshahab to build the temple. Part of this inscription reads:

> Behold, as for His Majesty, L.P.H. [Life, Prosperity, Health], he is vigilant in seeking every profitable occasion, by doing excellent things for his father, Horus, lord of He [a name of the locality of Abu Simbel], making for him his house of myriads of years, by excavating in this mountain of He, which no one did before except the son of Amon, Lord of . . . His might is in all lands; bringing for him multitudes of workmen from the captivity of his sword in every country.

The statement that no one excavated in the mountain except "the son of Amon, Lord of . . . " perhaps refers to Seti; but unfortunately the end of this sentence is obliterated, so we cannot be certain on this point. Nevertheless, it is significant; although the reference is peculiar if it applies to his father Seti.

Built, as we see from the building inscription, by prisoner-of-war labor, the monument was completed before the year 1259 B.C., and like many other temples in Nubia it was dedicated to the worship of Re-Harmachis, identified with the sun and usually represented as a man with a falcon's head wearing the solar disk. The whole purpose and position of the temple was devoted to the adoration of the sun at dawn, and it was only at sunrise at certain times of the year that the vast interior was illuminated, when the light penetrated the sanctuary. As it must have been for the ancients, so it is for the modern visitor an unforgettable experience to stand in the main hall at dawn and watch the life-giving light of the sun gradually reveal the splendour of this architectural masterpiece, finally penetrating into the Holy of Holies of an ancient

253

faith. But impressive as the spectacle is today, it can only be a shadow of what it must have been when the sculptured scenes on the walls were painted in brilliant colors, in the selection of which the ancient Egyptian artist was a master.

The main features of the exterior of the temple are the four gigantic statues of the king which have been carved out of the living rock of the hillside. The seated figures, two on each side of the entrance, are more than 65 ft. in height, and they represent Rameses wearing the double crown of Egypt. On either side of, and between the legs of, each statue are figures of Queen Nefertari and some of the royal children, themselves represented in statues of great size but dwarfed by the side of the colossi. Each of the four groups stands on a high pedestal on which are carved the cartouches of Rameses and groups of Asiatic and Negro captives; while the boxlike thrones on which the colossi are seated are decorated with conventional groups representing the union of the Two Lands. The façade which forms the background to the colossi is carved in pylon form with a cornice decorated with a row of baboons, their arms upraised in the worship of the rising sun. Over the entrance to the interior of the temple is a statue of the falcon-headed sun god Re-Harmachis.

The entrance to the temple leads directly into the great hall, the main features of which are two rows of four square pillars against whose fronts are colossal standing figures of the king, who is represented again wearing the double crown and holding the crook and flail scepters. The pillars and walls of the great hall, which measure 30 ft. in height, are covered with scenes and inscriptions relating to religious ceremonies and to the king's military exploits in his struggle with the Hittites in Syria and with the Kushites in the Sudan. The ceiling is decorated with a conventional design of cartouches and vultures with outstretched wings.

In the north and west walls of the hall, doors lead into a series of rooms which were probably used as vestries and stores for the priesthood. The reliefs on their walls are devoted entirely to religious subjects.

254   The central door in the west wall gives access to a smaller hall, the roof of which is supported by four square pillars, and here again the wall reliefs are entirely religious in character. Beyond this hall is the anteroom to the sanctuary, which has three doors

GREAT TEMPLE OF ABU SIMBEL

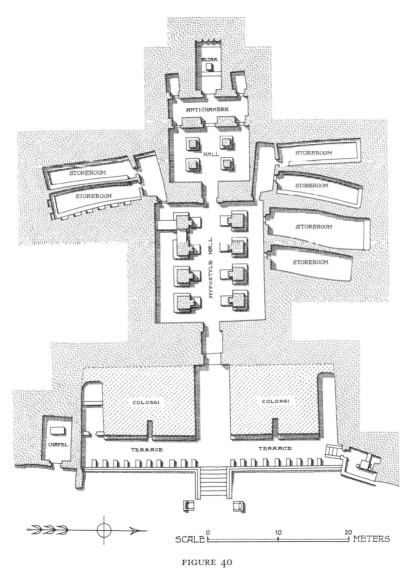

SCALE |————0————10————20————| METERS

FIGURE 40

255

in the west wall, two on either side leading to small uninscribed rooms and the central one on the direct axis of the temple, leading into the sanctuary. In the west wall of the sanctuary is a row of four seated statues carved in the living rock. These are the principal deities of the temple: Ptah, Amon, Rameses himself, and Re-Harmachis. In front of them, in the center, is a small uninscribed pedestal on which would rest the sacred boat of Amon, and it was here in this room that the sacrifice would have been made and the offerings placed, when the light of the rising sun illuminated the sanctuary at dawn. The faces of the four statues of the gods have been badly battered, probably by Christian iconoclasts; but in the strangely filtered dawn light they still present an awe-inspiring appearance to the beholder. As the late Arthur Weigall wrote more than fifty years ago: "At no other time and in no other place in Egypt does one feel the same capacity for appreciating the ancient Egyptian spirit of worship."

At a short distance to the north of the great temple, Rameses built a smaller rock-cut shrine for his queen Nefertari, who dedicated it to the worship of the goddess Hathor. Although overshadowed by the grandeur of the great temple, the Queen's monument still must be ranked as one of the finest structures of the period in Nubia. Two building inscriptions are found, one in the main hall, and the other on the façade. The first reads:

> Rameses, he made it as his monument for the Great King's wife Nefertari, beloved of Mut—a house hewn in the pure mountain of Nubia, of fine white enduring sandstone, as an eternal work.

The second inscription reads:

> Rameses-Meriamon, beloved of Amon, like Ra, forever, made a house of very great monuments, for the Great King's wife Nefertari, fair of face. . . . His Majesty commanded to make a house in Nubia hewn in the mountain. Never was done the like before.

The last statement that "Never was done the like before" must be taken as a purely conventional declaration, for it is obvious that the smaller monument was not built before the temple of Re-Harmachis, which, as already pointed out, was probably started by Seti I.

It would be interesting to know if the design of both structures was the work of the same architect, for the sculpture and relief carving are almost certainly by the same artists. The façade, 90 ft. long and 40 ft. high, is pylon-shaped and originally had the usual cavetto cornice. On each side of the doorway leading to the interior are three deep niches within which stand colossal statues, 33 ft. high, of the King and Queen, grouped as follows: on the north side of the doorway Rameses wearing the double crown, then Nefertari wearing the disk, horns, and plumes of Isis, then Rameses wearing the Atef crown. On the south side we have Rameses wearing the white crown, then Nefertari again with the headdress of Isis, and then Rameses wearing the white crown. At the sides of each colossal figure are two smaller statues representing the royal children, princes flanking the king and princesses the queen. The door to the interior leads directly into a hypostyle hall with its roof supported by six square pillars, each decorated in front with a design representing a sistrum, surmounted by the head of the goddess Hathor. The mural reliefs depict the king, accompanied by the queen, sacrificing a Negro before Amon and a Libyan before Re-Harmachis, with other scenes of religious character. More religious scenes decorate the walls of the antechamber and in the sanctuary: on the west wall in high relief, is a full-faced figure of Hathor in the form of a cow with a male figure, probably the king, standing beneath its head. On the north wall of the sanctuary the queen is represented in the presence of the goddesses Mut and Hathor, to whom she offers incense, and on the south wall the king is shown pouring a libation before statues of himself and Nefertari.

Rameses II's four other major monuments in Lower Nubia, the temples of Beit el-Wali, Gerf Hussein, Wadi es Sebua, and Derr, are all partly rock-cut, and although of rather crude con-   *257* struction, contain reliefs and inscriptions of interest relative to the history of Nubia.

The temple cut in the hillside at Beit el-Wali consists of an open forecourt, a hall supported by two fluted pillars and a sanctuary with a niche at the west end containing the remains of three rock-cut statues. Although these statues cannot be recognized, it is almost certain that they represented the deified Rameses and two other gods to whom the shrine was dedicated. The most important feature of the temple is the series of reliefs cut on the side walls of the forecourt, representing the king's Asiatic and Nubian wars. Although the Nubian campaigns were probably little more than military demonstrations, the reliefs here are of particular value, not only for the realism of the combat scenes but for the portrayal of the Nubian tribute. These reliefs were cast many years ago by Joseph Bonomi and the results of his work can be seen on the walls of the fourth Egyptian room at the British Museum. The casts are brightly colored from notes which Bonomi made before he applied his plaster, which when removed left no trace of the paint on the originals. The first scene depicts an attack on a Nubian village in the far south, and from a text over the enemy— " . . . those who transgress his boundaries"—it obviously refers to punitive action on the frontier. Rameses is shown in his chariot, followed by the two princes, Amenherunamf and Khaemwast, charging a mass of Negroes armed with bows and arrows, who break and flee to the refuge of their camp in a palm grove. A wounded Negro warrior is led away by two of his comrades, and the women and children run about in terror. In the next scene the king is seated on his throne under a canopy, receiving the tribute of Kush, presented to him by Egyptian nobles among whom is the Viceroy of Kush, Amenemopet, the son of the previous viceroy, Paser, who is rewarded for his services with gold chains. The tribute is varied, to say the least, consisting of gold rings, ebony and ivory furniture, panther skins, bows, myrrh, shields, ivory, ostrich feathers, and ostrich eggs. In addition to this there are live animals including monkeys, panthers, a giraffe, ibexes, a dog, oxen with carved horns, and an ostrich. But the most valuable gift is apparently a

258

splendid table, hung with skins and decorated with flowers, which is carried in by the viceroy himself. With the tribute are Negro captives, including two women, one carrying her children in a basket. There is also depicted a group of Nubian soldiers armed with spears, showing that colonial troops were now employed in punitive action in their own country—a sure indication of the security of Egyptian rule in the south at that time.

The temple of Gerf Hussein was apparently built towards the end of Rameses' reign, for the work was undertaken by Setaw, who was the last of his viceroys. Dedicated to the god Ptah and planned on the Abu Simbel model, it is poorly constructed and of little architectural interest. In front of the rock-cut temple is an open court surrounded on three sides by a covered colonnade with lotus pillars on the east side, and square pillars each faced with colossal statues of Rameses on the north and south sides. The roof of the hypostyle hall is supported by square pillars, in front of which are colossal statues of the king in Osirian dress. In the sanctuary there are badly damaged rock-cut statues of Ptah, the deified Rameses, Ptah-Tatenen, and Hathor. The reliefs and inscriptions throughout the temple are religious in character and of no historical value.

The temple of Wadi es Sebua, dedicated to Re-Harmachis and Amon, is built on a similar plan to that of Gerf Hussein; but the structure is in general better preserved and therefore more complete. Nevertheless the workmanship is shoddy, and we may judge that it was built during the latter part of the reign. Approached by an avenue of sphinxes and two colossal statues of Rameses, the pyloned entrance to the temple leads into a large open court flanked by colonnades of square pillars, in front of which are figures of the king. Beyond the court is the rock-cut part of the temple, consisting of the usual hypostyle hall with its roof supported by twelve square pillars, on the front of six of which are more colossal statues of Rameses. The inner rooms and the sanctuary are of the usual design, embellished with reliefs of a religious character, and on the east wall of the shrine are rock-cut statues of Amon, Rameses, and Re-Harmachis.

Unlike the temples of Gerf Hussein and Wadi es Sebua, the   *259* much ruined temple of Derr contains reliefs depicting scenes from Rameses' Nubian campaign which are of interest. Closely resembling the battle scenes on the walls of the temple of Beit el-Wali, they show Rameses charging panic-stricken Kushites who flee to their camp in the hills and trees. The wounded enemy are carried away by their comrades, who break the news of disaster to their womenfolk. All is confusion and panic, and the goats and oxen of the Negroes wander unattended while the prisoners are rounded up by the Egyptian soldiery. These reliefs on the east wall of the hypostyle hall obviously depict the same events as those portrayed in the temple of Beit el-Wali by another artist.

It is significant that in all these records of campaigns, Lower Nubia (Wawat) is never mentioned as an enemy, and it is obvious that the land was now regarded almost as a part of Egypt. The people were to a large extent Egyptianized and their chiefs and notables had Egyptian names. Moreover, Nubia was increasing in importance as a pawn in the internal politics of the homeland; she supplied a colonial army of outstanding prowess, and above all, she supplied gold. The office of Viceroy of Kush was fast becoming the most powerful in the land, and as we shall see, in the near future its holders would become strong enough to shake the throne itself.

When Rameses II died in 1232 B.C. he was succeeded by his thirteenth son Merenptah, who, confronted with the invasion of the Libyans and Mediterranean sea peoples, had little opportunity of attending to affairs in Nubia; but an inscription in the temple of Amada gives his speech to his southern subjects and suggests some form of military activity there after the termination of the Libyan war. But this was probably nothing more than the usual demonstration of strength on the southern frontier. With Merenptah's death in 1214 B.C., a dynastic struggle, similar to that of the Thotmosides of the previous dynasty, took place and the order of succession is still a matter of debate. The throne appears to have been usurped by Amenemeses, and the rightful heirs, Siptah and his queen Tausert, to have regained it largely with Nubian aid. He appointed a certain Seti as viceroy of Kush, and at the same time bribed officials of the Nubian administration perhaps to aid in their acceptance of his nominee. These events are recorded in an inscription of Neferhor in the temple of Hatshepsut at Buhen:

> Year 1 of the Good God, Rameses-Siptah, given life. Praise to thy *ka*, O Horus, Lord of Buhen! May he grant life, prosperity, health, fitness for service, favour and love, to the *ka* of the king's messenger to every country, priest of the Moon-god Thoth, the scribe Neferhor, son of Neferhor, scribe of the archives of Pharaoh, Life, Prosperity, Health, when he came with rewards for the officials of Nubia, and to bring the king's-son of Kush, Seti, on his first expedition.

The new viceroy remained loyal, and as "Superintendent of the Gold-country of Amen" he would be in a position to control one of the main resources of this powerful priesthood, thus obtaining its support for the king, and ultimately perhaps for himself; for on the death of Siptah he was succeeded by Seti II, who may well be identified with the powerful viceroy. However this may be, the reign of Seti II ended the Nineteenth Dynasty; the day when the viceroy and his Nubian soldiery would be able to interfere actively in Egyptian affairs was rapidly drawing nearer.

261

VII

The Twentieth Dynasty
and the Decadence in Egypt

c. 1184–751 B.C.

Sᴇᴛ-ɴᴇᴋʜᴛ, who became pharaoh in 1184 B.C., was far too occupied in restoring order in the homeland after the troubled period at the close of the previous dynasty to pay any attention to affairs in Nubia, and no records of his reign have so far been discovered in the south. His successor, Rameses III (1182–1151 B.C.), certainly conducted military operations in Kush, but these were probably little more than the usual demonstrations of strength, and the evidence of his Nubian campaign on the walls of his temple at Medinet Habu consists only of the usual pictorial record showing the king in battle against southern enemies. Beyond the names of captured geographical localities written in the usual city oval surmounted by the upper quarters of a bound captive, no written record accompanies these conventional reliefs.

How much of Kush remained in Egyptian hands at this time is uncertain, but the power of the pharaohs in the south was receding and it is doubtful if the frontier lay much beyond that of Senusret III. However, the name of Rameses III is found in the garrison temple at Semna, so we may conclude that the area of the Second Cataract was securely under Egyptian administration. Egypt depended more and more on her Kushite soldiers, and the staff of the viceroy included a "Commander of the Bowmen of Kush" who was certainly a person of considerable importance in pharaoh's palace. The last days of Rameses' life were troubled by the discovery of an assassination plot on the part of one of his

queens called Tiy, and among other high dignitaries involved was
the captain of the Kushite archers, called, in the record of the
trial, Binemwese. But this was not his real name, for the accused
were given fictitious names, indicative of the character attributed
to them; Binemwese means "Wicked in Thebes." This soldier had
been inveigled into the plot by his sister, who was one of the harem
ladies, and although no mention is made of this, it is not difficult
to imagine the value of such a man in command of Kushite troops
who probably had no particular loyalties. Unfortunately, the documents relative to this harem conspiracy are fragmentary and brief,
giving few details, so that we do not know if the Nubian troops
were actually garrisoned in the capital or were in the south. But
it gives a hint of Nubian military strength having become a formidable factor in the political affairs of the homeland. The viceroy
at the time was Hori, and it would appear that he was not involved in the affair, for his son, another Hori, succeeded to his
office and served under Rameses III's successor Rameses IV, who
came to the throne in 1151 B.C. Under him and his successor
Rameses V, we have no records of any activity in Nubia. Hori the
son of Hori continued to hold the viceregal office, but other than
this we know nothing of Nubian affairs, and it is not until the
reign of Rameses IV that we gain some insight into conditions in
Nubia. In the cliffs behind Aneiba, which under the name of Ma'am
was the capital of Nubia at that time, a certain Pennut built his
tomb. This rather simple rock-cut sepulcher is in many ways unique;
it was very rare indeed for a high official to arrange for his burial
in Nubia, and consequently few such monuments exist. Simple
rock tombs, crudely cut and undecorated, such as those at Buhen,
are fairly common, being made for minor Egyptian officials or
for native Nubians of some wealth; but the idea of burial far from
their homeland was abhorrent to those who could afford to make
the necessary arrangements. The question thus arises: was Pennut
a Nubian, like Djehuty-hetep who, in the reign of Queen Hatshepsut, constructed a similar painted tomb at Debeira?

Pennut's chief office was "Deputy of Wawat"; he was also "Chief
of the Quarry-service" and "Steward of Horus, Lord of Ma'am."   *263*

Another indication that Nubia was his native land was the fact that two of his relatives held the office of "Treasurer of the Lord of the Two Lands in Ma'am" and another was "Scribe of the White House and Mayor of Ma'am." However, tombs of these relatives, who obviously were equally important officials, have not been found in Nubia; so perhaps the family were Egyptians and Pennut was just eccentric in his wish to remain in Nubia after death. His claim to fame, which he recorded with pride on the walls of his tomb, was his distinction in receiving a gift of two silver vessels from the king, as a reward for his work in the erection of a statue of Rameses VI in the temple of Rameses II at Derr. The gift was presented to Pennut by the viceroy with considerable ceremony, he having received the vessels from the king himself with orders to give them to the Deputy of Wawat. Pennut also recorded in his tomb details of his domains in Nubia, which would furnish the income for the maintenance of the offerings to be presented to the statue of the king. In describing the boundaries of these lands, Pennut refers to the estate of Queen Nefertari and to the fields of the king, which indicates that much of the land in the vicinity of Ma'am was the private property of the royal family.

The priesthood of Amon, who by now held the gold lands of Nubia as possessions of the god, continued to increase their power, sometimes by influence and sometimes by rebellion. There is evidence suggesting that open revolt led by the High Priest of Amon occurred during the reign of Rameses IX, and from then on the royal house had to contend with sporadic civil war. Under the last king of the dynasty, Rameses XI, there was a rising in which the Libyan element in the population took part. This revolt was put down by the viceroy Panehesi and his Nubian troops, and from that time onward it would appear that he who controlled Nubia with its gold and soldiers controlled Egypt itself. Panehesi was succeeded as viceroy by the High Priest of Amon, Herihor, who also assumed the office of vizier; thus, with the wealth and military power of the south in his hands, he finally usurped the throne and became pharaoh in 1095 B.C. However, he was not able

264

to extend his rule over all Egypt, for following the civil wars which terminated the Twentieth Dynasty a certain Nesbanebdēdi had assumed the sovereignty of the delta, which he ruled from Tanis, so that Herihor was thus king only of Upper Egypt. But at his death the country became once more united under the Tanite kings, who became the Twenty-first Dynasty. Nevertheless, the high priests of Amon remained powerful princes and were more or less independent.

During this period of weakness and confusion there must have been a rapid decline of Egypt's domination in Nubia. Before his death Herihor had appointed his son Piankhy as viceroy of Kush, and it is significant that many years later the Kushite conqueror of Egypt also bore this name. Although conclusive evidence is not available, it would appear not improbable that the viceroy Piankhy transferred his allegiance to the south and was the ancestor of the royal house of Napata, who were ultimately to become the pharaohs of the Twenty-fifth Dynasty.

Egyptianized Lower Nubia (Wawat) probably remained a remnant of a lost empire, but Kush was by now semi-independent. For some time before this the priesthood of Amon had established a counterpart of Karnak at Gebel Barkal in the vicinity of Napata, where they built a great temple. Many Egyptians, priests, officials and traders settled there and intermarried with the native population, ultimately forming what might be termed a "government in exile," when in 950 B.C. the homeland was ruled by the kings of the Twenty-second Dynasty, who were of Libyan origin. Napata had become a great city embellished with temples and palaces in which a Kushite-Egyptian culture had evolved, full of vitality and with a definite character of its own. The products of Nubia's gold mines were probably flowing to the south instead of to the north, and above all, its chiefs considered themselves the legitimate rulers of the Nile Valley, assuming the age-old title "King of Upper and Lower Egypt." The stage was set for a reversal of the tide of conquest: Kush was to conquer Egypt.

VIII

The Twenty-fifth Dynasty

c. 751–656 B.C.

THE ROYAL house, perhaps descended from Piankhy, the son of Herihor, had long been established as the rulers of Kush before any attempt was made to establish their sovereignty in Egypt, and the great necropolis at Kurru had received their dead from as early a date as 860 B.C., more than a hundred years before the conquest of the north was achieved. The ancestors of the Twenty-fifth Dynasty were products of the gradual Egyptianization of what must originally have been a family with a purely Kushite background, perhaps descended from the ancient chiefs of Kerma. Sixteen predecessors of Piankhy, the conqueror of Egypt, were buried at Kurru, and the evolution of their burial installations tells the story of this change on sound archaeological evidence.

The earliest tombs consist of a pit grave under a circular earthen tumulus with the body slightly flexed on the right side and with the head to the north. Later, the tumulus is cased in stone masonry, which develops into a rectangular stone-built superstructure and finally into the typical Kushite pyramid. As the tombs become more elaborate and Egyptian in design, so the orientation of the burial changed from north-south to east-west. But even when Egyptian burial practices were adopted, one Nubian custom survived in many of the tombs: this was the bed burial in which the deceased was placed upon a bed in an attitude of sleep. This form of burial had been characteristic of both Upper and Lower Nubia from the earliest times, and we find it continued until Christianity swept away the last remnants of paganism in the sixth century A.D. But, in general, by the time of Piankhy's father, Kashta, the ruling

266

class of Kush had become Egyptian in art, architecture, religion, and culture, and even racially there were strong ties resulting from the intermarriage of generations of Egyptian settlers with the native stock. Kashta, who was King of Kush, died in 751 B.C., but before his death the conquest of Egypt had begun and he had already gained a large measure of control in Upper Egypt, whether by peaceful means or by open warfare is not known. But it is significant that in Lower Nubia (Wawat) no remains which might be attributed to this period have been found, and it would appear probable that it had once again become a battleground ravaged by contending armies. What vestiges of Egyptian power that remained there after the end of the Twenty-first Dynasty had long since disappeared, and resistance to the advance of Kush must have been negligible. In Lower Egypt rival dynasties contended for sole power, and nothing like a united front could be organized to check the Kushite encroachment; so that by the time of Piankhy's accession all the southern area of the country as far north as Herakleopolis was more or less controlled by Napata. Then came a potential Egyptian liberator in the person of Tefnakht, a delta prince, who succeeded in uniting Lower Egypt under his rule, assumed the rank of pharaoh, and advancing south, laid siege to Herakleopolis. This was the opening of the struggle that was to end with the victory of Kush and the foundation of the Twenty-fifth Dynasty. The record of these stirring events is contained on a large granite stela which Piankhy set up in the temple at Gebel Barkal, where it was found in 1863. Now in the Cairo Museum, this monument is one of the most important historical documents, which reveals to us, for the first time, ancient Nubia as a first-rate power that was soon, albeit unsuccessfully, to challenge the might of Assyria. The story it unfolds of Nubia's triumph is so dramatic and so well told that I have no hesitation in presenting extracts of Breasted's translation at some length.

The record on the stela starts with the date, year 21 of the King of Upper and Lower Egypt, Meriamon-Piankhy, when the monument was erected at Napata. This, presumably, would be shortly after the events it commemorates. An introduction follows, con-

267

taining the usual conventional boasts by the king of his prowess. Then comes the commencement of the epic:

> One came to say to His Majesty: A chief of the west, the great prince in Neter [a region in the central Delta] Tefnakht. . . . He has seized the whole west from the back-lands to Ithtowe, coming southward with a numerous army, while the Two Lands are united behind him, and the princes and rulers of walled towns are as dogs at his heels. No stronghold has closed its doors in the nomes [provinces] of the South; Mer-Atum [Medum], Per-Sekhemkheperra [probably Illahun, at the mouth of the Fayum], the temple of Sebek [Crocodilopolis, capital of the Fayum], Permezel [El-Bahnasa], Theknesh; and every city of the west; they have opened the doors for fear of him. He turned to the east, they opened to him likewise: Hatbenu [El-Hiba], Tozi, Hatseteni, Pernebtepih [Atfih]. Behold, he besieges Herakleopolis, he has completely invested it, not letting the comers-out come out, and not letting the goers-in go in, fighting every day. He measured it off in its whole circuit, every prince knows his wall; he stations every man of the princes and rulers of walled towns over his respective portion.

Piankhy received this news with indifference and we are informed that he laughed. As later events showed, he had perhaps reason to be amused, for he probably knew his strength, with Kush at the height of her power and Egypt in decay and riven by internal dissension. However, his Egyptian vassals thought otherwise and appeals for action came from the north. We are told that

> These princes and commanders of the army who were in their cities sent to His Majesty daily, saying: "Wilt thou be silent, even to forgetting the nomes of the Southland? While Tefnakht advances his conquest and finds none to repel his arm. Namlot, prince of Hatweret, he has overthrown the wall of Nefrus, he has demolished his own city, for fear that he [Tefnakht] might take it from him, in order to besiege another city. Behold, he goes to follow at Tefnakt's heels, having cast off allegiance to His Majesty [Piankhy]. He tarries with Tefnakht like one of his vassals in

the nome of Oxyrhyncus, and gives to him gifts, as much as he
desires, of everything that he has found."

The news of the defection of his vassal Namlot, who was a local
king of Hermopolis (El-Ashmunein), moved Piankhy at last to action, for it was obvious that the power of Tefnakht was moving
dangerously southward toward Thebes. The epic continues:

> Then His Majesty sent to the princes and commanders of the
> army who were in Egypt: . . . "Hasten into battle line, engage
> in battle, surround and capture its [Hermopolis] people, its cattle,
> its ships upon the river. Let not the peasants go forth to the
> field, let not the ploughman plough, beset the frontier of the
> Hare nome [the province of which Hermopolis was the capital],
> fight against it daily." Then they did so.

Having taken immediate action with his troops in Egypt, the king
gave orders for his army in Nubia to advance into Egypt, with
orders to

> . . . delay not day nor night, as at a game of draughts; but
> fight ye on sight. Force battle upon him from afar. If he says to
> the infantry and chariotry of another city, "Hasten," then ye
> shall abide until his army comes, that ye may fight as he says.
> But if his allies be in another city, then let one hasten to them;
> these princes whom he has brought to his support, Libyans and
> favourite soldiers, force battle upon them first. Say "We know
> not what he cries in mustering troops. Yoke the war horses, the
> best of thy stable; draw up the line of battle! Thou knowest that
> Amon is the god who has sent us."

After this exhortation to combat, Piankhy warns his soldiers that
even the mighty have no strength without the aid of Amon, and
he orders them, when they reach Thebes, to pray to the god: "Give
us the way, that we may fight in the shadow of thy sword." After
praising their king, we are informed that Piankhy's army "sailed
downstream, they arrived at Thebes, they did according to all that   *269*

His Majesty had said." Then, advancing northward, the Nubian army fought its first battle for the supremacy of the Nile Valley. Bypassing the rebel city of Hermopolis which they had already invested, the main Nubian army reached the vicinity of Herakleopolis. The record reads:

> They sailed downstream upon the river; they found many ships coming upstream bearing soldiers, sailors and commanders; every valiant man of the Northland, equipped with weapons of war, to fight against the army of His Majesty. Then there was made a great slaughter among them, whose number was unknown. Their troops and their ships were captured and brought as living captives to the place where His Majesty was (i.e., Napata).

After this naval victory the forces of Nubia advanced on Herakleopolis, still being besieged by Tefnakht and his allies, of whom the record gives a list, ending with the observation that "Every prince, the rulers of the walled towns in the West, in the East, and the islands in the midst, were united of one mind as followers of the great chief of the West, ruler of the walled towns of the Northland, prophet of Neit, mistress of Sais, the *sem* priest of Ptah, Tefnakht." It was certainly not the policy of Piankhy in this record to underestimate the power of the opposition and thus belittle his own great achievement in the conquest of Egypt.

The first stage of the two-day battle for Herakleopolis was fought on the river, ending with victory to the Nubians and with the withdrawal of Tefnakht's army to the west bank. Battle was joined again next day:

> When the land brightened early in the morning, the army of His Majesty crossed over against them. Army mingled with army; they slew a multitude of people among them; horses of unknown number; a rout ensured among the remnant. They fled to the Northland from the blow, and evil beyond everything.

The traitor King Namlot, learning of the threat to his capital Hermopolis by the Nubian army, at least had the courage, after

270

the disaster at Herakleopolis, to forego refuge with the retreating forces of Tefnakht. He made his way south and succeeded in avoiding the enemy and entering Hermopolis. When the Nubian commanders heard of his presence they invested the province more closely and the long siege commenced. When news of the progress of the war reached Piankhy, he was angry at what he considered a half-finished job.

> Have they allowed a remnant of the army of the Northland to remain? allowing him that went forth of them to go forth to tell of his campaign? not causing their deaths, in order to destroy the last of them? I swear: as Ra loves me! As my father Amon favours me! I will myself go northward, that I may destroy that which he [Tefnakht] has done, that I may make him turn back from fighting forever.

Having made his decision to take over the command, Piankhy was in no way mollified by news of the repeated military successes of his army when they captured Oxyrhyncus, Tetehen (Tenneh) and Hatbenu (El Hiba). The king reached Thebes, and after celebrating the new year feast of Amon, he sailed north to the besieged city of Hermopolis. We are told:

> His Majesty came forth from the cabin of the ship, the horses were yoked up, the chariot was mounted. . . . Then His Majesty went forth to hate his soldiers, enraged at them like a panther, saying "Is the steadfastness of your fighting this slackness in my affairs? Has the year reached its end, when the fear of me has been inspired in the Northland? A great and evil blow shall be smitten them." He set up for himself the camp on the southwest of Hermopolis and besieged it daily. An embankment was made to enclose the wall; a tower was raised to elevate the archers while shooting, and the slingers while slinging stones, and slaying people among them daily.

The intensification of the siege and the continuous assault soon had its effect, and we are told that "Hermopolis was foul to the   *271*

against it; let us elevate the ground to its walls. Let us bind together a tower; let us erect masts and make the spars into a bridge to it. We will divide it on this plan on every side of it, on the high ground and on the north of it, in order to elevate the ground at its walls, that we may find a way for our feet."

Piankhy decided to storm the city, and as a preliminary he captured the harbor with all its shipping intact; so that the plan to use the masts and spars of the ships as bridges to the top of the walls could be put into effect—a form of assault that the Venetians employed when they captured Constantinople in A.D. 1203. In this form of attack the ships had first to be marshaled, and we are told, that

> His Majesty himself came to line up the ships, as many as there were. His Majesty commanded his army, saying: "Forward against it! Mount the walls! Penetrate the houses over the river. If one of you get through upon the wall, let him not halt before it; so that the hostile troops may not repulse you."

He points out that it would be humiliating if, after conquering the south and reaching the north, they were to be checked on its threshold at Memphis and forced to face a siege.

However, the assault was successful, and we are informed:

> Then Memphis was taken as by a flood of water, a multitude of people was slain therein, and brought as living captives to the place where His Majesty was.

It is evident that the city was given over to pillage, but on the day following the capture the king restored order, sending officers into the town to protect the temples and install the priests in their various offices. The town was cleansed with natron and incense; then Piankhy proceeded to the temple of Ptah, where he received the recognition of the god.

When news of the fall of Memphis reached the provinces in
that area, the gates of their cities were opened, and their rulers

fled, or, like many of the princes of the northland, they submitted
to the Nubian conqueror and offered tribute. Finally, Piankhy proceeded to Heliopolis, and in the temple of Ra he was recognized
as king. But Tefnakht still resisted and with his remaining troops
he garrisoned a town called Mesed where, realizing that his situation was hopeless, he destroyed his ships and his supplies by fire.
Troops were sent against this last stronghold, and finally Piankhy
heard with satisfaction that "We have slain every man whom we
found there." However, Tefnakht was not among the dead, for he
had taken refuge in one of the islands in the delta swamps. From
here he sent a message of submission, asking that a representative
of the king should be sent to him to witness his taking an oath of
allegiance to the conqueror. Piankhy accepted his enemy's plea for
mercy and sent the chief ritual priest, Pediamenestowe, and the
commander of the army, Purme, to witness his oath. We are told:

> He [Tefnakht] presented him [Piankhy] with silver and gold,
> clothing and every splendid costly stone. He went forth to the
> temple, he worshiped the god, he cleansed himself with a divine
> oath, saying: "I will not transgress the command of the King. I
> will not overstep that which the King saith. I will not do a hostile
> act against a prince without thy knowledge; I will do according
> to that which the King says, and I will not transgress that which
> he has commanded." Then His Majesty was satisfied therewith.

How this great oath was kept we shall see later; but, as the epic
tells us, Piankhy was satisfied, and with the final submission of the
last princes and kinglets of the delta he was indeed pharaoh of all
the Nile Valley, from the southern borders of Kush to the coast of
the Mediterranean. The epic ends:

> Then the ships were laden with silver, gold, copper, clothing,
> and everything of the Northland, every product of Syria and all
> sweet woods of God's-Land. His Majesty sailed upstream, with
> glad heart, the shores on his either side were jubilating. West
> and east were jubilating in the presence of His Majesty; singing
> and jubilating as they said: "O mighty, mighty Ruler, Piankhy,

275

O Mighty Ruler, thou comest, having gained the dominion of the Northland. Thou makest bulls into women. Happy the heart of the mother who bore thee, and the man who begat thee. Those who are in the valley give to her praise, the cow that hath borne a bull. Thou art unto eternity, thy might endureth, O Ruler, beloved of Thebes."

There is no doubt that Piankhy considered himself the legitimate pharaoh, returning to claim that which was his by right. It is significant that throughout this record of his conquest the enemy is never described as Egypt but always as the northland. He was the son of Amon come to restore the power and prestige of the great god of the empire, and in this no doubt he had the support of many Egyptians and certainly that of the Theban priesthood. Although his army must have been predominantly Nubian, it must have had many Egyptians in its ranks, and so perhaps we must regard Piankhy's success not only as a Nubian conquest but as something in the nature of a restoration; for probably many Egyptians regarded it in that light.

On his return to Napata, Piankhy reconstructed the great temple of Amon and embellished it, no doubt, with much of the plunder he had gathered in his conquest of the north. He it was who probably moved the granite lions and rams from the time-honored temple of Amenhotep III at Soleb to Napata, the capital from which he intended to rule both Nubia and Egypt. It is strange that a man of Piankhy's obvious ability should follow so impracticable a policy; for to leave Egypt without a central administration situated within its boundaries, such as at Thebes or Memphis, was a fatal decision.

Forgetful of his oath, Tefnakht only waited for the Nubian withdrawal to throw off his allegiance, and eventually he was strong enough to assume the title of pharaoh. Ruling a large part of Lower Egypt, he was succeeded by his son Bekenrenef in 710 B.C.; while at about the same time the displaced princes of the Bubastite

276 family, Osorkon III and Takelot III recovered Thebes, which they

ruled until the return of the Nubians led by Shabako, the brother of Piankhy, whom he had succeeded in 716 B.C. Unfortunately no contemporary records of Shabako's reconquest of Egypt have been found, and we have only the account of Manetho, the Egyptian historian, writing some five hundred years after the event, of what must have been the culmination of his campaign. Manetho tells us that having captured Bekenrenef, the son of Tefnakht, he burned him alive. Profiting by the experience of his predecessor, Shabako moved his capital from Napata to Thebes, and with a united Nile Valley under his rule, he felt strong enough to challenge the might of Assyria, then at the zenith of her power in western Asia. Intriguing with Judah and encouraging this small nation to resist the advance of the Assyrians brought forth the insulting comment of Sennacherib which is recorded in the Book of Kings: "Now behold thou trustest on the staff of this bruised reed, even upon Egypt, on which if a man lean, it will go into his hand and pierce it; so is Pharaoh, King of Egypt, unto all that trust on him." Nevertheless, the "bruised reed" answered the call of an ally, and when Jerusalem was under siege by Sennacherib, Shabako dispatched his army to Palestine under the command of his nephew Taharka. However, an outbreak of plague forced the Assyrian army to withdraw, and the forces of Shabako and Sennacherib never made contact. But this was only a respite, and the threat of Assyrian aggression remained as formidable as ever, so that the whole foreign policy of Shabako and his successors must have been concentrated in this direction. Perhaps because of this, the administrative capital and royal residence of the Egypto-Kushite empire was established at Tanis in the western delta—Thebes and Napata retaining their importance as religious centers.

Shabako was succeeded by his nephew Shabataka (695–690 B.C.) who had already been associated with him as co-regent for two years. He, in his turn, appointed Taharka, his young brother, as his co-regent, and this important event took place when the young man was only twenty years of age. Shabataka died five years later, and Taharka became the sole ruler of both Kush and Egypt, in

689 B.C. In the opening years of his reign, fortune smiled favorably on the young king, and in both Egypt and Nubia there is ample evidence of his building operations which I will describe later.

At his coronation in Memphis, Taharka's mother, Abar, was present to see her son crowned "even as Isis saw her Horus on the throne of his father." In his youthful pride Taharka had sent for the queen-mother who had not seen her son since his departure from Nubia many years before. Nubia was now a world power and Taharka ruled the Nile Valley from the far south in the Sudan to the shores of the Mediterranean. But the power of Assyria was already casting its shadow over Egypt's northeastern frontiers; indeed there is reason to suppose that Taharka had already experienced battle with this formidable foe and had been worsted by Sennacherib at Elteheh in 701 B.C., when he was in command of the Egyptian-Nubian army sent by his uncle Shabako to aid Hezekiah of Judah. We have no knowledge of what preparations Taharka took to meet the Assyrian threat, beyond continuing residence at Tanis near his threatened frontier and seeking alliances with the buffer states in Palestine. In the time of impending war, the Nubian king was fortunate in having the loyalty of the prince of the Theban principality, Mentuemhat, a man of great ability who has left us a record—albeit a scanty and disjointed one—of the Assyrian aggression. Sennacherib, who died in 686 B.C., was succeeded on the throne of Assyria by Esarhaddon, who in 671 B.C. stormed and captured Memphis after a series of victories in the eastern delta. The Assyrian account of these events reads:

> In the tenth year in the month of Nisan, the army of Assyria went to Egypt. On the 3rd, 16th and 18th of Tammuz, three times, a battle was fought in Egypt. On the 22nd, Mimpi [Memphis] its royal city, was captured. Its king [Taharka] saved himself by flight. His brother was taken alive. Its booty was carried off, its people were plundered, its goods they carried away.

The Assyrians claimed to have overrun the whole of Egypt and to have invaded Nubia itself, for Esarhaddon tells us:

Baalu, King of Tyre, who relied on Tarku [Taharka], King of
Kusi [Kush]: all his cities and his property I took from him. I
conquered the land of Musri [Lower Egypt], the land of Paturisi
[Upper Egypt] and the land of Kusi, its King, five times with
the spear I fought and all his lands I ruled.

It is questionable if this claim is entirely justified; if the Assyrians really penetrated Nubia, they cannot have gone far, for
Taharka appears to have found safety in his southern homeland
and to have been ready for a return round in his struggle for the
sovereignty of the Nile Valley. However, there is no doubt that
they controlled Thebes, for Prince Mentuemhat's name figures as
one of the nobles who submitted to the conqueror and was apparently confirmed in his post. It would appear that Esarhaddon
considered that with the removal of the Nubians he could count
on the loyalty of the Egyptians, and as far as the latter were concerned his policy was placatory, for he tells us: "All the Nubians
I deported from Egypt, leaving not even one to do me homage.
Everywhere in Egypt I appointed new kings, governors, officers,
harbor overseers, officials and administrators." But his policy was
mistaken, for many, like Mentuemhat, remained in actual fact
faithful to Taharka, and after the conqueror's departure from Egypt
signs of revolt soon became apparent. Esarhaddon prepared to return to the Nile to make his conquest more secure, but on his
way back at the head of his army he died at Harran. Meanwhile
Taharka, gathering fresh forces in Nubia, had advanced north and
retaken Memphis and with it the control of Lower Egypt. Esarhaddon's successor Ashurbanipal did not take immediate action and
more than a year elapsed before the Assyrian army invaded Egypt
for the second time. They defeated Taharka at an unidentified
town somewhere in the delta, and once again he fled south to
Nubia leaving all Egypt in the hands of the invader. This was
the last time he was to see the northland, for he died at Napata
in 664 B.C. and was buried in his pyramid tomb at Nuri.

It is astonishing that in a reign so disturbed by war, Taharka
should have been able to indulge in so much building activity   *279*

both in Egypt and in his homeland. In the temple of Karnak he embellished the great court with a processional way flanked by huge columns of superb proportions, one of which survives, and it would appear probable that he was partly, if not wholly, responsible for the unfinished pylons which flank the main entrance to the temple. Apart from these major works, Taharka erected other buildings of lesser importance in the Karnak complex as well as at Medinet Habu on the west side of the Nile, and from inscribed material we may conclude that he built both at Tanis and Edfu. His building operations in his homeland were perhaps even more extensive, and at Napata he restored and embellished the great temple of Amon, and built a small rock-cut temple in the sacred mountain behind it. On the river side of the mountain, the face is so formed that it gives the appearance of an artificial façade consisting of four colossal figures, and it has been suggested that these are the remains of a rock-cut temple of the style of Abu Simbel and of even greater size. But many authorities doubt the existence of these rock-cut statues, and believe that they are merely chance formations of the natural rock. However, high up on the cliff, on the head of one of the supposed statues, cartouches of Taharka are claimed to have been seen; so we must consider the possibility that here at Gebel Barkal the great king built a monument that may at one time have rivaled Abu Simbel. But only extensive excavation at the foot of the cliff can prove or disprove this interesting theory.

Although the forts in the area of the First Cataract were at the time of Taharka largely ruined and unoccupied, he built at Semna a small temple within the fortress area, and at Buhen fragments of incised relief have been found which may well be ascribed to him and were probably additions to the existing fortress temple of Hatshepsut, or belonged to some adjacent building which has disappeared. His pyramid tomb at Nuri, near Napata, was the largest and the first of the great funerary installations in this royal necropolis, which he founded when the older burial ground at Kurru became too crowded.

280   Taharka was succeeded by his nephew Tanutamon (664–656 B.C.),

who after his coronation set forth to re-establish Nubian rule in
Egypt. He and his army descended the Nile to Thebes, where the
Prince Mentuemhat welcomed him and no doubt gave him additional support, so that he was soon able to invest Memphis and
occupy Lower Egypt, ultimately receiving the submission of the
delta chiefs who had become vassals of the Assyrian Ashurbanipal.
But this triumph was short-lived, for the great Assyrian conqueror
records that after the death of Taharka: "Tandamane [Tanutamon]
son of his sister, sat on his royal throne. Ni [Thebes] and Unu
[Heliopolis] he made the places of his strength and gathered his
forces to fight my army of Assyria, which was collected in Memphis.
He shut them in there and cut off their escape." Whether Tanutamon
succeeded in taking Memphis before the arrival of the Assyrian
monarch is uncertain, although the Egyptian account claims that
he did, and on the whole this appears probable. But in any case,
with the news of Ashurbanipal's arrival, he fled, without giving
battle, to Napata and once more an Assyrian army raged through
the Nile Valley.

Ashurbanipal's account of these events continues:

> On my second campaign, I directed my way to Musur [Egypt]
> and Kusi [Nubia]. Tandamane [Tanutamon] heard of my cam-
> paign and that I trod the soil of Egypt. He abandoned Memphis
> and fled to Ni [Thebes] to save his life. The kings, viceroys and
> burgraves [commander of town or fortress] whom I had set in
> Memphis, came to me and kissed my feet. After Tanutamon, I
> pursued my way and came to Thebes, the place of his strength.
> He fled to Kipkip [Napata?]. That city [Thebes] in its entirety
> I conquered with help of Ashur and Ishtar. Silver, gold, precious
> stones, all the possessions of his palace, many-colored clothing,
> linen, great horses, men and women attendants, two high obelisks
> of shining orichalcum [a brass alloy], 2,500 talents in weight,
> the doorposts of the temple door I took from their bases and re-
> moved to Assyria. Heavy booty, beyond counting, I took away
> from Thebes. Against Egypt and Nubia I let my weapons rage
> and showed my might. With my hands full returned I to Nineveh,
> my residence-city, in good health.

This rather matter-of-fact account of the sack of Thebes marks the end of one of Egypt's greatest cities, for it never recovered and modern excavations have revealed the remains of burnt houses at Karnak which are probably remains of the handiwork of the Assyrian soldiery when let loose in the captured metropolis. With the retirement of Ashurbanipal from the ruined city, the ever faithful Mentuemhat returned, and in his record tells how he purified the violated temples after the invasion of unclean foreigners in the southland.

After these disasters Tanutamon made no further attempt to return to Egypt, remaining in Nubia until his death shortly after, when he was buried in the necropolis of Kurru. Although his successors still called themselves kings of Upper and Lower Egypt, the death of Tanutamon marked the end of the Nubian supremacy in the northern Nile Valley. Lower Nubia between the First and Second Cataracts formed a barrier between the two nations, and exhaustive archaeological research in this region has found no trace of settled occupation during this period. There is little doubt that the land was more or less uninhabited.

IX

The Ptolemaic-Meroitic Period

c. 332 B.C.—A.D. 350

With the death of Tanutamon, Nubia's checkered domination of Egypt came to an end after a period of nearly seventy years of almost continuous warfare. Although gradual decadence and final destruction as a world power was to be the fate of Egypt, her people at this time must have indeed appreciated the no-man's-land of Lower Nubia which separated them from their warlike neighbors of the south. To what degree the Nubian "liberation" of Egypt was welcome is a matter of debate, and although the renaissance of the religion of Amon, with its promise of a rebirth of the glories of the Empire, must have gladdened the hearts of the people of Upper Egypt, these sentiments were certainly not held in the delta. Moreover, the Nubian liberators did not bring peace but almost continuous warfare with the presence of strange rulers and a foreign soldiery. Shortly after the expulsion of the Nubians, the Assyrian victors, hard pressed by the Babylonians and Medes in their homeland, were in their turn compelled to retire and Egypt was once more united under Psammetichos, a Lower Egyptian prince who founded the Twenty-sixth Dynasty.

Back in their own capital of Napata, the Nubian royal house continued to use the traditional royal titles of the Egyptian pharaohs; their claim to be the legitimate rulers of Egypt was not forgotten, and a further clash between the two powers was only a matter of time. But on this occasion Egypt struck first and in 590 B.C. Psammetichos II invaded Nubia with an army strengthened by Greek and Carian mercenaries. This would appear to have been in the nature of a preventive war, because, following Egyptian military reverses in Asia, the Nubians were preparing for another struggle with their northern rivals; at the time of the accession of their king Aspelta in 593 B.C. their army was already beyond the Second Cataract and from the no-man's-land of Lower Nubia was threatening Egypt. Victory remained with the Egyptians, however, and as a witness of this we have a group of Greek inscriptions carved on one of the colossi of the great temple at Abu Simbel. The longest of these texts reads:

> When King Psammetichos came to Elephantine, this was written by those who sailed with Psammetichos the son of Theocles, and they came beyond Kerkis as far as the river permits. Those who spoke foreign tongues were led by Potasimto, the Egyptians by Amasis.

An inscription at Karnak also refers to this expedition and states that it reached Pnubs (Tumbus) and that finally, after defeating the Nubians, it occupied "the land of Shas," identified by some authorities as the Dongola reach, which would include Napata. Apparently no attempt at permanent conquest was attempted and the invaders retired to the area of the Second Cataract; the names of Carian mercenaries presumably garrisoned there have been found on the walls of the temple of Buhen and on rocks of the hill of Sheikh Suliman at Kor.

Whether Napata was actually captured by the forces of Psammetichos is a matter of debate, and indeed it may have been little more than a raiding party. But it is significant that at about this time the political capital of the Nubians was moved south to Meroe, situated on the east bank of the Nile between the Fifth and Sixth Cataracts. Napata remained the religious capital, but as the influence of the powerful priesthood of Amon declined, so did the city, and with its decline came the end of what historians of the Sudan call the Napatan Period.

Following the defeat of the Egyptian king Psammetichos III at Pelusium by Cambyses, Egypt became a Persian province in 525 B.C., and after the pacification of the country, the great conqueror turned his attention to Nubia. We are indebted to Herodotus for an account of the events that followed. According to the Greek historian, Cambyses sent spies into Nubia and these men, posing as ambassadors coming with gifts, were received by the Nubian king in his capital at Meroe. But the Nubian was not deceived; having spurned the gifts, he told the Persian envoys:

> The King of the Persians sent you not with these gifts because he much desired to become my sworn friend—nor is the account which ye give of yourselves true, for ye are come to search out my kingdom. Also your king is not a just man—for were he so, he had not coveted a land which is not his own, nor brought slavery on a people who never did him any wrong. Bear him this bow and say—"The King of the Ethiops thus advises the King of the Persians—when the Persians can pull a bow of this strength thus easily, then let him come with an army of superior strength against the long-lived Ethiopians—till then, let him thank the gods that they have not put it into the heart of the Ethiops to covet countries which do not belong to them."

Such an answer had its inevitable result: a Persian army marched south, only to meet with disaster through lack of adequate preparation, particularly with regard to its commissariat, and Cambyses returned to Egypt with the starving remnants of his army, the greater part of which had died of starvation in the Nubian desert. This Persian fiasco was the last attempt at an invasion of Nubia from the north for many years, and with all connection with Egypt severed by the no-man's-land between the First and Second Cataracts, Egyptian civilization gradually declined in the south, to be replaced by a bastard culture which archaeologists have named after the new capital at Meroe. Although, particularly with regard to religious thought and art, Egyptian influence remained predominant in the new Meroitic civilizations, African and, later, Hellenistic elements had their place. The Egyptian hieroglyphic writing gradually became corrupted and it was obviously understood only by the priesthood and even in their case was only imperfectly known. The shapes of the signs became debased, and soon a native Meroitic

285

hieroglyphic and cursive character was developed, which in turn was to become the script for expressing the native language. This cursive Meroitic script has, through the efforts of various scholars, been successfully deciphered, but since it is in an unknown language its meaning is still unknown to us.

Free from foreign interference, the Meroitic state prospered and grew into a powerful empire whose rulers dominated the whole of the northern Sudan. Gradually, the power and influence of Meroe spread into Upper Nubia, until by the time of the reign of the Nubian king Arkamon (Ergamenes) the whole area as far north as Hierasykaminos had become a part of the Meroitic empire. The reach north of this to Philae was known to the Egyptians as "The Land of the Twelve Furlongs" and this was translated as the Dodekaschoinos by the Greeks. By this time the Dodekaschoinos had been entirely colonized by the Egyptians under their Ptolemaic pharaohs, and although at certain periods it came for a time under Meroitic rule, this was certainly of temporary duration and the archaeological remains are almost entirely Egyptian in character. However, during the reign of Ptolemy IV, it would appear that the rule of the Nubian king Arkamon extended over the whole of the Dodekaschoinos including Philae itself, for there are remains in the temple which bear his name, and at Dakka he built the inner shrine of the temple, the outer hall of which was added by Ptolemy IV, and the pronaos by Ptolemy IX when Egyptian rule was restored. It has been suggested that this curious mixture of monumental effort by the Nubian and Egyptian rulers was an amicable arrangement; something in the nature of an exchange of courtesies. But I think the more satisfactory explanation is that for a period Arkamon held the Dodekaschoinos and then lost it. But, in general, relations between the two countries appear to have been friendly, and south of the Egyptian Dodekaschoinos Meroitic settlement of Lower Nubia developed undisturbed. This happy state of affairs continued until the death of Cleopatra (30 B.C.) made Egypt a province of the Roman empire.

Roman interest in Lower Nubia was soon aroused, and under the emperor Augustus the great temple of Kalabsha was built and

286

additions made to the existing shrines at Debod, Dendur, and Dakka. Dedicated to the Nubian god Mandulis, the temple of Kalabsha is one of the finest and best preserved in Nubia (Figure 41). The site on which it was built was always of religious importance, and there is evidence that an earlier sanctuary was built there in the Eighteenth Dynasty by the pharaoh Amenhotep II which was refounded by one of the Ptolemaic kings. Such building operations instigated by the Romans so soon after their conquest of Egypt show the importance they attached to Nubia, and at that time it is obvious that they intended to extend the frontier far south of the territory which had satisfied the Ptolemaic kings.

In 29 B.C. the Roman prefect Cornelius Gallus signed a treaty with envoys of the Meroitic king, whereby the whole of Lower Nubia should be made a Roman protectorate, although it would still remain a part of the Meroitic empire. Such an agreement could only have been accepted under considerable political pressure and there can be little doubt that the rulers of Meroe could only wait for favorable circumstances which would enable them to retaliate. They had not long to wait, and when in 23 B.C. Roman rule in the Near East was embarrassed by the failure of the third prefect Aelius Gallus in his Arabian expedition, the Nubians struck back and with an army of 30,000 men they defeated three Roman cohorts forming the garrison at the First Cataract and occupied Syene (Aswan). According to the Roman account of these events, the Meroitic army was led by their queen, whom they called Kandake; but in fact Kandake is the Meroitic word for "queen," and this warlike lady is perhaps to be identified with Queen Amanirenas, who ruled the Nubian empire at that time. Her triumph was short-lived, for the new Roman prefect Gaius Petronius hurried with a force of 10,000 infantry and 800 cavalry, and drove her ill-armed soldiers before him to Pselkis (Dakkeh), where he inflicted a disastrous defeat on them. The remnants of the Nubian army retreated to Primis (Kasr Ibrim) and there in this mountain fortress they endeavored to make a stand. Petronius, however, stormed this stronghold, which, had it been defended by a well-equipped and disciplined force would have been impregnable. But the re-

287

THE TEMPLE OF KALABSHA

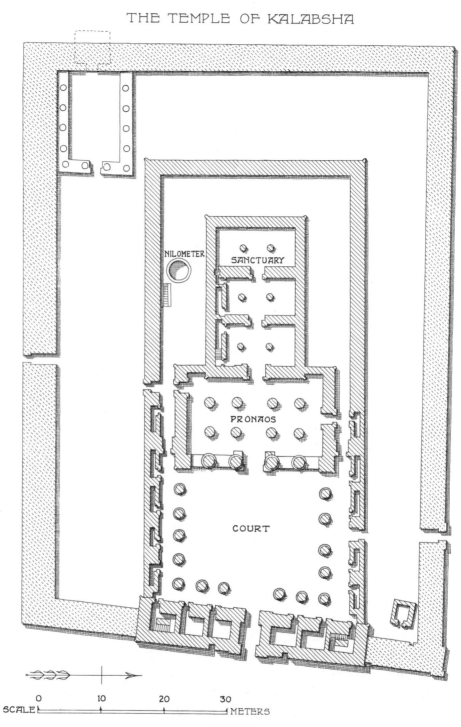

NILOMETER

SANCTUARY

PRONAOS

COURT

SCALE
0   10   20   30
METERS

FIGURE 41

treating Nubians, broken in morale, could put up only a feeble resistance, and Primis soon fell before the Roman onslaught. After this second reverse, their retreat became a rout that ended with the capture and sack of Napata, the religious center and second city of the Meroitic empire. The Nubian queen sued for peace, and captives and spoil from early successes were surrendered to Petronius, who returned to Egypt leaving a garrison of 400 men at the fortress of Primis, which then marked the southernmost frontier of the Roman empire. But within two years Petronius had to return to relieve his garrison that was besieged by a strong Nubian army, once again sent to invade the north. The relief of Primis forced the Nubian queen to offer to negotiate, and she was ordered to send her envoys to deal directly with the emperor at Samos. Strangely enough, they were favorably received by Augustus, and the Roman frontier was withdrawn to the former boundary of the Dodecaschoinos at Hierasykaminos. But the Meroites never really recovered from their struggles with Rome and although the rest of Nubia was nominally part of their empire, their control gradually declined. The towns and settlements which had not been destroyed in the struggle were impoverished, and many parts of the country became uninhabited. In such important centers of Meroitic culture as Karanog, little remains that can be dated later than the early part of the first century, and this also applies to the numerous Meroitic cemeteries, where the richer type of burial can certainly be dated to a period prior to the invasion of Petronius. Poorer graves of a later date exist in fairly large numbers, but they all show every sign of the rapid decline from the prosperous years before the advent of Rome.

The richer type of Meroitic tomb found in Nubia is usually a miniature copy of the burial installations of the kings and nobility in the royal necropolis of Meroe itself. Such tombs consist of a large rectangular pit with a ledge or shelf on which rests a leaning barrel vault of mud brick faced with mud plaster. Sometimes this ledge is replaced with mud brick vertical walls as a support for the vaulted roofing of the pit. Entrance to this shallow vaulted substructure is usually from a small stairway situated at the east end. The superstructure above the tomb, built either of brick or   *289* dressed, was apparently a steep-sided pyramid with a small brick-built niche or shrine made to receive the ba statue and table of offerings (Figure 42).

Tombs of the more humble citizens were usually of two sorts: one consisted of a ramp which led down to a rock-cut burial chamber, the door of which was blocked with brickwork and rough stone blocks. Above the burial chamber was a small brick-built pyramid. The second type simply consisted of an oblong pit with a lateral niche for the actual burial on the west side.

The Nubian of the Meroitic period buried his dead in an extended position lying on the back with the head to the west. There was no attempt at mummification, but the body was wrapped in garments of linen or woolen cloth. In the richer burials it was customary to place the so-called ba statue and a table of offerings. The latter is understandable, for it was a continuation of the Egyptian custom of placing a small altar outside the tomb on which offerings of food and drink could be placed for the dead; but the significance of the ba statue still remains uncertain, for we have no exact counterpart in the old Egyptian funerary ritual. Some of these statues represent a human-headed bird, while others portray a complete human figure with the wings of a bird. Their resemblance to the Egyptian representations of the ba, which was the soul of man, fleeing to heaven at death but returning at intervals to give comfort to the remains of the deceased left behind in the tomb, caused Egyptologists to identify these unique Meroitic statues with it. This may be so; nevertheless we must consider the possibility of their being actual portrait statues and more in the nature of the ka statues of the Egyptians.

But very few tombs of the Meroitic period have been found intact in Nubia; the majority have been plundered in both ancient and modern times. Yet in the few cases in which they have been discovered intact, the funerary equipment gives every indication of a prosperous and indeed luxurious standard of living. Apart from beadwork of considerable variety, bronze and glass vessels, toilet equipment, iron tools and weapons, etc., the contents of the tombs

TYPE OF MEROITIC BURIAL

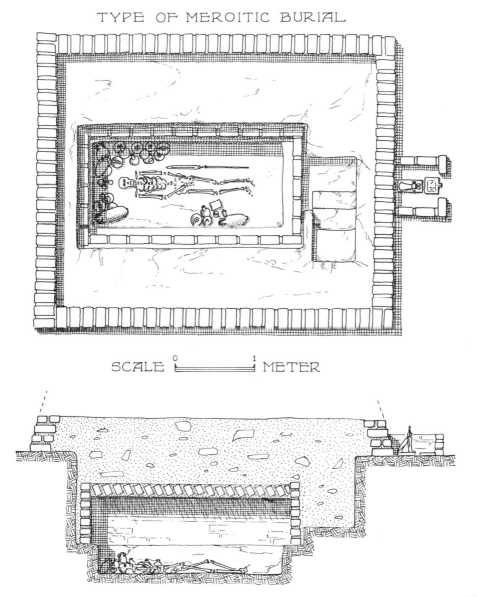

SCALE 0 1 METER

FIGURE 42

291

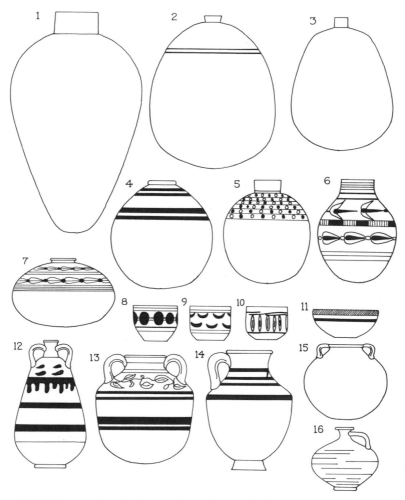

TYPES OF MEROITIC POTTERY

FIGURE 43   *1–3.* Red ware; *4.* Red ware with painted black bands; *5.* Red ware with painted red and black decoration; *6.* Red ware with painted black and white decoration; *7.* Red ware with painted black and purple decoration; *8.* Cream ware with painted black decoration; *9* and *10.* Cream ware with painted red and black decoration; *11.* Red ware with painted red and black decoration; *12.* Red ware with painted red and yellow decoration; *13.* Red ware with painted red and black decoration; *14.* Red ware with painted red and black decoration; *15* and *16.* Red ware

292

are remarkable for the very fine pottery which they contain (Figure 43). Much of it, particularly jugs and flasks and amphorae, is Egyptian Ptolemaic in origin, or at least has been copied from designs of northern type; but the bulbous jars and so-called biscuit-ware cups are purely Meroitic and unique to this culture. The cups of fine cream ware with painted designs in red, black, and orange are particularly attractive. Such urban centers as Faras (Pakhoras), Kasr Ibrim (Shimale), and Karanog (Akin) all bear witness to the high degree of culture which existed in Nubia before the withdrawal of Meroitic control in the north which preceded the decay and final destruction of the center of the empire in the middle of the fourth century A.D.

X

The X-Group Period

c. A.D 200–550

THE MEROITIC empire never really recovered from the disastrous defeat inflicted on it by the Romans under Petronius in 23 B.C., and although Nubia enjoyed many years of prosperity under Roman administration in the Dodekaschoinos in the north and the nominal rule of Meroe in the south, another period of great change was fast approaching. This was a period when Nubia was to be occupied by two warring peoples and was to witness the final struggle between Christianity and paganism. The culture of this period, which was the direct descendant of the Meroitic, is called by archaeologists X-Group, because we are still uncertain as to which of these two people it belonged.

There is little doubt that up to the middle of the third century Nubia south of the Dodekaschoinos was still a part of the declining Meroitic empire, although it was largely occupied by a people known to the Romans as Blemyes. It is still a matter of debate who exactly these people were, or how they came to penetrate into Nubia, or indeed where they came from. Another question complicates the matter of the identification of these intruders: this is the possibility that Roman and Christian writers used the term Blemyes to denote all the inhabitants of Nubia in much the same way as the British at the time of the struggle with the Mahdi at the end of the last century classed every racial variety of their Sudanese opponents as "dervishes."

As we shall see, during the period between the third and sixth centuries A.D., when the X-Group culture flourished, Nubia was occupied by two distinct nationalities, Blemyes and Nobatae, and although most authorities believe that the X-Group are to be identified with the Nobatae, I consider, on purely archaeological evidence, that this culture belonged to their opponents whom the Romans called Blemyes.

The Meroitic empire comprised many subject peoples, and Strabo mentions that among these were the Blemyes. Eratosthenes (*c.* 19 B.C.) tells us that they lived along the east bank of the Nile and that they were subjects of the Ethiopians (Meroites) and neighbors of the Egyptians. We do not know how far to the south the country was occupied, but the fact that they were "neighbors of the Egyptians" is supported by the mention in a Ptolemaic document of two men who were reproached for neglecting the worship of Isis and for having drunk wine with the Blemyes.

Gradually, the Blemyes appear to have occupied the whole of Nubia, and although perhaps still subject to Meroe, were by the middle of the third century strong enough to attack the Roman frontier during the reign of Decius, and although they were driven back, no punitive measures appear to have been taken against them. It was at this time that Meroe had its last contact with Rome, for in A.D. 253 an embassy led by one Pasmun, son of Paese, was sent by the Meroitic king Teremen to Trebonius Gallus, with gifts to the temple of Isis at Philae. It has been suggested that the main purpose of this embassy was to appeal for aid against the barbarian tribes of the Black Noba, who were threatening Meroe itself, and who were ultimately to cause its downfall. Although at this period the archaeological remains in Nubia are purely Meroitic, the Blemye vassals of Meroe may well have attained their independence owing to the weakened state of the central government. At any rate we find them in A.D. 261 again attempting to invade Egypt, and although they were repulsed by Julius Aemilianus at the First Cataract, the area of the Dodekaschoinos appears to have remained in their possession.

In A.D. 272 the Blemyes took advantage of the Palmyrene invasion of Egypt and the Egyptian rebellion led by a Greek named Firmus who had trade relations with them. Thus allied with the

295

enemies of Rome, they invaded Upper Egypt and advanced north as far as Ptolemais (El-Menshiyeh) and Koptos (Kuft), which they held until the defeat of Firmus and the Palmyrans by the emperor Aurelian. The emperor then left Egypt under the command of Probus, who had to deal with the Blemyes, and it was only by degrees that he drove them back to Nubia in A.D. 274.

This reverse does not appear to have seriously affected the fighting powers of the Blemyes, for they again invaded Upper Egypt after Probus had been made Emperor in A.D. 276. Once more they occupied Ptolemais and Koptos, but were finally defeated by Probus, who was able to restore the old frontier of the Roman empire to its former position at Hierasykaminos (Maharraga). It is not improbable that the Egyptians of Upper Egypt were largely in sympathy with the Blemye invaders, and certainly the citizens of Ptolemais were allied to them, for Zosimus records that "Ptolemais of the Thebaid, having rebelled, started a war which was at first successful. Probus crushed both Ptolemais itself and the Blemyes who had been its allies."

But the holding of the area of the Dodecaschoinos remained a difficult task and eventually in A.D. 297 the emperor Diocletian decided that it was not worth the maintenance of the large protective force necessary to keep the warlike Blemyes in check. He therefore withdrew the Roman frontier to the First Cataract and invited a people called the Nobatae to occupy the abandoned territory in northern Nubia, in the belief that they might form a buffer state between Egypt and the Blemyes, who by this time probably inhabited the rest of Nubia. So, for the next 250 years Nubia was occupied by two distinct races, and it is to one of them that the X-Group culture belongs, on the question of whose identity, as already mentioned, archaeologists are still divided in their opinions.

Procopius gives the following account of Diocletian's policy and of the events which resulted from its implementation:

> From the city of Auxomis [Abyssina] to the border of the
> Roman Empire in Egypt, where is the city called Elephantine

[Aswan], there is a journey of thirty days for the fast walker. There, beside many other races are established the Blemyes and the Nobatae, extremely numerous peoples. But the Blemyes are established in the middle of that country, while the Nobatae occupy the part along the Nile. Formerly that was not the end of the country under Roman rule, but the limit was seven more days' [journey] further on. But when the Roman Emperor Diocletian, having come there, noticed that the tribute paid by these countries was insufficient by reason of the fact that the land there happens to be very narrow and within a short distance of the Nile the rocks which rise very high occupy the rest of the country, that an important force of troops had been established there for a long period whose expense was a very heavy burden on the treasury, and also that the Nobatae established round the city Oasis [Kharga?] constantly plundered everything in that country, he persuaded these barbarians to give up their habitations and to settle along the river Nile, having promised to give them big cities and a large country much better than the one in which they previously lived. He thought that by that means they would no longer harass the regions of the Oasis and that having changed to a land they would obviously drive out the Blemyes and other barbarians. And after the Nobatae had accepted these conditions, they immediately started to move to the regions to which Diocletian had ordered them to go, and they occupied the Roman cities on both sides of the Nile, starting from Elephantine. Then the king decided to give them and the Blemyes every year a fixed sum of gold, on condition that they would not plunder the Roman frontier any more, which sum they still receive. But none the less they raid the countries in that region, so impossible is it to make any barbarians keep faith with the Romans except by fear of soldiers. And still the emperor having found an island in the river Nile somewhere near the city of Elephantine, and having established in this island a very strong garrison, he built there some shrines and altars common to the Romans and to those barbarians, and he established priests of each nation in that stronghold, thinking that the friendship between them would be strengthened by the fact of having a common priesthood and for that reason he called the place Philae.   *297*

> Both these people, Blemyes and Nobatae, adore all the other
> gods which the Greeks adore and also Isis and Osiris and above
> all Priapus, besides which the Blemyes are accustomed to sacri-
> fice men to the sun.

Procopius' statement that the Blemyes were established in the
middle of Nubia and that the Nobatae lived on the banks of the
Nile has been put forward by some authorities as evidence that
the Blemyes were confined to the desert areas and that their enemies were more civilized people living in the fertile parts of the
land. But that this referred only to the Dodekaschoinos is shown
by his later reference to Diocletian ordering the Nobatae to occupy
the Roman cities on both sides of the Nile, starting from Elephantine; Roman cities did not exist south of the Dodekaschoinos.
The historian's statement that the Blemyes were accustomed to
sacrifice men to the sun is of interest in view of the fact that the
discovery of the tombs of the X-Group kings at Ballana and Qustol
showed that wholesale human sacrifice was a custom of these people. The nationality of the Nobatae is uncertain, and we can only
accept Procopius' statement that at that time they were a warlike
people occupying the areas of the oasis of the western desert. It has
been suggested that they were a branch of the Noba who, shortly
before the commencement of the Christian era, had moved north
from their original homeland in Kordofan to the desert oasis, leaving the main group of their race to invade the Gizera and finally
to destroy the Meroitic empire in the fourth century A.D. Alternatively, they have been identified with the Berbers of Libya and
again as coming from Napata the ancient capital of Kush. Who-
ever they were, the Nobatae appear to have served their purpose
as far as Diocletian's policy was concerned, and we have no records
of serious aggression against the Roman frontier until the introduction of Christianity by Constantine I (A.D. 323–337) laid the foundations of the final struggle in which the Blemyes stood foremost as
the champions of the ancient paganism. In A.D. 390 Theodosius I
issued the edict for the compulsory Christianization of Egypt and
298 for the closing of the temples, which would of course include the

sanctuary of Isis on the island of Philae, where both Blemyes and Nobatae were accustomed to worship. Such action could only result in war and in Nubia becoming the last refuge of the ancient faith.

It was about this time that the territory of the Blemyes was visited by the Greek historian Olympiodorus, who, being a pagan, received a hospitable welcome. The record of this visit is of particular value, for it shows that Upper Nubia was the land of the Blemyes at a period when archaeological evidence proves that the X-Group culture was flourishing in all that area and that the X-Group kings were ruling from a capital somewhere in the vicinity of their tombs at Ballana and Qustol. This important record tells us:

> The historian says that while he was in the region of Thebes and Syene [Aswan] doing historical research, the pagarchs and prophets of the barbarians, that is to say the Blemyes of the region of Talmis, conceived the idea of meeting him by reason of his reputation. And they took me, he says, as far as Talmis itself, so that I studied also those places which are five days' journey from Philae as far south as the city of Prima [Ibrim] which was in the first city of the Thebaid one would meet from the country of the barbarians, and for that reason it was called by the Romans in the Roman language Prima, that is to say the first, and it still retains that name although it has for a long time been occupied by the barbarians with other cities Phoinikon, Chiris, Taphis and Talmis. He says that in those countries he heard that there were emerald mines from which the emeralds were plentiful for the Egyptian kings, and those mines he says the prophets of the barbarians allowed me to see but that was not possible without the royal permission.

Olympiodorus' reference to the Blemyes of the region of Talmis (Kalabsha) suggests that by this date (A.D. 407–425) the area of the Dodekaschoinos was in their hands, and perhaps allied to the Nobatae, the Blemyes had commenced their northward pressure in answer to the Christian challenge. Another important statement by the historian is his mention of the necessity for royal permission for his visit to the emerald mines; this shows that the Blemyes were   *299* by no means a conglomeration of desert tribes, as some authorities believe, but an organized monarchy with control over a vast area. In their struggle with Christianity the Blemyes were at first successful and by the middle of the fifth century they had overrun the Thebaid, besieging the harried Christian communities in the monasteries. Appion, Bishop of Elephantine, appealed to the emperor Theodosius for aid, and he mentions both Blemyes and Nobatae; it is evident that the two peoples were now united in their common antagonism to Christianity. No doubt they were aided by the pagan elements in the population of the invaded territory which enabled them to establish some form of civil government of which we have evidence from three documents written in bad Greek; these, believed to have been found at Gebelen, are now in the Cairo Museum. A translation of one of these letters throws an interesting sidelight on the abject condition of the Romans in the Thebaid at this time; it reads:

> I Charachen, Kinglet of the Blemyes, write to the children of Charadun, Charapatkur and Charahiet, that by my order I have given [you] the administration of the island called Tanare and according to my orders nobody should hinder you. And if the Romans make difficulties and do not pay the ordinary tribute, neither Phylarch nor the Hypotyrannos will prevent you from compelling the Romans to pay the ordinary tribute of my island.
>
> Charachen, Kinglet.
> Laize, Domestikos. Witness.
> Tuitikna, Domestikos. Witness.

A second letter sent by another Blemye kinglet named Pachytimne appoints a priest called Poae as administrator of the island called Tanare, which was probably situated in the Gebelen district.

But the turn of the tide was not long delayed, and in A.D. 452 the emperor Marcianus took belated steps to protect his Egyptian subjects. His general Maximinus marched against the combined forces of the Blemyes and Nobatae, inflicting such reverses on them that they were compelled to plead for peace. We are indebted to

Priscus for the account of the humiliating terms which they were
forced to accept:

> The Blemyes and the Nobatae having been defeated by the
> Romans sent to Maximinus ambassadors from both nations de-
> siring an armistice in order to make peace. And said that they
> would keep that peace as long as Maximinus would remain in
> the Thebaid, and as he would not accept a truce for that period
> of time, they said they would not take up arms as long as he
> lived. And as he did not welcome even the second proposition
> of the embassy, they made a truce of peace for a hundred years
> in which it was decided to release the Roman prisoners without
> ransom, whether they had been taken in that campaign or another,
> and to give back the cattle which had been driven away. And
> to refund the expenditure which had been incurred and to give
> as hostages those of them who were of good family so as to in-
> sure the observance of the truce. And they would according to
> former custom have free crossing to the temple of Isis. The Egyp-
> tians would have charge of the river boat used for taking the
> statue of the goddess, because the barbarians at a certain period
> take the statue to their own land and having used it for the
> purpose of an oracle, bring it back to the island. It seemed suita-
> ble to Maximinus to ratify the treaty in the temple of Philae.
> Some representatives [of the Romans] were sent to Philae and
> were also present those of the Blemyes and the Nobatae, who
> would ratify the truce on the island. And having written down
> those who had approved, the hostages were given, they who were
> ancient rulers or the children of ancient rulers, a fact which had
> never happened previously in that war, for never did the children
> of the Nobatae and the Blemyes be given as hostages to the
> Romans. And it happened that Maximinus was in bad health
> and died, and having heard of the death of Maximinus the bar-
> barians took back the hostages and raided the country.

That Maximinus, a Christian, should have found it politic to
permit the continuance of pagan worship at Philae shows that his
military successes cannot have been in any sense overwhelming; it   *301*

is obvious that the Blemyes were still a force to be reckoned with. Further indication of this is the fact that following the death of Maximinus, Florus, Procurator of Alexandria, thought it wise to overlook the matter of the rescued hostages and to content himself with driving back the raiders from Egyptian territory.

But paganism and its Blemyes were doomed, for the gradual infiltration of Christian belief among the Nobatae had made them the friends of Rome, and, beyond minor raids, the peace of Maximinus appears to have been preserved for over eighty years.

The signal for the final struggle was given about A.D. 540, when the king of the Nobatae was converted to Christianity by the monophysite missionary Julian who had been dispatched to Nubia for this purpose by the empress Theodora. The temple of Philae was closed, and the statues of the gods were sent to Constantinople; the inevitable result was war with the Blemyes. Details of this struggle are not known, but the ultimate destruction of the Blemye power in Nubia is recorded in an inscription in barbaric Greek on the wall of the temple of Kalabsha (Talmis) by Silko, a king of the Nobatae, who was perhaps the monarch converted by Julian. Translations of this difficult text vary and the interpretation is very difficult, but one fact is certain: that Silko undertook various campaigns against his pagan adversaries, and ultimately destroyed them.

> I Silko, kinglet of the Nobatae and all the Ethiopians, went to Talmis and Taphis. Twice I made war with the Blemyes and God gave me the victory. After the three times I was victorious again and occupied their cities; I established myself there with my armies. The first time I conquered them and they supplicated me; I made peace with them and they swore to me by their idols, and I trusted their oath as I believed them to be honest men. I went back to my upper regions. When I became a kinglet I did not follow behind other kings but in the very front of them, for those who seek a quarrel against me I do not let them sit in their country unless they beseech me and supplicate me, for I am a lion in the lower country and I am an oryx [?] in the upper country. I made war with the Blemyes from Primis to

Telelis once and [with] the other Nobatae in the upper country.
I ravaged their countries because they sought a quarrel with me.
The lords of the other nations who quarrel with me, I do not
let them sit in the shade but outside in the sun, and they did
not drink water inside in their house, for my enemies I carry off
their women and their children.

To what extent Silko was aided by the Romans is not known,
but that his victories resulted in their destruction of the Blemyes as
a nation is certain, and with them passed the last lingering religious beliefs and traditions of pharaonic Egypt. It is significant,
in connection with the possible identification of the Blemyes with
the X-Group, that at the time of Silko's conquest archaeological
research shows that the X-Group culture decayed and eventually
disappeared, to be replaced by a Christian-Nubian culture from
which it was quite distinct.

Let us examine the remains of the X-Group culture so far discovered in Nubia. Because the towns and villages of this period
were usually situated adjacent to the river, little trace of them
has survived, for they were either overbuilt by later generations or
destroyed so that the land on which they stood could be turned
over to cultivation. The fertile areas of Nubia are so limited that
every yard of cultivable ground is of great value; consequently
when a settlement, through war or politics, became depopulated,
the abandoned buildings were ruthlessly leveled and the district
used for the cultivation of much needed crops. However, in some
cases the X-Group people built their towns on barren ground behind the thin line of productive land which bounded the edge of
the Nile. The excavation of such settlements as those discovered
at Karanog and the Wadi-el-Arab have revealed the foundations of
houses belonging to this period which are well built and designed
and show every indication of a well-organized and civilized society.
The fortress town of Ibrim (Primis) although originally built by
the Meroites must have remains of buildings erected by the X-Group
people; but if such exist they have been so overbuilt by later occupants that they are impossible to identify. However, the excava-

303

tions of the Egypt Exploration Society that are now being conducted on the site may reveal buildings which can be definitely attributed to them.

Although the tombs of the X-Group kings and higher nobility have been discovered at Ballana and Qustol (see pages 52–91) no trace of their capital city has been discovered, although it must

A ROYAL TOMB OF THE X~GROUP PERIOD

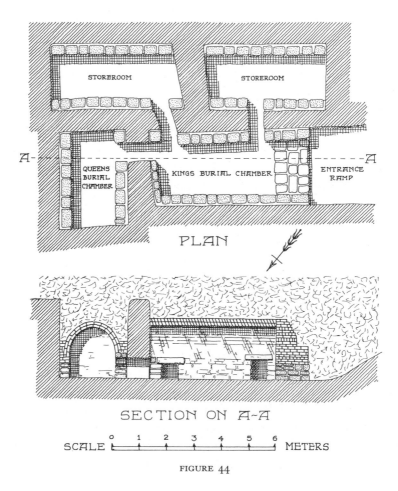

PLAN

SECTION ON A~A

SCALE METERS

FIGURE 44

to the dead in the afterlife. The body was usually wrapped in garments of linen or wool and in some cases was laid on a carpet or a low wooden bed. In the case of more humble people, the

TYPE OF X-GROUP BURIAL

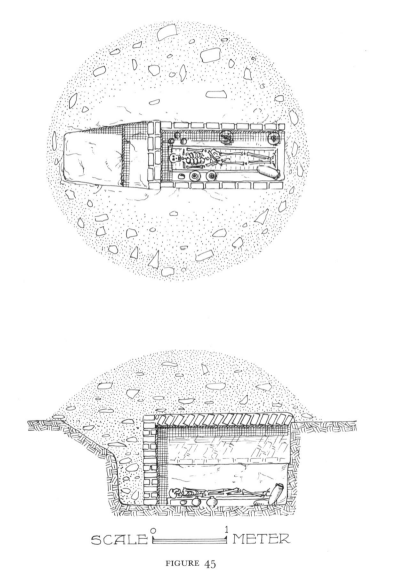

SCALE 0 ⊢━━━━━━┥ 1 METER

FIGURE 45

have existed somewhere in the vicinity of the royal necropo:
When the discovery was made, scanty remains of buildings we
found near the river bank at Ballana, but these proved to be of
later date than the X-Group period and were probably Christi
in origin. A short distance north of Qustol is the fortress tow
of Addeh; built on a hill and surrounded by a vast burial groun
this may be the lost capital of these people, but like Ibrim whi
it closely resembles, it is very much overbuilt by later structure
and it also awaits excavation. However, in the adjacent cemete
there are many small mound burials which appear to be of X-Grou
origin; so there is some reason to suppose that Adda was th
residence of the kings who ruled Nubia during the fourth, fift
and sixth centuries B.C.

Apart from the vast tumuli tombs of the X-Group kings whic
I have described in Part Two, Chapter III, very many cemeteries
this people have been excavated throughout Nubia (Figure 44
Consequently we have a wide knowledge of the design of the
tombs and their contents, which again give every indication
a well-organized people with rigid funerary customs which sho
little or no variation over an area of the Nile Valley more tha
300 miles long. Although the superstructure of the X-Group tomb
differs from their Meroitic predecessors in that the built pyrami
gave place to circular tumuli of earth or boulder stone, the sub
structure remained the same in almost every detail and there can b
little doubt that one was the direct descendant of the other. The
tumuli-covered tombs of the ordinary citizens were of three types
these are shown in Figures 45, 46, and 47. The orientation of the
body varies considerably and this also applies to the burial position.
for although the majority of interments are contracted or flexed,
those extended on the back or side are not uncommon. The contents of the tomb consists mainly of pottery vessels varying from
large amphorae to small cups with gaily painted decoration, cruder
but similar to the Meroitic biscuit ware (Figures 48 and 49). In
the richer tombs we find bronze lamps and vessels, toilet implements, and ivory inlaid wooden caskets, glass vessels, iron tools and
weapons, in fact every variety of equipment that would be of service

funerary equipment usually consisted of pottery flasks and drinking
cups with bowls or dishes containing the remains of food.

To return to the vexed question: who were the X-Group people

TYPE OF X-GROUP BURIAL

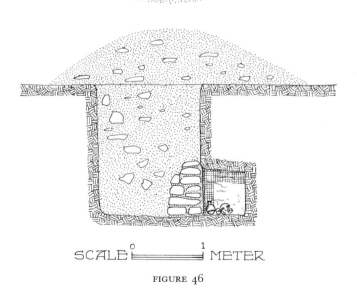

SCALE ⊢━━━━┥ METER

FIGURE 46

307

—Blemyes or Nobatae? It is not my intention to write in detail on this subject, which is still a matter of controversy among archaeologists, and on which fresh evidence may be revealed at any moment by the pick of the excavator. However, I do not think it would be out of place at the present juncture to summarize what we do know of the X-Group people from the results of recent archaeological research:

TYPE OF X-GROUP BURIAL

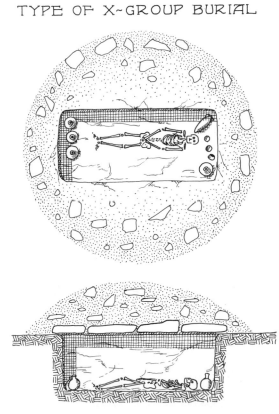

SCALE 0 ━━━━ 1 METER

FIGURE 47

1. Racially they were of mixed stock, akin to the Meroites but with an even stronger Negroid element.

2. They occupied the greater part of Upper and Lower Nubia from about A.D. 250 to 550.

3. Their kings were buried in the great tumuli tombs at Ballana and Qustol.

4. Their center of government was probably in the vicinity of Ballana and Qustol.

5. Their biggest centers of population were at Kalabsha (Talmis), Kasr Ibrim (Primis), Adda (Adwa), Faras (Pachoras), Gammai, Firka, Sai, and Wawi.

6. The greatest concentration of their burials is around the district of Kasr Ibrim.

7. Their burials at Kasr Ibrim, Ballana, and Qustol must cover a period of at least 250 years.

8. They were the settled inhabitants of Kasr Ibrim (Primis) at the time of the visit of Olympiodorus (A.D. 407–425), who described them as Blemyes.

9. Their burials at Kasr Ibrim continue to a later date than those at Ballana and Qustol.

10. They were pagans, worshiping the gods of Meroe and ancient Egypt.

11. Their culture followed directly after that of Meroe, from which it was undoubtedly descended.

12. Their kings assumed the crowns and emblems of Meroitic royalty.

13. The design of their tombs shows a direct descent from the Meroitic pattern.

14. Their pottery, with the exception of the imported variety, shows distinct Meroitic influence.

15. Their tomb furniture shows both Meroitic and Byzantine influence and manufacture.

16. In warfare they were accustomed to the use of leather armor and bull-hide shields, while their weapons were the stabbing spear, sword, ax, and bow and arrows.

17. They had little or no knowledge of a written language.   *309*

TYPES OF X~GROUP POTTERY

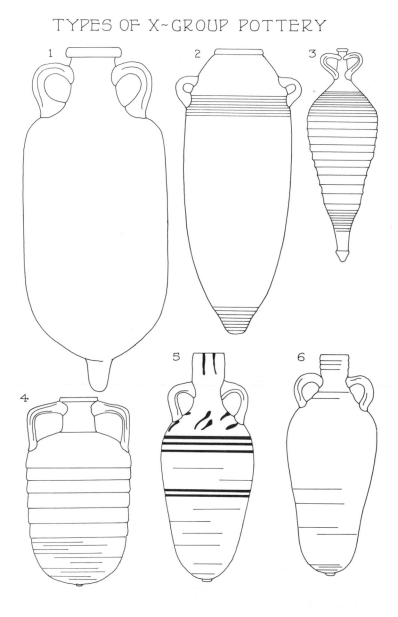

FIGURE 48   *1.* Red ware; *2* and *3.* Brown ware; *4.* Red or buff ware with cream
310   wash; *5.* Red ware with black painted decoration; *6.* Red ware with a pink wash

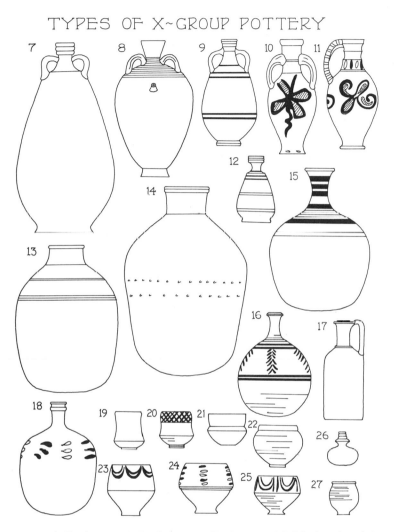

TYPES OF X~GROUP POTTERY

FIGURE 49   *7.* Red ware; *8.* Buff ware; *9.* Red ware with black painted decoration; *10* and *11.* Buff or pink ware with painted decoration in black and red; *12.* Buff ware; *13.* Red ware with painted decoration in black and red; *14.* Red ware; *15* and *16.* Red or buff ware with painted decoration in red and black; *17.* Red ware; *18.* Red or pink or buff ware with painted decoration in white, black, and red; *19.* Cream "biscuit" ware; *20.* Cream "biscuit" ware with painted decoration in red or black; *21* and *22.* Red ware; *23–25.* Red ware with painted decoration in black or white; *26.* Brown ware; *27.* Red ware

In my official report on the discovery of the royal tombs at Ballana and Qustol which was published in 1938, I outlined my reasons for identifying the X-Group people with the Blemyes, and our excavations during 1962–1963 in the necropolis of Primis (Ibrim) have given me no reason to modify this opinion. Without going into detail, which I think would be out of place in this book, the facts summarized above are in my view strongly indicative of the view that the X-Group culture did indeed belong to the people whom the Romans called the Blemyes, and whom they recognized as the last champions of the outworn religious beliefs of pharaonic Egypt in the Nile Valley.

APPENDIX

METRIC TABLE

10 millimeters (mm.) = 1 centimeter (cm.) = 0.3937 in.

10 centimeters = 1 decimeter (dm.) = 3.937 in.

10 decimeters = 1 meter (m.) = 39.37 in. or 3.28 ft.

10 meters — 1 decameter (dkm.) — 393.7 in.

10 decameters = 1 hectometer (hm.) = 328 ft. 1 in.

10 hectometers = 1 kilometer (km.) = 0.62137 mi.

10 kilometers = 1 myriameter (mym.) = 6.2137 mi.

BIBLIOGRAPHY

ARKELL, A. J. *Early Khartoum*. Oxford, 1949.

———. *Shaheinab*. Oxford, 1953.

———. *A History of the Sudan*. London, 1955.

BATES, O. "Excavations at Gemmai," *Harvard African Studies*, VIII (1927), 11 ff.

BLACKMAN, A. M. *The Temple of Dendur*. Cairo, 1911.

. *The Temple of Derr*. Cairo, 1913.

———. *The Temple of Bigeh*. Cairo, 1915.

BREASTED, J. H. *Ancient Records of Egypt*. Chicago, 1906.

———. *A History of Egypt*. London, 1951.

BUDGE, E. A. W. *The Egyptian Sudan*. London, 1912.

———. *A History of Ethiopia*. London, 1928.

CHAPMAN, S. E., and DUNHAM, DOWS. *The Royal Cemeteries of Kush*, III. Boston, 1952.

CLARKE, SOMERS. "Ancient Egyptian Frontier Fortresses," *Journal of Egyptian Archaeology*, III (1916).

CROWFOOT, J. W. "Christian Nubia," *Journal of Egyptian Archaeology*, XIII (1927).

DAVIES, NINA DE G., and GARDINER, A. H. *The Tomb of Huy*. London, 1926.

DE VILLARD, U. M. *La Nubie Médiévale*. Cairo, 1935.

DUNHAM. DOWS. *El Kurru*. Boston, 1950.

———. *Nuri*. Boston, 1950.

———. *Semna Kumma*. Boston, 1960.

———. "Excavations at Gemmai," *Harvard African Studies*, VIII.

EDWARDS, A. B. *A Thousand Miles up the Nile*. London, 1877.

EMERY, W. B. "Two Nubian graves of the Middle Kingdom at Abydos," *Liverpool Annals of Archaeology and Anthropology*, X (1922).

———. *The Royal Tombs of Ballana and Qustol*. Cairo, 1938.

———. *Nubian Treasure*. London, 1948.

———. Preliminary Reports on the Excavations of the Egypt Exploration Society at Buhen.

Kush, Vol. VII, 1959.

Vol. VIII, 1960.

Vol. IX, 1961.

Vol. X, 1962.

EMERY, W. B., and KIRWAN, L. P. *The Excavations and Survey between Wadi Es Sebua and Adindan.* Cairo, 1935.

FAIRMAN, H. W. Preliminary Reports on the Excavations at Amara West.
Journal of Egyptian Archaeology, XXIV (1938).
Journal of Egyptian Archaeology, XXV (1939).
Journal of Egyptian Archaeology, XXXIV (1948).

FAIRSERVIS, W. A. *Ancient Kingdoms of the Nile.* New York, 1962.

FIRTH, C. M. *The Archaeological Survey of Nubia.* Reports, Cairo, 1912, 1915, 1927.

GARDINER, A. H. "The defeat of the Hyksos by Kamose." *Journal of Egyptian Archaeology,* III, 1916.

———. "An Ancient List of the Fortresses of Nubia," ibid., III, 1916.

———. *Egypt of the Pharaohs.* Oxford, 1961.

GARSTANG J. SAYCE, A. H., and GRIFFITHS, F. L. *Meroë, the city of the Ethiopians.* Oxford, 1911.

GAUTHIER, H. *Le Temple de Kalabchah.* Cairo, 1911.

———. *Le Temple Ouadi es-Sebouâ.* Cairo, 1912.

———. *Le Temple d'Amada.* Cairo, 1913.

GREENER, L. *High Dam over Nubia.* London, 1962.

GRIFFITH, F. L. "Oxford Excavations in Nubia," *Liverpool Annals of Archaeology and Anthropology* (1921–1922–1923, 1928).

———. *Catalogue of the Demotic Graffiti of the Dodecaschoenus.* Oxford, 1935.

HAL, H. R. *The Ancient History of the Near East.* London, 1932.

JUNKER, H. *Bericht über die Grabungen der Akademie der Wissenschaften im Wien auf den Friedhöfen von El-Kubanieh Nord.* Vienna, 1920.

———. *Bericht über die Grabungen der Akademie der Wissenschaften im Wien auf den Friedhöfen von Ermenne.* Vienna, 1925.

KEATING, R. *Nubian Twilight.* London, 1962.

KIRWAN, L. P. "A Survey of Nubian Origins. *Sudan Notes & Records,* XX (1937).

———. *The Oxford University Excavations at Firka.* Oxford, 1939.

LEPSIUS, C. R. *Denkmäler aus Aegypten und Aethiopien.* Berlin, 1849–1859.

LITTLE, T. *High Dam at Aswan.* London, 1965.

MACADAM, M. F. L. *The Temples of Kawa.* Oxford, 1949.

MACQUITTY, W. *Abu Simbel.* London, 1965.

MASPERO, G. *Les Temples immergés de la Nubie.* Cairo, 1909–10, 1911.

MICHALOWSKI, K. Polish excavations at Faras, 1961, *Kush* X, 1962.

PORTER, B., and MOSS, L. B. *Topographical Bibliography of Ancient Egyptian Hieroglyphic Texts, Reliefs and Paintings,* Vol. VII. Oxford, 1951.

POSENER, G. "The location of the Land of Kush during the Middle Kingdom," *Kush,* Vol. VI, 1958.

RANDALL-MACIVER, D., and WOOLLEY, C. L. *Areika.* Philadelphia, 1909. *Karanog.* Philadelphia, 1910. *Buhen.* Philadelphia, 1911.

REISNER, G. *The Archaeological Survey of Nubia.* Report for 1907–8. Cairo, 1910.

———. "The Viceroys of Ethiopia," *Journal of Egyptian Archaeology,* London (1920).

———. "Excavations at Kerma." *Harvard African Studies,* V and VI. Cambridge, Mass. (1923).

———. "The Meroitic Kingdom of Ethiopia," *Journal of Egyptian Archaeology,* London (1923).

———. "Clay sealings of Dynasty XIII from Uronarti Fort," *Kush* III, 1955.

———. "The Egyptian Forts from Halfa to Semna," *Kush* VIII, 1960.

ROEDER, G. *Debod bis Bab Kalabsche.* Cairo, 1911. *Der Tempel von Dakka.* Cairo, 1913.

SÄVE-SÖDERBERGH, T. *Ägypten und Nubian.* Lund, 1941.

———. "A Buhen Stela from the Second Intermediate Period," *Journal of Egyptian Archaeology,* London (1949).

———. "The Nubian kingdom of the Second Intermediate Period," *Kush,* IV (1956).

———. "Preliminary Report of the Scandinavian Joint Expedition," *Kush,* X (1962).

SCHIFF GIORGINI, M. Reports on the Excavations at Soleb. *Kush,* VI, 1958. VII, 1959. VIII, 1960. IX, 1961. X, 1962.

SMITHER, P. C. "The Semnah Despatches," *Journal of Egyptian Archaeology,* London, (1945).

STEINDORFF, G. *Aniba.* Cairo, 1935–7.

TRIGGER, B. C. *History and Settlement in Lower Nubia.* New Haven, 1965.

VERCOUTTER, J. "Kor est-il Iken?" *Kush* III (1955).

———. "Upper Egyptian Settlers in Middle Kingdom Nubia." *Kush,* V (1957).

———. "The gold of Kush," *Kush,* VII (1959).

WEIGALL, A. E. P. *Report on the Antiquities of Lower Nubia.* Cairo, 1907.

INDEX

Figures in bold type refer to illustrations

Abar (mother of Taharka), 278

Abisko (town), 188

Abkanarti, excavations at, 101

Abu Hammad, 201, 227, 230

Abu Simbel, 9, 51, 53, 103, 247; façade, **252**; plan, **255**; UNESCO project, 12, 100, 123–25, **163, 164, 165**; temples, 12, 33, 249, 251–57, 284

Abydos, **182**

Adda (fortress), 12–13, 209; excavations at, 103, 247, 305

Adindan (place), 4, 12, 43, 51, 103

Aelius Gallus (Roman prefect), 287

Afyeh (district), excavations in, 100

Agilkia (island), 123

A-Group (people), 35, 38, 98, 100; culture, 170, 173; burials, 170, **171**

Ahmose (admiral), 225–26, 228

Ahmose I (pharaoh), 223–24, 225, 226, 243

Ai (pharaoh), 247

Akhenaton (Amenhotep IV, pharaoh), 96, 97, 245

Akin (modern Karanog), 293

Akita (modern Wadi el Alaki), 104, 201, 230, 240, 249–50

Aksha: temple at, 98, 99, 250

Alabaster: bracelets, 214; grinding stones, 170; jars, **182;** kohl pots, 222, 234; palettes, 170; studs, 72

Amada: temple at, 38, 99, 100, 242, 243, 260

Amanirenas (Meroitic queen), 287, 289

Amara, 249; temple at, 96–97, 250

Amasis (military leader), 284

Amenemhat I: pharaoh, 189, 190–91; prince, 101

Amenemhat II (pharaoh), 206

Amenemhat III (pharaoh), 209

Amenemhat IV (pharaoh), 209

Amenemopet (viceroy), 258

Amenherunamf (prince), 258

Amenhotep (viceroy of Tutankhamen), 246

Amenhotep I (pharaoh), 226

Amenhotep II (pharaoh), 120, 242, 242–43, 287

Amenhotep III (pharaoh), 96, 243–44, 248, 276

Amenhotep IV (Akhenaton, pharaoh), 96, 97, 244–45

American Research Center (Cairo), 103

Amethyst: beads, **143;** bracelets, 72, 88, **141, 145;** earrings, 72, **145;** scarabs, 222

Amon (god), 237, 238, 247, 253, 256, 257, 259, 269, 271, 272, 276, 280,

Amon (*cont.*)
283; priesthood of, 264–65, 284
Amulets, 214, 222, 234
Aneiba (ancient Ma'am), 9, 12, 35, 49, 51, 94, 199, 263; excavations at, *see* Ma'am
Anklets, 88
Antiquities law: in Egypt, 22, 23; in Sudan, 23–24
Antiquities Services, *see* Egypt; Sudan
Anubis (god), 239
Apepi (Hyksos king), 223
Appion (bishop of Elephantine), 300
Arabic, 121
Archaeological Surveys: First (1907–1911), 18, 31–39, 44; Second (1929–1933), 18, 30, 31, 36, 40–51, 56, 91, 182, 200; Third, 90
Archaic Period: history of Nubia during, 169–73
Archers and archery: bows and arrows, 230, 258, 262, 309; bracers, 78, 83; Egyptian, 230; looses, 78, 83; Nubian, **166;** quiver, 69, **151**
Areika: excavations at, 94
Argentina: excavations by, 98
Argin: excavations at, 101
Argo (island), 218
Arkamen (pharaoh), 237
Arkamon (Nubian king), 286
Armant (place), 40
Armor; breastplate, 69; *see also* Shields
Army: Egyptian, 230–33; Nubian, 202–4
Ashurbanipal (Assyrian king), 279, 281–82
Askut (fort), 104
Aspelta (Nubian king), 284
Assyria, 277, 283; invasion of Egypt, 278–79, 281–82
Aswan (ancient Syene), 6, 122, 178, 205, 206, 287
Aswan Dam, 6, 15–16, 27, 28, 39, 78, 122, 123; first raising, 10, 16, 30, 31; second raising, 12, 18, 40
Aswan High Dam (Sadd el Aali), 4, 18–20, 31, 115, 122, 123; map, **19**
Asyut: tomb of Prince Hepzefa, 187, 204–5
Atef: crown, 257; plumes, 81
Atfih (ancient Pernebtepih), 268
Aton (god), 245, 247
Augustus (Roman emperor), 241, 286–87, 289
Austria; excavations by, 98
Axes and axheads, 59, 85, 175, 230, 234, 309

Bahan: cemetery at, 169
"Baki" (fortress), *see* Kubban
Baki, Abdel, 41
Ballana, royal tombs: description of by Amelia Edwards, 54–55; discovery and excavation of by Emery, 53–55, 74–76, 77–89, **132,** 304–5; doorway to burial chamber, **133;** effects of discovery, 53, 89–90; Tomb 3, 74–76; Tomb 6, 78; Tomb 47, 87–88; Tomb 80, 80–86, **82;** University of Chicago excavations, 103
Baraba people, 6
Barkal, 241, 244; temple at, 237, 265, 267, 280
Ba statues, 120, 290
Bates, Oric, 32–33, 36
Batn el Hagar (Belly of Stones), 13–14, 191, 229
Batrawi, Dr. Ahmed, 41, 67, 68
Beads: amethyst, **143;** carnelian, 71, 88, **142, 143,** 171, 175; coral, 72; faïence, 68, 72, 88, **143,** 175, **182;** gold, 76, **141;** jasper, 88, **143;** ob-

sidian, 88, **143;** olivine, 88; quartz, **143;** shell, 67, 171, 175; silver, 72, 88, **142;** steatite, 88, 171

Bega tribe, 61

Beit el Wali: temple at, 103, 250, 257, 258–59, 260

Bekenrenef (pharaoh), 276, 277

Belgium: field work by, 98–99

Bells: bronze, 67

Beryls: bracelets, 72, 88, **141, 145;** earrings, 72; medallions, 67; rings, 72

Bes (god): carved knife handle, 62, **146**

B-Group (people), 38; burials, 174–75, **175;** culture, 173–74; pottery, 117, 118, 174, 175, **176**

Biga (island): fortress, 201; temple, 10, 37, 123

Binemwese (Kushite captain), 263

Blackman, Aylward, 32, 37–38, 97

Blemyes (people), 28, 36, 294–96, 297– 303; identification as X-Group, 308–9, 312

Bonomi, Joseph, 258

Boston Museum of Fine Arts–Harvard University Expedition, 96, 181

Bracelets: alabaster, 224; beadwork, 183, 214; ivory, 183, 214; gold, 224; shell, 170, 183, 214; silver, 72, 83, 88, **141, 145,** 214

Brass: bowls, 72

Breasted, James H., 93

British Museum, 112, 244

Bronze: bells, 67; brackets, 83; censer, 85, **147;** door hinges and plates, 68; earrings, 234; flagon, 65; lamps, 68, 76, 85, 120, **146, 148, 149,** 305; mirrors, 214, 222; rings, 234; saddle mount, 70; spearheads, 234; tables, 85, **147;** vessels, 83, 85, 120, **134, 146, 147,** 290, 305

Brown University: expedition, 103

Bubastite family, 276

Bucheum (place), 40

Buhen, 14, 35, 94, 188, 190, 207; defense system, 107–10, **155,** 198–99; dismantling and moving of, 102, 115, **156, 157;** Egypt Exploration society House, **131;** fortress, 99, 105–18, **109, 153, 154,** 173, 191, 197–99, **198,** 202, 219, 226, 227, 229, 236; Governor's residence, 112–13; history, 106–7; plan, **238;** reconstruction of West Gate, **110;** temple (Hatshepsut), 107, 114, 237–39, 242, 248, 261, 280; temple of Horus, 114, 219–20, 238, 243, 284; town site, 116–18, **158,** 174

Burckhardt, J. L., 55

Cairo, University of, 102

Cairo Museum, 63, 73, 90–91, **135,** 267, 300

California, University of: expedition, 104

Cambyses (Persian king), 284–85

Camels, skeletons in tombs: Ballana, 83, 84; Qustol, 60, 64, 70

Cameo: in medallions, 67

Caminos, Dr. Ricardo, 115, 120

Canada, National Museum of, 99

Canals: of Senusret III, 206–7, 225, 228, 240; of Uni, 177

Carnelian: amulets and scarabs, 234; beads, 72, 88, **143,** 171, 175; crowns, 78, 79, 84, **139, 140;** earrings, 72, 234; necklaces, 81, 234; scarabs, 222; studs, 72

Cataracts of the Nile: Fifth, 284; First, 4, 8, 9, 10, 34, 36, 92, 122, **128,** 169, 170, 177, 189, 206, 207, 218, 222, 228, 240, 243, 280, 282, 285, 287, 295, 296; Fourth, 241; Second, 4, 13, 39, 92, 93, 95, 96, 101,

Cataracts of the Nile (*cont.*)
102, 105, 106, 171, 177, 181, 187,
188, 190, 191, 192, 196, 209, 226,
229, 250, 262, 282, 284, 285;
Sixth, 284; Third, 95, 204, 227
Censer, 85, **147**
C-Group (people), 38, 69, 94, 100, 101;
burials, 181, 183, **184,** 210–14,
210, 211, 213, 215, 220–22, **221;**
culture, 180–87, 209–17; pottery,
180–81, 182, 183, 185, **186,** 214,
216, 220–22
Champollion, Jean-François, 92, 105,
248
Charachen (Blemyes kinglet), 300
Charles University, Czechoslovakia, 99
Chest: inlaid wooden, 71, 72–73, **152**
Chicago, University of: Oriental Insti-
tute, excavations by, 102, 103
Christianity, 298–303; antiquities of,
51, 98, 100, 101, 103, 104, 107,
119, 121
Clarke, Somers, 93
Cleopatra (queen), 286
Colorado, University of: expedition, 104
Columbia University: expedition, 103
Constantine I (Roman emperor), 298
Copper: borers, 170; implements, 175;
mining and smelting at Buhen,
116–18, 174
Coptic, 121
Coral: anklets, 88; earrings, 72, 88, **145**
Cornelius Gallus (Roman prefect), 287
Cosmetics, 72, 214, 222, 234
Coxe, Eckley B., Expedition, 94
Crocodilopolis (ancient Sebek), 268
Crowns, 257; silver, 77–78, **79, 80,** 81,
84, 87, 88, **139, 140**
Crystal: necklace, 83
"Curbing-the-countries" (fortress), *see*
Shalfak
Cusae, 219

Czechoslovak Institute of Egyptology,
99

Dabarosa: excavations at, 104
Dabnarti (fortress), 104, 195, 196
Daggers, 222, 234
Dahabeahs: of Emery, 41, 53, 56, **126,
130;** of Weigall, 30
Dakka (modern Pselchis), 35, 36–37,
287; temple at, 11, 36, 38, 102,
237, 286, 287
Dal Cataract, 101
Daraw-Kurkur, 178
Darfur, 177
Debeira, 13, 101, 263; excavations at,
100
Debod, 10, 100; temple at, 11, 38, 100,
102, 287
Decius (Roman emperor), 295
Dedun (god), 240, 242
Dehmit, 100, 102, 103
Deir el Bahri: temple at, 237
Dendur, 9; temple at, 37, 102, 287
Denmark, *see* Scandinavian Joint
Expedition
Derr, 11, 12, 13; temple at, 11, 37, 102,
250, 260
Derry, Douglas, 33, 35, 36
De Villard, Monneret, 51
D-Group (people), 38
Dice and dicebox (pyrgus), 62-63, 77
Diocletian (Roman emperor), 296, 297
Diorite, 176
Djadefra (pharaoh), 176
Djadkasa-Isisi (pharaoh), 176
Djehuty-hetep (official); tomb of, 263
Documentation Center for the History
of Art and Civilization of Ancient
Egypt (Cairo), 121
Dodekaschoinos (area), 286, 289, 294–
95, 296, 298, 299

Dogs, skeletons in tombs: at Ballana, 83; at Qustol, 64, 67

Dongola, 4, 6, 14, 245; reach, 227, 228, 229, 284

Donkeys, skeletons in tombs: at Qustol, 60, 64, 70

Dorganarti (fortress), 103

Dudy-mose (pharaoh), 219

Dunbar, J. H., 97

Dynasties, 38 (*table*), *see also* specific numbers

Earrings, 72, 88, **145**, 183, 214, 234

Ebony: chest inlay, 73; game pieces, 62–63

Edfu (place), 280

Edwards, Amelia: descriptions of Ballana and Qustol area, 54–55

Egypt: cultural periods and dynasties, 38 (*table*)

Egypt Antiquities Service, 30; activities in Nubia, 37–38, 94, 99, 102; maps, 119; plan for joining Biga and Agilkia, 123; publication on rock drawings and inscriptions, 97; Second Survey, 31

Egypt Exploration Society, 23, 104–5; Armant, 40; Buhen, 14, 99, 102, 105–18, **131**; Ibrim, 91, 103, 120–21, 302; "Iken," 197; Sesebi and Amara West, 96–97; survey of Nile River area, 103, 118–19

Eighteenth Dynasty, 10, 94, 106, 217, 225–47, 287; antiquities of, 107, 112; Army, 230–33

El-Ashmunein (ancient Hermopolis), 269, 270, 271–72

El-Bahnasa (town), 268

Elephantine: fortress, 201, 284; island, **128**, 240, 296; road, 177–78

Eleventh Dynasty, 187–88

El-Hiba (ancient Hatbenu), 268, 271

El Kab (ancient Nekhen), 225, 228, 245

El Leisiya: temple at, 242

El Malki (village), 11

El-Menshiyeh (ancient Ptolemais), 296

Elteheh (place), 278

"Embracing-the-two-lands" (fortress), 199

Emery, Walter B.: director of Second Archaeological Survey, 40–41; excavations, *see* Ballana, Bucheum, Buhen, Kubban, Qustol

Eratosthenes, quoted, 4, 295

Ergamenes (Nubian king), 286

Esarhaddon (Assyrian king), 278–79

Esna (place), 9

Ewers, 74, **145**

Faïence: amulets, 222, 234; beads, 68, 72, 88, **143**, 175, **182;** carrings, 88; scarabs, 67, 214

Fairman, H. W., 97

Faras (ancient Pakhoras), 95, 199, 247, 293; excavation by Poles, 100–1; temple at, 239, 247

Fayum, 268

Fifth Dynasty: antiquities of, 118; pharaohs, 118, 176

Finland, *see* Scandinavian Joint Expedition

Firka (place), 90, 96, 309

Firmus, 295

First Dynasty, 170, 171, 173; antiquities of, 169; rise of, 169

First Intermediate Period, 38, 180–87

Firth, Cecil, 32, 34, 35, 36, 37, 40–41, 43, 44, 50

Flasks, 72, **144,** 307

Flint: implements, 169; knives, 85

Florus (procurator of Alexandria), 302

Fortresses, 96, 105, 192–200; *see also* names, i.e., Adda, Askut, Baki, Biga, Buhen, Dabnarti, Dorganarti, Elephantine, "Embracing . . . ," Ibrim, Iken, Ikkur, Kor, Kumma, Ma'am, Mirgissa, Qirtas, Semna, Serra East, Shalfak, Uronarti

Fourth Dynasty: pharaohs, 118, 176

Fourth and Fifth Dynasties, 174; antiquities of, 102, 117, 118, 174; pharaohs, 118, 176

France: excavations and field work by, 92, 99, 100

Frankfort, Dr. H., 40

French Institute for Oriental Archaeology, 99, 102

French National Excavations Commission, 98, 99

French National Geographic Institute, 99

Frescoes: at Faras, 100–1

Gaius Petronius (Roman prefect), 287, 289, 294

Galena, 183

Gamai, 308; survey of, 101

Gaming board, 62

Garnets: bracelets, 72, 88, 141, **145;** lamp, 68, **146;** medallions, 67; rings, 72, 85

Gauthier, Henri, 37, 38

Gazelles, 220

Gebel Adda, *see* Adda

Gebel Barkal, *see* Barkal

Gebelen (place), 300

Gebel esh-Shems (mountain), 55

Gebel Sheikh Suliman, *see* Sheikh Suliman

Gematon (modern Kawa), 96, 245

Gerf Hussein: temple at, 102, 104, 250, 259

German Archaeological Institute

(Cairo), 49, 100

Germany: expeditions by, 93–94; Democratic Republic of, 104; Federal Republic of, 100

Ghana: excavations by, 100

Ginari (town), 35

Gizera (place), 298

Glass: amulets and scarabs, 234; beads, 72, 88, 234; vessels, 120, 290, 305

Gold: beads, 88, **141;** bracelets, 214; mines, 201, 230, 240, 249–50, 264, 265; necklaces, 76, **141,** 234; rings, 85, 234

Golenisheff, V., 55

Griffith, F. Ll., 94–95, 96, 199

Hapu (official), 206

Harvard University: expedition with Boston Museum of Fine Arts, 96, 181; survey with National Museum of Canada, 99

Hassenein, Mohammed, 41

Hatbenu (modern El-Hiba), 268, 271

Hathor (goddess): temple of, 239, 256, 257, 259

Hatseteni, 268

Hatshepsut (queen), 237, 242, 263; temple at Buhen, 107, 114, 237–39, 242, 248, 261, 280; dismantling and moving of, 102, 115, **156, 157;** plan, **238**

He (name for Abu Simbel), 253

Heh (place), 206, 208

Hekanefer (Prince of Ma'am), 104, 246

Heliopolis, 275

Hepzefa, Prince, 204–5

Herakleopolis, 267, 268, 270, 272

Herihor (viceroy, vizier and pharaoh), 264–65, 266

Herkhuf (official of Mernera), 177–79

Hermes: figure on plate, 76, **144**

Hermopolis (modern El-Ashmunein),

269, 270, 271–72

Herodotus (Greek historian), 285

Hezekiah (Judean king), 278

Hierasykaminos (modern Maharraga), 286, 289, 296

Hik-khase, *see* Hyksos

Hinkel, Dr., 115

Holland: experts' study of joining islands of Biga and Philae, 123; field work by, 100

Hor Aha (pharaoh), 171

Horemheb (pharaoh), 248

Hori (viceroy) and son of Hori (viceroy), 263

Horn: knife handles, 62, 71

Horse harness and trappings, **135, 136–37;** bit, 59 60, 66, **135, 136, 138;** bridles, 64, 65, 66, 90–91, **135, 137;** collar, 67, **136;** head stall, 66; reins, 66; saddles, 60, 64, 70; trappings, 60, 64, 65, 70, **135, 138**

Horse skeletons in tombs: at Ballana, 84; at Buhen, 111–12; at Kurru, 272; at Qustol, 60, 64, 65, 66, 67, 70

Horus (god), 242, 253, 261, 278; temple at Buhen, 114, 219–20, 238

Human sacrifices, 60, 67, 68, 83, 84, 87, 95, 204

Humboldt University, 115; expedition, 104

Husni, Mohammed, 41

Huy (viceroy of Tutankhamen), 245–47; tomb of, **246**

Huyot, Jean-Nicolas, 92

Hyksos (people): invasion of Egypt, 106, 112, 218–19, 222–23, 225, 230

Ibrim, Kasr (fortress), 12, 49, 91, 120, **158, 159,** 242–43, 287–88, 293, 303, 309; necropolis, 103, 119–20, 310;

town site, 103, 120–21, **158,** 299

Ico, Kasr: excavations at, 101

"Iken" (fortress), 196–97, 208

Ikhmindi: explorations at, 100

Ikkur (fortress), 35, 50, 187, 200–1, 229

Ikonarti, 226

Illahun (ancient Per-Sekhemkheperra), 268

India: excavations by, 100

Inebu-Amenemhat, 204–5

Iron: axheads, 59, 85; chair, 83; ingots, 85; knives, 62, 71, **146;** satchel handles, 71; spears, 62, 70, 78, 85, **150,** 290; swords, 65, 83, **151;** tools, 85–86, 290, 305

Irtet (tribal area), 177, 179

Isis (goddess): emblems in decoration, 70, 78, 89, 257; temple at Philae, 10, 16, **19,** 27–28, **29,** 122–23, **160, 161, 162,** 295, 299, 301; worship, 28, 238, 278, 295, 298

Italy: excavations by, 100

Ivory: bracelets, 183, 214; casket, 69; comb, 62; game pieces and dice, 62–63; inlays, 73, 120, **152,** 305; knife handles, 62, **146;** medallions, 66

Jasper: amulets and scarabs, 234; beads, 88; earrings, 234; necklaces, 83, **143**

Jones, Wood, 33, 35

Josephus (historian), 219

Julian (missionary), 302

Julius Aemilianus (Roman general), 295

Kakai (pharaoh), 117, 174

Kalabsha (ancient Talmis): excavations at, 102, 103; temple at, 11, 38, 100, **162,** 241, 242, 286, 287, 302, 309; plan, **288**

Kalat Adda, 55

Kamose (pharaoh), 222–24

Kandake, *see* Amanirenas

Karanog (ancient Akin): excavations at, 94, 289, 303

Karnak, 284; temple at, 265, 280

Kashta (king of Kush), 266–67

Kasr Ibrim, *see* Ibrim

Kasr Ico, *see* Ico

Ka statues, 290

Kawa (ancient Gematon), 96, 245

Kerma, 218, 266; culture, 181–82, 187, 217; excavations, 95–96, 181, 204–5; pottery, **182, 216,** 217, 231

Kertassi: temple at, 102

Khaemwast (prince), 258

Khafra (pharaoh), 118, 174

"Khakaura-justified-is-powerful" (fortress), *see* Semna

Khaneferra Sebekhotep (pharaoh), 218

Kharga Oasis, 178, 297

Khartoum Museum, 99, 102, 103, 115

Khasekhemui (pharaoh), 173, 174

Khnum (god), 240

Khufu (pharaoh), 176

Kirwan, L. P., 41, 54, 96

Knives, 62, 71, **146**

Kohl pots, 72, **182,** 222, 234

Konosso, 243

Koptos (modern Kuft), 296

Kor (fort), 102, 105, 284

Kordofan (place), 298

Korosko (place), 6, 11

Kubban ("Baki" fortress), 35, 36, 50–51, 243, 249; excavations, 100, 104, 201, 202, 209, 227, 228, 229, 230; plan, **201**

Kuft (ancient Koptos), 296

Kumma ("Warding-off-the-Bows," fortress), 14, 192–93; plan, **194;** temple, 99, 103, 241

Kurgus, 227

Kurru: necropolis at, 266, 272, 280, 282

Kush (Upper Nubia) and Kushites, 3, 4, 6, 14, 95, 106, 111, 182, 183, 188, 190, 191, 202, 204, 205, 206, 207, 209, 217, 218, 219, 220, 222, 226–27, 228, 231, 236–37, 240, 243, 244, 245, 246, 247, 249, 250, 254, 260, 265, 298; conquest of Egypt, 266–76

Lamps: hand, 68, 70, **146;** hanging, **149;** standard, 76, 85, **148, 149**

Lapis lazuli: medallions, 66

La Plata, University of, 98, 99

Late Period, 38

Leather: armor, 309; arrow quiver, 69, 151; breastplate, 69; burial garments, 214; clothing, 182, 214; documents, 121; horse collar, 67; saddles, 60, 64; satchel, 71–72; shields, 61–62, **150**

Leiden Museum, 100

Leningrad Institute of Archaeology: excavations by, 104

Lepsius, Karl Richard, 93

Libya, 4, 178

Lower Nubia, *see* Wawat

Luxor, 39, 40

Lyons, Capt. H. G. (Sir Henry), 28, 31

Ma'am (modern Aneiba): fortress, 94, 199–200, 229–30, 236, 242, 243, 263–64; plan, **200**

Macramallah, Neguib, 41

Maharraga (ancient Hierasykaminos), 296; explorations at, 100, 102

Mandulis (god), 287

Manetho (historian), 219, 277

Marcianus (Roman emperor), 300

Masai tribe, 62

Masmas: excavations at, 101

Maspero, Sir Gaston, 30, 37

Maximinus (Roman general), 300–2

Mayanarti (island), 101, 196

Medallions, 66, 67, **136**

Medinet Habu, 108, 280; temple, 262

Medju (tribal area), 177

Medum (ancient Mer-Atum), 268

Memphis, 177, 219, 222, 249, 272–74, 276, 278, 279, 281

Menkaura (pharaoh), 118, 174

Mentu (god), 190, 238, 247

Mentuemhat (prince), 278, 279, 281

Mentuhotep (general), 190, 191

Mentuhotep II (pharaoh), 188

Merenptah (pharaoh), 260

Meriamon-Piankhy (pharaoh), 267

Mermose (viceroy), 243

Mernera (pharaoh), 176–77, 178

Meroe (city), 4, 284, 285, 287, 289

Meroites (people), 36, 44, 309

Meroitic Empire, 38, 237, 286–87, 294–95, 298; antiquities of, 96, 100, 103, 104, 107, 119, 120, 210, 289, 290, 292; burials, 289–90, **291;** culture, 285–86; pottery, **291, 292**

Mesed (town), 275

Middle Kingdom, 38, 176, 197, 210, 228, 230; antiquities of, 6, 36, 95, 96, 99, 103, 106, 107, 111, 114, 115, 116, **182,** 190, 199; soldiers, **166**

Milan, University of, 100

Mines: copper, 116–18, 174; gold, 201, 230, 240, 249–50, 264, 265

Mirgissa (fortress), 99, 195–96; plan, **197**

Mond Excavations, 40

Moneim, Abdel, 41

Moonstones: medallions, 67

Musawwarat es Sufra: excavations at, 104

Mut (goddess), 256, 257

Namlot (king of Hermopolis), 268, 269, 270–71, 272

Napata, 242, 245, 265, 267, 270, 277,
281, 283, 284, 289, 298; temple at, 276, 280

Necklaces, 68, 72, 76, 88, **141, 142, 143,** 171, 183, 214, 234

Neferhor (scribe), 261

Neferhotep (pharaoh), 218

Neferirkara (pharaoh), 117, 118

Nefertari (queen), 264; temple at Abu Simbel, 123–25, **164,** 254, 256–57

Nefrus (town), 268

Nehi (viceroy), 239, 240, 242, 243

Nekhen (modern El Kab), 225, 228, 245

Nesbanebdedi (pharaoh), 265

Netherlands, *see* Holland

Neuserra (pharaoh), 118

New Kingdom, 38, 181, 206, 225–65; antiquities of, 12, 44, 49, 96, 103, 107, 108, 111, 114, 115, 116, 195; burials, **231, 232, 233,** 233–36; pottery, 234 (*chart*), **235**

New Mexico, University of: expedition, 103

Nile River and Valley, 4, 9, 10–14; archaeological surveys of, 99, 101, 103, 118–19; map, **5;** *see also* Cataracts

Nilometer, 218

Nineteenth Dynasty, 97, 248–61

Noba, Black (tribe), 295

Nobatae (people), 28, 294–95, 296–303

Norway, *see* Scandinavian Joint Expedition

Nubia, 3–14; cultural periods, 38 (*table*); description, 9, 10–14; history, outline of, 168–312; language, 6; location, 4; map, **17;** name, 4, 6; present population, 9

Nubians: background, 6–7; as workers, 7–9

Nubian Surveys, *see* Archaeological Surveys

Nuri: tomb of Taharka at, 279, 280

Obsidian: beads, 88, **143**

Old Kingdom, 38, 173, 176; antiquities of, 50, 117

Olivine: beads, 88

Olympiodorus (Greek historian), 299, 309

Onyx: bracelets, 88, **141;** medallions, 67

Osiris (god), 298

Osorkon III (pharaoh), 276

Ostraca, 117, 118

Oxen: skeletons in tombs at Qustol, 68

Oxford Expedition, 94–95, 96

Oxyrhyncus (town), 269, 271

Pachytimne (Blemye king), 300

Pakhoras (modern Faras), 95, 100–1, 199, 309

Palmyrene invasion of Egypt, 295–96

Panehesi (viceroy), 264

Pan Grave culture, 181–83, **182,** 217

Paper scrolls, 121

Papyri, 113, 117, 118, 121, 174, 189, 190

Paser (viceroy), 247, 248, 258

Pasmun (Meroitic ambassador), 295

Pediamenestowe (priest), 275

Pefnedibast (ruler of Herakleopolis), 272

Pelusium (town), 284

Pennsylvania, University of: expeditions, 94, 104, 105, 246

Pennut (official), 263–64

Pepi I (pharaoh), 176, 177

Pepi II (pharaoh), 178, 179

Pepi-nakht (general), 179

Permezel (modern El-Bahnasa), 268

Pernebtepih (modern Atfih), 268

Per-Sekhemkheperra (modern Illahun), 268

Persians: invasion of Egypt and Nubia, 284–85

Petrie, Sir Flinders, 30, 32

Philae: area map, **19;** island, **129,** 286, 297; plan, **29;** temple of Isis, 10, 16, 27–28, 122–23, **160, 161, 162,** 295, 299, 301, 302

Piankhy (viceroy of Kush), 265, 266; conquest of Egypt, 268–76

Pisa, University of: expedition, 104

Plenderleith, Dr. H. J., 115

Plumley, Prof. J. Martin, 91, 120

Pnubs (modern Tumbus), 284

Poae (priest), 300

Poland: expeditions at Faras, 95, 100–1, 199

Polish Center of Mediterranean Archaeology (University of Warsaw), 100–1

Potasimto (military leader), 284

Pottery: A-Group, 171, **172;** B-Group, 117, 118, 174, 175, **176;** C-Group, 180–81, **182,** 183, 185, **186,** 214, 216, 220–22; Kerma, **216,** 217; Meroitic, 119, **291,** 292; Meydum Bowl, 117; New Kingdom, 234 (*chart*), **235;** X-Group, 57, 61, 75, 77, 85, 119, **134**

Predynastic Periods, 38; Early, 169; Late, 170; Middle, 170

Priapus (god), 298

Primis (modern Ibrim), 287, 289, 299, 309

Priscus (Roman historian), 301

Probus (Roman general), 296

Procopius (historian), 296–98

Prussian Expedition to Egypt and Nubia, 93

Psammetichos I (pharaoh), 283

Psammetichos II (pharaoh), 283–84

Psammetichos III (pharaoh), 284

Pselchis (modern Dakka), 36, 287

Ptah (god), 247, 256, 259, 270, 274

Ptah-Tatenen (god), 259

Ptolemaic-Meroitic Period, 283–93

Ptolemais (modern El-Menshiyeh), 296

Ptolemy II (pharaoh), 237

Ptolemy IV (pharaoh), 286
Ptolemy IX (pharaoh), 286
Ptolemy XIII (pharaoh), 10
Purme (army commander), 275
Pyrgus (dicebox), 63

Qirtas: fortress, 99; temple, 11
Quibell, James, 191–92
Quartz: necklaces, 81, 88, **143**
Queens College, Oxford, 103
Qurta: temple at, 241–42
Qustol: excavations by University of Chicago, 103; royal tombs: discovery and excavation of by Emery, 13, 52, 56–74, 89, **132,** 304–5; Tomb 2, 59, 74; Tomb 3, 57–58, 61 63, 67 69; Tomb 14, 71–73

Ra (god), 72, **144,** 241, 247, 256, 271, 275
Rameses I (pharaoh), 248
Rameses II (pharaoh), 249–60; chapel at Ibrim, 120; temples, 251–60, 264; temples at Abu Simbel, 11, 12, 53, 100, 123–25, **163, 164, 165,** 249, 251–57; façade, **252;** plan, **255**
Rameses III (pharaoh), 262–63
Rameses IV (pharaoh), 263
Rameses V (pharaoh), 263
Rameses VI (pharaoh), 264
Rameses IX (pharaoh), 264
Rameses XI (pharaoh), 264
Rameses-eshabah (official), 253
Ramesseum, 192, 199, 201
Randall-MacIver, David, 94, 105
Recording: at base camp, 48; in the field, 44–48; record cards, **46, 47**
Re-Harmachis (god), 242, 253, 254, 256, 257, 259
Reisner, George: First Archaeological Survey, 31–32, 33, 34, 36, 44, 93, 96, 204; Kerma excavations, 95–96, 182
Rekhmire (vizier), 247
"Repelling-the-Inu" (fortress), *see* Uronarti
"Repelling-the-Mezaiu" (fortress), 199
"Repressing . . ." (fortress), 192
Rings, 214, 234; silver, 72, 88
Roeder, Gunther, 37
Roman Province, Egypt as, 286–89 294–303
Rome Center for the Preservation of Ancient Monuments, 115
Rossellini, Niccolo, 92

Saad, Zaki Yusef, 41
Sabagura: excavations in, 100
Sahura (pharaoh), 118, 174, 176
Sai (island), 91, 228, 309; temple, 241
Saite period, 67
Sakkara, 23, 32, 40, 41, 85
Samos (island), 289
Sarenpuwt (governor), 205–6
Sarras, 194
Satis (goddess), 238, 242, 247
Sayala: excavations in, 98
Scabbards, 83, **151**
Scandinavian Joint Expedition: field work by, 101
Scarabs, 214, 222, 234; medallions, 67
Schiff Giorgini Expedition, 104
Sealings, 112, 117, 118, 174
Sebek: temple at, 268
Sebek-neferura (queen), 209, 218
Second Dynasty, 170, 173; antiquities of, 117
Second Intermediate Period, 38, 95, 217, 218–24
Sedenga: temple at, 244
Sehel (island), 207
Seiyala, 9
Sekhemkara (pharaoh), 218

Sekhemrekhutowi (pharaoh), 218

Semenkhkara (pharaoh), 245

Semna ("Khakaura-justified-is-power-ful," fortress), 14, 101, 192, 204, 207, 218, 243–44, 262, 280; plan, **193**; temple at, 98, 103, 240–41

Sennacherib (Assyrian king), 277, 278

Sennuwy (wife of Hepzefa), 204

Senusret I (pharaoh), 36, 50, 189, 190, 191, 192, 194, 199, 201, 202, 203, 204, 205, 206, 230

Senusret II (pharaoh), 206

Senusret III, 36, 50, 192, 194, 206–9, 225, 228, 240–41, 242, 262

Sepedher (soldier), 219–20

Serra East (fortress), 103

Sesebi: excavation of, 96–97; temples at, 245

Setaw (viceroy), 259

Seti (viceroy of Kush), 260, 261

Seti I (pharaoh), 97, 249, 250, 253, 257; rock inscriptions at Ibrim, 120

Seti II (pharaoh), 261

Set-nekht (pharaoh), 262

Seventeenth Dynasty, 222–24

Shabako (pharaoh), 277, 278

Shabataka (pharaoh), 277

Shalfak ("Curbing-the-countries," fortress), 194–95; plan, **196**

Sheep: skeletons in tombs of Ballana and Qustol, 64

Sheikh Suliman: inscriptions at, 171, **173**, 284

Shell: bracelets, 183, 215; earrings, 183, 214; necklaces, 67, 171, 175, 234

Shellal, 4, 8, 9–10, 35, 37, 53, 103, 118, 207

Shields, 61–62, **150**, 203, 231, 246, 309

Shimale (modern Ibrim), 293

Sieglin, Ernst, 49

Sihather of Abydos, 206

Silko (king of Nobatae), 302–3

Silsileh: chapel at, 248

Silver: anklets, 88; arrow looses and bracers, 78, 83, **151**; beads, 72, 88, **142**; bowls, 76; bracelets, 72, 83, 88, **141, 145**, 214; casket, 76; crowns, 77–78, **79, 80,** 81, 84, 87, 88; cups, 76; earrings, 72, **145**; ewers, 74, **145**; flagons, 65; horse harness and trappings, *see* Horse harness and trappings; ingots, 246; medallions, 66, 67, **136**; necklaces, 72, 88, **142**; plates, 76, **144**; rings, 72, 88; scabbards, 83, **151**; spoons, 76; studs, 72; torque, 88, **142**; water skin, 65

Siptha (pharaoh), 260–61

Sixth Dynasty, 181; pharaohs, 176–77

Smith, Elliot, 33, 35, 36

Smith, H. S., 118, 197

Sneferu (pharaoh), 118, 174, 189

Soldiers: Egyptian, Middle Kingdom, **166**; Nubian archers, **166**; Nubian forts, 202–4

Soleb: temple at, 241, 244, 276

Spanish National Committee for Nubia: excavations by, 101

Spears, 62, 70, 78, 83, 85, **150,** 230, 234, 309

Steatite: beads, 88, 171; plaque, 218; scarabs, 214, 222, 234

Steindorff, Dr. Georg, 50, 94

Stelae, 120, 190, 194, 206, 207–9, 219, 220, 227, 241, 242, 243–44, 249–50, 267–76

Strabo, 4

"Subduing-the Oasis-dwellers" (fortresses), *see* Dabnarti, Mirgissa

Sudan Antiquities Service: Batn el Hagar, 14; Buhen, 105, 115; excavations and use of UNESCO archaeologists, 101

Sulb: excavation of, 104

Sweden, *see* Scandinavian Joint Expedition

Swiss Institute for Archaeological Research on Ancient Egypt, 99, 102, 103

Swords, 65, 83, **151,** 230, 231, 309

Syene (modern Aswan), 287, 299

Tafa: excavations at, 99; temple, 11, 102

Tahdrka (pharaoh), 277–80; temple at Kawa, 96

Takelot III (pharaoh), 276

Ta-kens, ancient name of Nubia, 4

Talmis (modern Kalabsha), 299, 302, 309

Tamit: excavations in, 100

Tanare (island), 300

Tanis, 265, 277, 278, 280

Tanutamon (pharaoh), 280–81, 282

Tausert (queen), 260

Tefnakht (prince), 267; campaign against Piankhy, 268–75; pharaoh, 276

Temehu (people), 178

Tenneh (ancient Tetehen), 271

Teti (pharaoh), 176

Thames (dahabeah), 41

Thebes, 108, 187–88, 192, 219, 222, 223, 242, 243, 249, 269, 271, 272, 276, 277, 299, 300, 301; fall of, 281–82

Thehmann (Nubian soldier), 188

Theknesh (town), 268

Theodora (Roman empress), 302

Theodosius I (Roman emperor), 298, 300

Thirteenth Dynasty, 218–19

Thoth (god), 261

Thotmose (viceroy), 245

Thotmose I (pharaoh), 227–28, 230, 236, 237

Thotmose II (pharaoh), 236–37

Thotmose III (pharaoh), 237–42, 247; chapel at Ibrim, 120

Thotmose IV (pharaoh), 243

Thuwre (viceroy of Nubia), 226–27, 228, 229

Tiy (queen), 263

Toilet articles, 62, 72, **144,** 214, 222, 234, 290, 305

Tombos, 227, 228

Tomb robbers: Ballana, 76, 87; Firka, 96; Kasr Ibrim, 119–20; Qustol, 56–69

Tools: bone, 175; iron, 85–86, 290, 305

Torque, 88, **142**

Toshka, 176; tomb at, 104, 246

Tozi, 268

Trebonius Gallus (Roman), 295

Tumas, 11, 12, 13; excavations at, 101, 176

Tumbus (ancient Pnubs), 284

Turin Museum of Egyptology, 100

Tutankhamen (pharaoh), 22, 23, 33, 245–47

Twelfth Dynasty, 189–217; antiquities of, 35, 50, 94, 106

Twentieth Dynasty, 107, 262–65

Twenty-fifth Dynasty, 244, 265, 267

Twenty-first Dynasty, 265

Twenty-second Dynasty, 265

Twenty-sixth Dynasty, 283

Tyi (queen of Amenhotep III), 244

Uni (official of Mernera), 177, 179

Union of Soviet Socialist Republics: excavations by, 104

United Arab Republic: excavations and field work by, 102

United Kingdom: excavations and field work by, 94–96, 102–3, 104–21

United Nations Educational, Scientific and Cultural Organization (UNESCO): archaeologists supplied to Sudan Antiquities Service, 101; International Campaign to Save the Monuments of Nubia, 10, 12, 14, 20–21, 24; field work result-

UNESCO (*cont.*)
   ing from, by nations, 98–121 (*see also* names of countries and organizations); results, 98–125; summary of accomplishments, 121
United States: excavations and field work by, 93, 94, 96, 102, 103–4
Uronarti ("Repelling-the-Inu" fortress), 193–94, 195, plan, **195**
Userkaf (pharaoh), 118, 174

Veronese, M. Vittorino, 20
Vienna, University of, 98
von Seiglin Expedition, 93–94

Wad-ba-Nagaa, 243
Wadi el Alaki (ancient Akita): excavations at, 104; gold mines at, 201, 230, 240, 249–50
Wadi-el-Arab: excavations at, 303
Wadi es Sebua, 6, 10, 11, 16, 30, 37, 39; temple at, 38, 99, 102, 250, 259
Wadi Halfa, 8, 9, 11, 13, 18, 105, 115, 199
"Warding-off-the-Bows" (fortress), *see* Kumma
Warsaw, University of, 100–1
Wawat (Lower Nubia), 4, 6, 177, 179, 182, 183, 187, 189, 190, 202, 206, 207, 209, 217, 220, 222, 231, 234, 239, 241, 243, 246, 250, 260, 264, 265

Wawi (town), 309
Weapons, *see* Archers and archery, Axes and axheads, Daggers, Knives, Scabbards, Spears, Swords
Weigall, Arthur, 30, 54, 55, 256
Wesersatet (viceroy), 242–43
Woolley, Leonard, 94, 105

X-Group (people), 38, 90, 91, 100, 102, 103, 303–12; antiquities of, 102, 103, 104, 119, 120, 304–7, 310–11; burials, 52–91, 304–7, **304, 306, 307, 308,** 309 (*see also* Ballana, Qustol); crowns, 77–78, **79, 80,** 81, 84, 87, 88, **133, 139, 140;** culture, 294, 296, 299; identity of people as revealed by research, 308–9, 312; kings, 51, 81–82, **133, 140;** pottery, 57, 61, 75, 77, 85, 119, 305, 307, 309, **310, 311;** queens, 87–88, **139**

Yale University: expedition, 104, 246
Yam (country), 177–78
Yugoslavia: field work by, 104

Zati (district), 188
Zenit el Nil (dahabeah), 41–42, **126, 130;** plan, **42**
Zer (pharaoh), 171–72, **173**
Zosimus (Greek historian), 296